Karen Kraska
740-369-5162

Praise for

THE DHARMA IN DIFFICULT TIMES

"Inspiring, beautifully written, uplifting, tough, and tender. A powerful book to raise your spirits and help you navigate these uncertain times with a clearer vision and a loving heart."

– **Jack Kornfield**, best-selling author of *A Path with Heart*

"If I could hand-deliver a copy of this book to everyone, I would do it. What a brilliant and–more importantly–necessary contribution to the wisdom of our collective soul. Please read this book."

– **Caroline Myss**, best-selling author of *Anatomy of the Spirit* and *Intimate Conversations with the Divine*

"Masterful storytelling . . . Inspiring accounts of leading figures in human history are woven together with the relevance of ancient Indian philosophy and the contemplative practices of yoga and meditation. This book is an essential read for anyone who is facing life challenges and hopes to grow spiritually through them—in other words, everyone."

– **Sat Bir Singh Khalsa, Ph.D.**, Assistant Professor of Medicine, Harvard Medical School; Director of Yoga Research, Yoga Alliance; Editor-in-Chief, *International Journal of Yoga Therapy*

"When faced with a life event that shakes you to the core, what is your response? Stephen Cope points to the Bhagavad Gita and people throughout history to show the way in his latest book: The Dharma in Difficult Times. *Written with charm and introspection, it takes us on a journey to learn just how deep we can go when faced with the things that knock us down. You will want to read every last bit, savoring the fascinating research and compelling connections."*

– **Sharon Salzberg**, best-selling author of *Lovingkindness* and *Real Change*

*"Cope masterfully combines storytelling with substance. That mastery was on full display in his first book about dharma–*The Great Work of Your Life. *In this new book, he takes us even deeper into the mysteries of dharma, distilling wisdom from the lives of both ordinary and extraordinary human beings who have been challenged in the deepest possible ways. He leaves us with very useful tools for our own journey through difficult times."*

– **Dr. Suneel Gupta**, Harvard Medical School faculty and best-selling author of *Backable*

"Stephen Cope is at the height of his considerable powers as mystic, scholar, and master storyteller. To say that this is the right book at the right time would be an understatement. Illuminated by the ancient wisdom of the Bhagavad Gita, Cope has laid out a clear path for how to utilize difficult times to deepen life purpose, sense of meaning, and capacity for mature compassion. In the lineage of all great mystics, he both invites and implores us to fully comprehend that when we face our greatest difficulties as opportunities for spiritual growth, this not only saves us, it also saves the world. With this audacious and brilliant book, Cope has thrown down the gauntlet: Will you fully take up your dharma in these difficult times?"

– **Gail Straub**, co-founder of The Empowerment Institute and author of *The Rhythm of Compassion*

"In this outstanding exploration of what makes us brave in tumultuous times, Stephen Cope goes to the heart of the question that haunts our lives: How can we rise to the challenges of this unprecedented, uncertain era? Cope looks at the lives of heroes and saints who've lived these sacred principles, tracing the roots of their courage, vision, irascibility (in the case of Thoreau), and transcendence through stories that uplift and enlighten. He shows that Arjuna's struggle is the one we all face; and that we, too, can break through our chains, enter the battle, rise up to live another day. A wonderful reminder of human greatness."

– **Mark Matousek**, best-selling author of *Sex Death Enlightenment* and *When You're Falling, Dive: Lessons in the Art of Living*

"An alarm may go off, and you see how long you've been sleeping. That alarm may be a book like Stephen Cope's The Dharma in Difficult Times. *The depth of the author's psychological, spiritual, and historical understanding informs his contemporary reading of the Bhagavad Gita, one of the world's most profound scriptures. Cope walks us through the 'disorienting dilemma'—the traumas great and small that blast through our lives. I can't read Cope without feeling the ground shift beneath my feet, the fog lift in my mind, and a deep listening within to learn how it will change me."*

– **Amy Weintraub**, founder, LifeForce Yoga Healing Institute, and best-selling author of *Yoga for Depression*

"I celebrate Stephen Cope's book The Dharma in Difficult Times. *This work gifts us with stories from the paths of accomplished notables, citing their rise from dilemma to dharma. Interwoven throughout the text are teachings from the Bhagavad Gita. Through reading this work, I have reacquainted my spirit with perspectives on loss, praise, change, action, and the sacred. It reminds one that the Gita's teachings lie within; practice, the sacred, and self-awareness will awaken these teachings as we strive to live our dharma. A wonderful read!"*

– **Maya Breuer**, Vice President for Cross-Cultural Advancement, Yoga Alliance, and co-founder, Black Yoga Teachers Alliance

"This is a book of inspiration, not because of happy endings, but because in this book we meet people who had to dig deep to find and live their dharma. Cope offers us no platitudes, no simple formulas, but does offer us what we truly need: enormous doses of truth and painfully won wisdom. Here is a book that shows us how to walk through these difficult times and the difficult times that are surely to come."

– **Diane Cameron**, author of *Out of the Woods* and *Never Leave Your Dead*

"The Gita never disappoints and neither does this book. A blend of wisdom and inspiration, the perfect recipe for these times. In order to meet the moment we are collectively facing, we need to draw from a deep well. This book brings the Gita alive and into your heart. May we all live these teachings as we serve and find collective healing and wholeness."

– **Robert Mulhall**, Chief Executive Officer, Kripalu Center for Yoga and Health

"Brilliant! Enthralling! Mind-blowing! Revelatory! . . . More than an excellent read, this book is truly a work of art, a call-to-action to discover and live unapologetically our own 'idiosyncratic dharma.' Stephen Cope reminds us, inspires us, and gives us all permission to be ourselves and offer our unique gift to the world while we still can. In this timely work, Cope skillfully weaves together spirituality, history, social justice, and the issues of our time, sourced in the historical lives of real heroes and philosophers, all beautifully blanketed in the ancient text of the Bhagavad Gita. I felt as though Cope saw right through me, drawing me into the deepest question about my own life: To what extent am I living my dharma, living on purpose? For all spiritual seekers, yogis, meditators, deep thinkers, and anyone searching for a deeper purpose in the world–this book is a must-read!"

– **Todd Norian**, acclaimed yoga teacher, founder of Ashaya Yoga, and author of *Tantra Yoga: Journey to Unbreakable Wholeness, A Memoir*

"Anyone who has followed the writing life of Stephen Cope knows that his work explores every angle on what it takes to live a vibrant, fulfilling, and spiritually connected life. I see him as a luminary in the line of Swami Kripalu, another exquisite transmitter of the ancient science of skillful living that the yoga tradition calls dharma. Picking up his latest book, The Dharma in Difficult Times, *I was immediately reminded of how hungry I was for more of Stephen's writing. Putting it down left me aware of how dearly I need this kind of insightful inspiration in my life."*

– **Richard Faulds**, former President, CEO, and Board Chair of Kripalu Center for Yoga and Health; author of *Kripalu Yoga: A Guide to Practice On and Off the Mat*

The DHARMA in DIFFICULT TIMES

ALSO BY STEPHEN COPE

Books

The Great Work of Your Life

Soul Friends (published in paperback as *Deep Human Connection*)*

Will Yoga and Meditation Really Change My Life?

The Wisdom of Yoga

Yoga and the Quest for the True Self

DVDs

Yoga for Emotional Flow (Sounds True)

Kripalu Yoga Dynamic (Kripalu)

Your True Calling: Essential Teachings of Yoga to Find Your Path in the World (Sounds True)

Gentle Yoga Kit: A Kripalu Program (Padma Media)

*Available from Hay House
Please visit:

Hay House USA: www.hayhouse.com®
Hay House Australia: www.hayhouse.com.au
Hay House UK: www.hayhouse.co.uk
Hay House India: www.hayhouse.co.in

The DHARMA in DIFFICULT TIMES

Finding Your Calling in Times of Loss, Change, Struggle, and Doubt

STEPHEN COPE

HAY HOUSE, INC.
Carlsbad, California • New York City
London • Sydney • New Delhi

Published in the United States by: Hay House, Inc.: www.hayhouse.com® • ***Published in Australia by:*** Hay House Australia Pty. Ltd.: www.hayhouse.com.au • ***Published in the United Kingdom by:*** Hay House UK, Ltd.: www.hayhouse.co.uk • ***Published in India by:*** Hay House Publishers India: www.hayhouse.co.in

Cover design: Julie Davison • *Interior design:* Nick C. Welch

Indexer: J S Editorial, LLC

Grateful acknowledgment is made for permission to reprint previously published material:

Lines from *The Bhagavad Gita: Translated for the Modern Reader*, translated by Eknath Easwaran (Tomales, CA: Nilgiri Press, 2007), used by permission of Nilgiri Press.

"My life closed twice before its close," "I measure every grief I meet," and "The brain is wider than the sky," from *The Poems of Emily Dickinson: Reading Edition*, edited by Ralph W. Franklin, Cambridge, Mass.: The Belknap Press of Harvard University Press, Copyright © 1998, 1999 by the President and Fellows of Harvard College. Copyright © 1951, 1955 by the President and Fellows of Harvard College. Copyright © renewed 1979, 1983 by the President and Fellows of Harvard College. Copyright © 1914, 1918, 1919, 1924, 1929, 1930, 1932, 1935, 1937, 1942 by Martha Dickinson Bianchi. Copyright © 1952, 1957, 1958, 1963, 1965 by Mary L. Hampson. Used by permission. All rights reserved.

Four lines of #29 from Tao Te Ching by Lao Tzu. Translation copyright © 1988 by Stephen Mitchell. Used by permission of HarperCollins Publishers.

Cataloging-in-Publication Data is on file at the Library of Congress

Hardcover ISBN: 978-1-4019-5726-1
E-book ISBN: 978-1-4019-5727-8
Audiobook ISBN: 978-1-4019-5729-2

10 9 8 7 6 5 4 3 2 1
1st edition, January 2022

Printed in the United States of America

SFI label applies to the text stock

For Sandy, beloved twin sister and friend:
"a pearl of great price."

Sometimes crisis alone, without any preparatory training, is sufficient to make a man forget to be his customary self and become, for the time being, something quite different. Thus the most unlikely people will, under the influence of disaster, temporarily turn into heroes, martyrs, selfless labourers for the good of their fellows. Very often, too, the proximity of death produces similar results.

— Aldous Huxley,
The Perennial Philosophy

CONTENTS

PROLOGUE

The Disorienting Dilemma

My life closed twice before its close;
It yet remains to see
If Immortality unveil
A third event to me,

So huge, so hopeless to conceive
As these that twice befell.
Parting is all we know of heaven,
And all we need of hell.

— Emily Dickinson

Has your life ever been turned completely upside down?

Has your world ever been blown up by the unforeseen events of a single day—or perhaps through a slow, grinding ordeal of weeks and months? I wonder if you have ever sat stunned—as I have—staring at the wall for days on end, pondering how you can possibly put your life back together after a devastating event? Pondering, perhaps, if you can even go on?

Emily Dickinson's life, apparently, was blown up at least twice. "My life closed twice before its close," she wrote, midway through her difficult life journey. Scholars disagree about which events she was referring to in her now famous poem, but it seems likely that they were the untimely death of her best friend and the loss of a romantic love attachment.

My own life has been blown up three times. So far. Once through a difficult divorce. Once when my best friend died suddenly and tragically smack in the middle of his youth. And once when I encountered a three-year-long career nightmare that forced me to radically rewire my life.

Psychologists now call these world-rattling events "disorienting dilemmas." What a great phrase. A disorienting dilemma is an event that so turns your life upside down that all you can do for a while is sit and stare at the wall. "So huge, so hopeless to conceive," wrote Emily after one of her "events." The world is a different place than you had thought. You are stunned into inaction. You sit in shattered amazement: "I had no idea this could happen to me."

By one account:

> A "disorienting dilemma" usually occurs when people have experiences that do not fit their expectations or make sense to them and they cannot resolve the situations without some change in their view of the world.

Yes, that's it: some change in our very conception of the world is required.

Or by another account:

> A disorienting dilemma is an experience within which a current understanding is found to be insufficient or incorrect and the learner struggles with the resulting conflict of views. This dilemma is also sometimes descriptively referred to as creating a state of "disequilibrium" for the learner.

A wife comes down the stairs in the morning and announces—seemingly out of the clear blue—that she wants a divorce. Do you suppose her husband will be disoriented for a while? How will he make sense of this?

A baby falls into the pool and drowns. A beautiful, intelligent nineteen-year-old boy "with everything to live for" dies in an urban alley of a heroin overdose. A young woman arrives home from the doctor ashen-faced: she will almost certainly die of cancer within months.

We hear these tales all the time, of course. Sometimes we hear them told by a storyteller who is still haunted and dazed. They often start in exactly the same way: "I didn't see it coming at all." The storyteller looks off into the far distance as if in a trance. "It was a perfectly normal day when the two army men knocked on the door, with a telegram in their hands."

And then, inevitably, as the narrative proceeds, comes some version of this: "We were completely numb for a while. We just put one foot in front of another."

When the great American philosopher Ralph Waldo Emerson's first wife died suddenly on February 8, 1831—only fourteen months into their marriage—he felt disoriented for a long time. He struggled to come to terms with death. How *could* she be gone? Where, indeed, *had* she gone? One evening he walked from the then small city of Boston to the neighboring town of Roxbury, where his dead wife lay entombed. In a moment of desperation, he pried open the door of her mausoleum and lifted the lid of the coffin itself. He stared at the remains. He needed to see her body. Was she really dead? And what, exactly, did death look like?

There it is. The disorienting dilemma.

Sometimes we suffer these catastrophic blows as part of our society itself, don't we? The African American man is brutally murdered by a police officer in broad daylight as terrified bystanders film the tragedy. Can this really be happening in America? Oh, yeah. And worse.

A pandemic grips the world. The economy collapses, and the social order is in chaos. The world is sunk into depression, and our family loses the little money we've managed to save. No one has a job. We garden in the backyard to grow tomatoes and squash. We wait, aghast, in food lines.

During these times, we struggle to make meaning. We ask: How could this happen to me? To us? How can the world be this unfair? Why did God allow this chaos, this tragedy?

How does any of us make sense of a world turned upside down? Well, how you make sense of it depends upon who you are, I suppose. Christians may read the Book of Job—the Bible's handbook for disorienting dilemmas. The Book of Job raises what is called, in scholarly circles, "the theodicy problem." Simply put, the theodicy problem is this: Is God just? And if God is, in fact, "just," then how exactly do we explain human suffering? How can a just God allow an innocent child to die? How can She allow whole races of people to be oppressed?

Jews read the Book of Job as well, by the way, when they are wrestling with the disorienting dilemma—though I must say that Jews are by and large much better at speaking back to God than my own Protestant crew is. God, you screwed up. Jews at the Auschwitz concentration camp during the Second World War established a court in the prisoners' barracks and put God on trial. He was found guilty of high crimes.

Hindus read the Katha Upanishad—a stunning dialogue narrated by Death herself. "Death," in this ancient text, turns out to be quite wise. She actually comes up with some pretty compelling answers.

2

Here's an interesting fact: it turns out that no great spiritual hero has avoided a confrontation with a disorienting dilemma. Indeed, most great spiritual writing begins with our hero or heroine laid low precisely by some such conundrum. Have you noticed? Job, of course, has been heaped with suffering by a God who turns out to be playing games with him. (It's shocking when one really understands how God has toyed with Job.) Old Testament Abraham is commanded to sacrifice his only son. The Buddha was continually tempted by Mara—the evil, ill-willed one. The gentle St. Thérèse of Lisieux had her mean-spirited co-religionists. Mother Teresa of Calcutta had her terrifying periods of spiritual aridity. And so on.

In every instance, of course, the confrontation with difficulty forces the emerging spiritual adept to dig more deeply into her spiritual quiver. To look more closely at the whole mess. What does it all mean? What *are* the laws of God—precisely? Can I jerry-rig my view of reality to include even this world-shattering event? Is there any true order in the Universe?

These questions can preoccupy us for a very long time. Disorienting dilemmas can undo us for years. One of my own three dilemmas—divorce—took ten years to resolve in my heart, mind, and soul. (My many divorced friends say the same thing.) I know people who have never recovered. After her husband left her for another woman, my great-aunt Beatrice closed the blue velvet drapes of every window in her house and never reopened them again during the rest of her long life.

But here is the fascinating part: it is precisely in confronting the most disastrous disorienting dilemma that our classic spiritual hero finds God. This hero—this Job, this Mother Teresa, this Buddha, this Muhammed—learns to turn the wound itself into effulgent light. Really? These spiritual heroes, not *in spite of*, but *as a result of* the successful negotiation of their plight, reach the highest possibility of the human condition.

3

A few paragraphs back, I asked if you'd ever been caught up in a dilemma that rattled your world.

I think I already know the answer to that question, since you are, presumably, a human being, and therefore have lived through the recent pandemic, social upheaval, and political chaos in America, as I have. (And by the way, aren't we all living with global warming? If that doesn't qualify as a disorienting dilemma, I don't know what does.)

If you think about it, too, you will realize that from time to time *entire countries* encounter their own particular disorienting dilemmas. Countries sometimes encounter conflicts that go to the very heart of their existence as a political and social entity. The Roman Empire, for example, went through a disorienting dilemma as its citizens struggled with the conflict between their republican institutions and the false enticements of demagoguery. Which would it be?

And here's one closer to home. Since its birth, our very own United States of America has lived with a disorienting dilemma, hasn't it? On the one hand, our founding documents declare, stirringly, that "all men are created equal." And at the same time, this very freshly born government accepted and institutionalized human slavery. All men are created equal? Truly? Then how can slavery be acceptable within the borders of such a country?

It is said that there are three kinds of dilemmas: dilemmas that are like lines drawn in water ("Should I buy the organic apples or the regular ones?"); dilemmas that are like lines drawn in sand ("Should I keep this job or risk taking that new one?"); and dilemmas that are like lines etched in rock ("Can democracy survive an apparently robust hunger for autocracy in our current-day America?").

The problem of slavery and its ghastly consequences have been for America like a dilemma etched in rock. Everywhere you turn, there it is. It has stained our life as a country from the very beginning. It has been denied, fought over, pushed underground, tolerated. But we should learn from Rome. Rome discovered: unless you resolve a dilemma like this, it will destroy you.

As always, there is some good news too. For the United States, for example, there is this: since our founding, the Original Sin of slavery has been seen for what it is by a small cadre of people and has called forth from them some of the highest and best of human instincts. You will read about eight of these exemplars in this book.

4

Now here is another interesting fact: if you look closely at your history books, you will see that dilemmas-etched-in-rock are quite common in societies throughout human history. And since this is so obviously the case, where are the treatises about precisely how to deal with these dilemmas? What have we learned—as a species—about these challenges to our well-being? There must be libraries full of such tomes, right? Unfortunately, no.

Luckily for us, there *is* one treatise that tackles this very problem head-on. It's an ancient treatise, yes, but still remarkably relevant. It is a brilliant examination of how human beings might behave in the midst of an apocalyptic disorienting dilemma. It was written somewhere on the subcontinent of India about 2,300 years ago. It's a scripture called the Bhagavad Gita, or the Song of God, and it turns out to be one of the world's greatest tales of conflict, disorientation, recovery, and transformation.

5

Have you read the Bhagavad Gita, I wonder?

The Bhagavad Gita—or just "the Gita," as it is fondly called in India—is the story of a young warrior named Arjuna who is confronted by an earth-shattering dilemma. His own country, the kingdom of Kuru, is riven by a conflict between a ruling family who governs with fairness, wisdom, and equity, and a competing family who aspires to rule by fear, selfishness, and greed. As the story opens, this conflict has come to a head and war threatens to destroy the kingdom. Our young friend Arjuna finds himself at the very center of this war—a fateful war, says the Gita, that is predicted to "tear the fabric of the Universe."

Our hero, Arjuna, is terrified, and completely undone by the dilemma that confronts him. The heart of his dilemma is this: he is not sure what his *duty* is in the face of his disintegrating world. Is it his duty to fight in this upcoming battle? Or should he walk away and find another way to contribute? In the midst of his country's fierce struggle, he is caught on the horns of his own personal dilemma. To fight, or not to fight?

Have you ever been paralyzed in the face of an impossible life dilemma? Torn? Split in half? Then you know what Arjuna is experiencing.

On the night before the great battle, Arjuna and his best friend and charioteer, Krishna, sit side by side at the edge of the battlefield. They talk through the entire night. Luckily for Arjuna, his wise charioteer—whom we later find out is a human incarnation of God—knows how to help him regain the balance of his mind and to think clearly about his existential tangle. The wise Krishna shows Arjuna how to expand his perspective until his view of the dilemma itself is transformed. And over the course of eighteen short chapters, Krishna guides our confused friend through a conversation about major life decisions—an immortal dialogue that has already enlightened generations of wobbly human beings.

The dialogue recounted in this ancient treatise has been known by almost every Indian villager for the last two thousand years. And since its translation into English in the latter part of the 18th century, it is also now well known and loved in the West. The Gita was one of the first books Henry David Thoreau took with him to Walden Pond. Thoreau, who himself faced several major dilemmas in his life, tells us that the Gita was the closest thing to a Bible he ever had. Mahatma Gandhi was never without his own frayed copy, and he consulted it at every crossroads in his life—very often when he was locked up in a British jail for months on end. British women's rights activist Annie Besant used its teachings as the very basis of her work. The American astronaut Sunita Williams carried her copy with her to the International Space Station. Some of us today, having perhaps studied the Gita in school or heard about it from a friend, dig into it when we're in emotional extremis.

6

What exactly does Krishna teach to our friend Arjuna? Well, Krishna hangs his entire guidance on an ancient Indian concept known as "dharma."

Dharma is a Sanskrit word that has many layers of meaning. In ancient Hindu and Buddhist texts, the word often means "path," or "truth," or "law," or "teaching." In this particular treatise, however—in the Bhagavad Gita—the word *dharma* always means "sacred duty," or "true calling."

Krishna's view is that we each have a sacred duty in this life. No exceptions. And he teaches that in every moment of our lives, no matter how difficult, there lies buried deep within our souls a *knowledge* of this duty—a mystic knowledge.

You have a dharma too, you know. You have a sacred duty that you cannot escape, as much as you might like to. When the Old Testament prophets were confronted by their God—by Yaweh—with their particular sacred duty, they often took the first boat out of town. Like, for example, the prophet Jonah. *No! I don't want to do it! Not that! Please God, don't ask me to do that!* Of course, Jonah was swallowed by a whale, wasn't he, and was returned to the vocation that was calling out to him. Can't escape it! On the other hand, some of these Old Testament prophets relished "the call." They already had a deep inner knowing about who they were supposed to be in this lifetime.

Where do you fall on this spectrum? Do you know what your dharma is on this earth—and especially in this difficult and conflicted time of ours? Do you know why you were put here and set here in this time and place, and in this particular body? Well, you need to find out. Because if you do not, it will be pretty much impossible for you to find your way through the inevitable maze of disorienting dilemmas life has in store for you. If you do not know who you are, how can you possibly decide what actions to take in this life? Why do you get up in the morning?

The ancient authors of the Bhagavad Gita intentionally make Arjuna a colorful, flawed, and neurotic character. Why? Because that makes him just like us. So, in hearing the fantastic tale of the Gita, we are fated to identify with him. Arjuna, of course, does not understand his dharma at all as the story opens. He doesn't know who he is. He doesn't understand his true nature. And as a result he cannot make wise choices about how to proceed. The guy is a mess.

As it turns out, though, Arjuna can become a great model for us because he (even he!) *does* eventually work his way slowly through his own dilemmas. Over the course of the eighteen brief but intense chapters, we watch as Arjuna—with Krishna's help—transforms his own disorienting dilemma into a transcendent experience of awakening. Krishna lays out a clear path for the troubled warrior. And perhaps for us. We would do well—like those millions of Indian villagers—to have this story tucked into our back pocket, just in case life knocks us off our blocks.

7

For many years, I have been the Scholar in Residence at Kripalu Center for Yoga and Health—the largest yoga center in America. Here, high up in the Berkshire Hills of western Massachusetts, our staff of almost 500 ministers to 50,000 retreatants a year. We teach yoga and meditation retreats, of course, and personal growth workshops of all kinds. But most of our guests are, in fact, coming to our safe haven to investigate their own disorienting dilemmas. Kripalu, for this reason, is a kind of great pilgrimage center, like Lourdes—Lourdes for a new age. (Unlike Lourdes, very few people leave their crutches here at Kripalu.) We host pilgrims of every conceivable religion and spiritual tradition: Christians, Jews, Muslims, Sufis. They all come eventually. Because if you're wrestling with a disorienting dilemma, you must be persistent. You must check out every lead. Run every ground ball to the fence.

For twenty years now, I have been teaching the wisdom of the Bhagavad Gita—the story of Krishna and Arjuna—to rooms full of these pilgrims at Kripalu. These are mostly Westerners who have come into contact with the wisdom of the Gita for the first time, but who are intrigued to find a two-thousand-year-old treatise that speaks so vividly to our difficult times.

By and large, these students are grateful to soak in Krishna's wisdom. As a follow-up to our weeks or months together, they often send me postcards and e-mails from around the globe to explain to me how they are, in fact, living the path of dharma taught by Krishna, and how well things are working out for them—or not.

Several years ago, I wrote a book on dharma—titled *The Great Work of Your Life*. In that particular book, I lay out the Four Pillars of Dharma in quite a bit of detail. And of all my books, this book on the Gita seems to have become the most popular. Krishna's wisdom seems to help quite a bit.

8

But now comes a new time. As I write this, the world has been turned upside down even more than usual. The entire globe is caught up in a series of common disorienting dilemmas.

This is not the placid, scholarly middle age I had expected to live through. No. We live in a world saturated with loss, change, struggle, and doubt. So, in recent months, I have turned back to my well-worn copy of the Bhagavad Gita. And I've found, of course, that there is, embedded in this ancient text, a prescient strategy for transforming our individual and collective disorienting dilemmas into a kind of doorway into an expanded life. The Gita speaks directly, immediately, to our time. It is a distant mirror into which we might now look.

And so I offer up this new book, *The Dharma in Difficult Times*, in order to bring the distant mirror of the Gita into today's struggles—both personal and societal. I will focus on the four simple facets of Krishna's teaching that speak directly to our time. We might almost call the book "Krishna's Four Lessons for Tough Times."

1. First, says Krishna, "Take refuge in me." In other words: take refuge in God. Take refuge in your highest spiritual resources. This is where we begin. All disorienting dilemmas are really spiritual crises.
2. Then, teaches Krishna, look carefully through the chaos of an upside-down world for the hidden signs of dharma. These will often be obscure in difficult times, but they are surely there, hiding in plain sight. Signs and omens and hunches point the way. Your work is set out in front of you.
3. Next, having homed in on your precise sacred calling, see how—almost miraculously—when you trust in your dharma, your own highest fulfillment and the common good arise together. It turns out, teaches Krishna, that the thriving of the self and the thriving of the whole people are inextricably linked.
4. Fourth, understand that when you fully surrender to your dharma, you are "not the Doer." The Divine spirit moves and acts through you and guides you with a consciousness you alone could never possess.

9

In every age and time there are women and men who have discovered Krishna's principles. In this book, I have chosen to tell the stories of a handful of inspiring human beings who have turned to the principles of the Gita precisely because they were in the midst of some disorienting dilemma. Some of these folks you will know: Mohandas Gandhi, Sojourner Truth, Marian Anderson, Henry David

Thoreau, Harriet Beecher Stowe. Others you may not know: Ruby Sales, Charles Russell Lowell, Jonathan Daniels.

You will probably notice right away that this book has a subtext. In order to keep our investigation in sharp focus, I have chosen to examine the Gita's wisdom in the light of America's most persistent disorienting dilemma: American chattel slavery and its ongoing ghastly consequences. This is fitting, for it turns out that there is no book of wisdom that has been more influential in healing racism and xenophobia worldwide than the Bhagavad Gita. In America, this influence began with Henry David Thoreau's reading of the Gita at Walden Pond in the 1840s, and his subsequent writing of the great essay "Civil Disobedience." From there its influence moved in a straight line to Mahatma Gandhi's work in South Africa and India in the late 19th and early 20th century, and then to the inspiring work of Annie Besant for women's rights and for Indian and Irish home rule. From Thoreau, Gandhi, and Besant, the power of the Gita exploded into the work of Dr. Martin Luther King Jr. and his many followers. The Bhagavad Gita has provided a narrative for understanding and healing the hate, racism, and xenophobia that has so torn our world apart in the 20th and 21st centuries.

Henry David Thoreau said that we only connect with the Divine through the particular—that is, through the real and idiosyncratic lives of people struggling right here on planet Earth. I have chosen eight stories of real human struggle and transformation sparked by the Gita and its tenets. I hope that these stories will inspire you, as they have me. I have found that in each case the stories I chronicle here point the way through the maze of loss, change, struggle, and doubt by following the principles of transformation laid out in the ageless Bhagavad Gita.

LESSON ONE

TAKE REFUGE

"I see only disaster here, dear friend," says Arjuna. He walks nervously back and forth beside the chariot, which is now parked at the edge of the battlefield. His horse paws the ground and whinnies.

"How can this possibly end well?" says Arjuna. "You know this is true, Krishna: even if we win, we will lose." Arjuna brings his hand up to his forehead, massaging his furrowed brow for a moment.

Arjuna and his friend and mentor, Krishna, are having a conversation at the side of the great plain of Kuru. For a moment, they stand together in the sunset, surveying the field where the battle will take place the next morning at first light.

The plain of Kuru is dusty and dry. The soil is a reddish brown. As the sun sinks into the horizon, the red hues in the field begin to glow. The evening is clear and cool, and a light breeze disturbs the broad leaves of a nearby grove of neem trees. The two friends can see the campfires of the opposing army gleaming in the twilight just a mile away.

Both Arjuna and Krishna have heard the predictions of the Soothsayers, who have said that this coming battle will "tear the fabric of the Universe." The battle itself will usher in a Dark Age: the Kali Yuga. Civilization itself is threatened.

Krishna, the charioteer, has driven the chariot up to the edge of the field so the two friends can ponder what is to come. They have brought food and water with them, and wood for a fire. They will talk through the night about the meaning of the battle ahead.

Arjuna is a mere twenty years of age, and though he is known to be the most skillful archer in the kingdom, he has not yet really experienced a battle such as this. He is dark-skinned, handsome—with only the wisps of a beard yet showing. His black hair is piled high on his head, and he wears the gold-embossed leather wristbands that denote his royal lineage—the lineage of the Pandava family. Arjuna is not only a skilled archer, he is a prince, and much loved by the people of the kingdom.

Arjuna's dark eyes dart back and forth across the field. He knows that arrayed against him on the other side of the battle will be his own cousins, friends, and peers. He is pretty sure, too, that one of his greatest archery mentors is there.

Krishna takes a step toward Arjuna and puts his hand reassuringly on his friend's shoulder, but says nothing. Krishna is a much older man, although his exact age is something of a mystery to everyone. He is full foot taller than Arjuna. He is a commanding presence. In the twilight his fair skin looks almost blue. He is also adorned with the insignia of the Pandavas, who employ him to mentor their son, Arjuna. He wears a leather chestplate with the Pandava crest embossed in gold. As Krishna tightens his grip on Arjuna's shoulder, he can feel that Arjuna's entire body is shaking, and that he's breathing heavily.

Finally, Arjuna turns full on toward Krishna: "Krishna, the world is falling apart. This is a battle like no other in history. I feel totally lost. I'm not sure what my duty is. Is this really my battle to fight? Must I really wage war against my own kin? I simply do not understand. I'm damned to Purgatory if I do fight, and damned if I do not."

Krishna bows his head for a moment. He does not answer. He knows that Arjuna is undone. But he knows, too, that his friend is undone not by fear of injury and death so much as he is by the massive *moral dilemma* that now confronts him. Arjuna knows that arrayed against him in the morning will be many of his own kin. He knows, too—excellent marksman that he is—that if he brings his whole self to the battle, as he must, he will likely kill many of his own people. For this sin, he will die many inward deaths. He will spend eons in Purgatory. On the other hand, if he shirks his true calling as a warrior, he will likewise suffer dire consequences: humiliation, ostracism from society, and, yes, again, Purgatory.

"Even if we win, we will lose," Arjuna mutters again, as if to himself.

Arjuna has come to the most important crossroads in his young life. And he is stuck. He confronts a dilemma that seems to have no good answer. And yet he must make a decision—and quickly. Finally, Arjuna's emotions rise up. He can no longer contain the conflict within. Arjuna drops to his knees in front of Krishna, and cries out:

My will is paralyzed, and I am utterly confused. Tell me which is the better path for me. Let me be your disciple. I have fallen at your feet; give me instruction. (Gita 2:7–8)

2

Let me be your disciple?

How is it that young Arjuna, the very prince of the kingdom, is asking to surrender himself to his own charioteer?

Who is this man to whom the prince of the kingdom kneels? Well, of course, Arjuna does not know it yet, but Krishna is an avatar of God. Krishna is an avatar—an earthly and fleshly emanation—of Lord Vishnu, one of the three most important gods of ancient India. What Arjuna *does* know for sure, however, is that Krishna is his most trusted companion and aide. He knows that he has always been able to rely on Krishna's wisdom and love and strength. Indeed, over the ten years they have been together, Krishna has become his most beloved friend.

In the very first chapter of the Bhagavad Gita, we find our very human hero, Arjuna, engulfed by sorrow and depression. And finally, at the end of Chapter 1, as emotions overwhelm him, Arjuna succumbs to the inner disorganization that comes with his awful dilemma. He falls to the floor of his chariot and calls out to Krishna.

Conflicting sacred duties confound my mind . . . I cannot fight this fight! (Gita 2:7, 2:9)

3

Krishna takes Arjuna fully into his arms now, and holds him for a long moment.

When Krishna speaks, his voice is deep, calm, and soothing. "Arjuna, my dearest boy. Take refuge in me. Take refuge in my love for you. Take refuge in my wisdom. Hide yourself for a while in the shadow of my abiding care."

Then Krishna whispers into his ear an instruction that Arjuna does not at first understand. The whispered guidance is a harbinger of things to come—a foreshadowing of the great secret Krishna will eventually share with his friend.

Fill your mind with me; love me; serve me; worship me always. Seeking me in your heart, you will at last be united with me. (Gita 9:34)

This is Krishna's instruction: "Take refuge in me." And he will repeat it over and over again. Indeed, "Take refuge in me" is perhaps the most oft-repeated advice that Krishna gives to Arjuna throughout the text of the Gita.

Arjuna allows himself to be held for a moment in Krishna's strong arms. He allows his belly to relax. He allows himself to trust his friend.

"Take refuge in me!" What, precisely, does Krishna's instruction mean? Who or what is this God who Krishna seems to represent? And how will finding safe harbor in God help Arjuna resolve his great dilemma?

This will be our inquiry in Lesson One.

CHAPTER 1

MOHANDAS K. GANDHI I

First, Take Refuge

Drop Thy still dews of quietness,
till all our strivings cease;
take from our souls the strain and stress,
and let our ordered lives confess
the beauty of Thy peace.

— One of the Christian hymns sung at Gandhi's ashram (Words by John Greenleaf Whittier)

In January of 1915, a large throng of well-wishers gathered on the teeming docks in the port city of Mumbai, India. The air was electric. What was happening? Who was arriving? The crowd had assembled at the magisterial "Gateway of India," built years earlier to welcome England's King George V. But on this day in 1915, it was not the King this crowd was here to welcome. Rather, all of the excitement was for a small Indian barrister who was just returning from South Africa, where—far from his homeland—he had become one of India's most distinguished sons. The crowd was awaiting the arrival of Mohandas K. Gandhi.

Before Mr. Gandhi disembarked, he was met onboard by a deputation of some of India's most prominent royalty and political leaders, who were decked out in their glittering jewels and finest regalia. The group garlanded Gandhi with flowers and escorted him to the gangplank. And, as the little barrister became visible in the hot Indian sun for the first time, the crowd roared its approval.

One young fan remembers the moment she first set eyes on Mr. Gandhi:

> I caught a glimpse of him in the midst of silks and brocades, frills and sparkling jewels. He was dressed in a coarse *khadi dhoti* and looked like a small-town tailor who had wandered in by mistake. I lost my heart to him. He became my father, my mother, my girlfriend, my boyfriend, my daughter, my son, my teacher, my guru.

As it turned out, this young woman spoke for much of India.

2

Mohandas Gandhi had been away from his homeland—from India—for almost twenty years, living and working as a barrister among the subjugated Indian population of South Africa. There, he had become well known and loved for his nonviolent approach to resisting South Africa's deeply entrenched racism and the horrors of colonial oppression. The name on his passport read, simply, Mohandas K. Gandhi. But, already foreseeing great things for him upon his return to India, the peninsula's greatest poet, Rabindranath Tagore, had renamed him. Henceforth, he would be *Mahatma* Gandhi. (Mahatma, or *maha atma*, is Sanskrit for "great soul.")

Could this man live up to such a title? Many people thought that he could. Indeed, some of Gandhi's fellow Indians had great plans for him. He was known among India's political class for having brought a remarkable new sense of empowerment to the Indian community in South Africa—and for lighting a spark that led to serious reforms there. It was expected, now that he was home, that he might do the same in India. Jawaharlal Nehru, the head of the influential Indian

National Congress (INC) party, and a host of other political operatives, implored him to get to work, to take up the fight in India, to start organizing the masses for what must be India's eventual liberation from three hundred years of colonial occupation by the British.

But Mr. Gandhi had other plans.

Gandhi, the expatriate, was now desperate to reacquaint himself with his homeland. He longed to plunge himself into what he remembered as the greatness of Mother India. To bathe in Her soul. And he wanted to see the country as the poorest of Indians would see it. So he traveled. By train. Third class. Without pretense. For seven months, Gandhi traveled the length and breadth of India—rumbling along the tracks of the impressive rail infrastructure created by the British Raj. Stopping for a day or two in a village. Staying with a local family. For the most part, he traveled in packed, sweltering, and filthy railway cars. Or in animal-drawn carts. Sometimes, indeed, he traveled on foot. His evening accommodations—when he took them—were routinely stinking, sweltering, chaotic.

3

If you had been traveling on a crowded third-class railway coach almost anywhere in India in 1915, you might well, without knowing it, have sat next to this Mr. Gandhi. He must have been a curious sight. He was a small man, with a unique set of features that we know so well from the many sepia-toned photos we've seen: the small head and the large, protruding ears; those big, questioning eyes; the ever-present round and oversized spectacles. In 1915, as he traveled, Gandhi would have been wearing a clean, white *dhoti*—loose, flowing wraparound pants; a starched *kurta*—a traditional three-quarter-length collarless tunic; and a white turban. There would have been an unfalteringly polite, calm, and refined air about him: self-contained; at ease with himself; clearly someone special. *What is this obviously highly educated and cultured little man doing traveling in the squalor of third class?* his fellow passengers must have wondered.

Gandhi was looking. Feeling. Touching India. He was talking with Her natives, his countrymen. He was drinking it all in. He was home, finally.

4

We now know that Gandhi was devastated by what he saw in his seven months of travel across the length and breadth of India. It was well beyond his worst fears. His twenty-year-long experience in South Africa had already opened his eyes to the suffering of a colonial underclass. Now, in the land of his birth, he saw a downtrodden, desperately poor country. Most of India's almost 300 million citizens were at that time involved in some form of subsistence agriculture. The majority were dirt poor, and many were hungry much of the time. Most could not read or write.

As he traveled, Gandhi became increasingly upset, and he alternated between despair and anger. What enraged him most, according to his own account, was not just the poverty but the lethargy and despair that he encountered everywhere. He felt deeply the plight of a colonized people, many of whom had given up—had completely surrendered to increasingly heavy-handed British rule. Had his people forgotten the spiritual genius of their ancient culture? Everywhere he went, Gandhi found a lack of self-esteem, of basic cleanliness, of pride of workmanship, and of place. He found a people sunk into a sense of helplessness. This is what colonialism does to the colonized, of course. It engenders a lack of self-respect. A lack of what we would today call "agency." A lack of empowerment.

Gandhi was seeing his once noble—and once spiritually refined—culture in ruins. It's hard to overstate how shattered he was by the sight. Disgusted. Repelled. Sorrowful. Horrified.

5

Upon his return from seven months of traveling, still seething and deeply upset, Gandhi gave a blistering speech in February 1916 at the opening of the Hindu University Central College in Banaras. It must have been an unforgettable scene. The viceroy of India was there, in all his vice-regal splendor, and so were dozens of bejeweled maharajas, maharanis, Indian princes and princesses and high officials—all in their dazzling tribal dress, with mountains of jewels. Here were some of the same dignitaries who had welcomed Gandhi home just seven months earlier.

The mood was celebratory as the crowd gathered. A number of the most important attendees sat on the dais behind the speaker's platform. There was a good deal of preening going on at the head of the room. And then the diminutive figure of Gandhi appeared, dressed in the clothes of a peasant. He walked solemnly through the audience and ascended the podium.

The well-bedecked crowd of dignitaries did not have a clue what they were in for. This Gandhi—this little tiger—was seriously pissed off. He spoke without notes, and with unexpected flashes of anger. He described his trip across India: What he had seen. The lack of self-esteem. The spiritual torpor. The filth. Nothing enraged him more than the filth, by the way, which he saw as an outward and visible sign of spiritual decay.

"We spit anywhere on the carriage floor," he exclaimed to the assembly, "irrespective of the thought that it is often used as sleeping space. We do not trouble ourselves as to how we use it; the result is indescribable filth in the compartment."

Gandhi described his visit to a once glorious but now degraded temple: the Vishwanath Temple in Banaras. "If a stranger dropped from above onto this great temple," said Gandhi with outrage, "and he had to consider what we as Hindus were, would he not be justified in condemning us? Is not this great temple a reflection of our own character?"

He railed against the bejeweled maharajas, who stood in shock as this force of nature spoke directly to them, as if to shake them to the core: "There is no salvation for India unless you strip yourselves of this jewelry and hold it in trust for your countrymen in India," he shouted. No salvation for Mother India! "That wealth you wear around your neck came from our farmers!" He railed against the British Raj—also in attendance—whom he described directly to their faces as "overbearing, tyrannical and thoughtless." And, most shockingly to some, he deplored his own countrymen, the many Indians who had become "unbearably sycophantic" around their British masters.

Slowly, most of the proud dignitaries put their heads down and exited the stage, creeping away in shame or embarrassment. Finally, Mrs. Annie Besant, the well-known British aristocrat-turned-Theosophist and founder of the Hindu University Central College, had to abruptly adjourn the meeting. It ended with a whimper, not a bang.

After the talk, Gandhi remained angry. And profoundly saddened. In his autobiography, he reports feeling overwhelmed by all of this. Mohandas K. Gandhi was now encountering the most profoundly disorienting dilemma of his life. He had seen firsthand the magnitude of India's problems. He had felt it personally. He wondered: What could his duty—his dharma—possibly be in this clearly impossible situation? How can one person make even a dent in a situation of this scale? How could he apply all that he had learned in the much smaller field of South Africa to this drastically more complex set of circumstances? His head spun. The suffering of India had blown apart any preconceived notions he had about how he might proceed with his dharma of civil disobedience and nonviolent change that had been so successful in South Africa.

6

As Mohandas Gandhi faced the greatest dilemma of his life—the liberation of Mother India from its many shackles—he turned to his frayed copy of the Bhagavad Gita. While working in South Africa, Gandhi had become profoundly devoted to the Gita. He carried his much-annotated copy with him everywhere (especially to jail, where he spent many months during his campaigns of civil disobedience) and consulted it on any occasion—but particularly when he was overcome with doubt and division. And now he found that he identified over and over again with Arjuna's dilemma: Was he called to fight this particular fight? And if so, how in the world could he do it?

Gandhi referred to the Gita as his "spiritual reference book." As his longtime secretary, Mahadev Desai, would write later, "Every moment of Gandhi's life is a conscious effort to live the message of the Gita." Throughout his life, Gandhi repeated this sentiment to friends and students: "If you want to see how a life appears when lived according to the principles of the Gita, look to my life."

So, of course, at this particular crossroads of his life, Gandhi dove into his spiritual reference book. He found himself focusing on one passage in particular: Krishna's teaching about anger. Krishna is crystal clear on this point. He teaches Arjuna:

> *Anger clouds the judgment: you can no longer learn from past mistakes. Lost is the power to choose between what is wise and what is unwise, and your life is utter waste. (Gita 2:63–64)*

Lost is the power to choose between what is wise and what is unwise. *Lost is the power of discernment.*

In this passage and in many other similar passages throughout the text of the Gita, Krishna teaches Arjuna that "anger disturbs the mind" so that one cannot hear the still small voice of wisdom within. Gandhi really had to wrestle with this issue. He is well known to have had a mammoth temper. On the one hand, he understood that his anger had some good qualities. It brought him a certain kind of energy. It drew clear lines. It created power. And he did not want to blunt this power. But Gandhi—taught by the Gita—also learned that anger is like a forest fire that burns up its own fuel, and that eventually destroys its host. And he realized that if he based his liberation work on anger and ill will, he could not be successful. Rather, he would himself be immolated by the anger and would thereby violate every principle he held dear. Indeed, a central principle of his work in South Africa had been that it was conducted *without hatred of any kind.* Without malice.

7

Gandhi, in the critical weeks after his arrival home from his seven-month-long journey, was Arjuna on the edge of the battlefield. He pondered the battle to come. Like Arjuna, his "knees shook, and hair stood on end." And, like Arjuna, a part of him wanted to run from the fight.

Gandhi's friends and associates urged him to get to work immediately. "Channel your anger and disappointment into action," Nehru counseled him. Nehru and others talked of a national strike. Of a massive campaign of civil disobedience. They implored him to attack the British colonial establishment with all the force he had used in South Africa.

But Gandhi knew that he would have to resolve his seething ill will and anger before he could take any action. He knew he would have to regain the balance of his mind, because he realized that the highest powers of his mind and soul would be required in the coming battle.

And what, indeed, did Gandhi do?

He shocked his peers and supporters. The Mahatma went into retreat.

8

Instead of diving into the political maelstrom, the Great Soul—to the dismay of the political class—spent most of his time creating and organizing a spiritual community. He called it an "ashram," a kind of classic Hindu spiritual monastery (though as we shall see, it was by no means typical). Gandhi's new spiritual community would be called Sabarmati Ashram, and it would become the base from which he would operate for the rest of his life. Indeed, it would become the chrysalis out of which the new Gandhi would eventually emerge. I say "the new Gandhi" because he understood, after his seven months on the road, that a transformed Gandhi would indeed be required in order to take up the sacrificial calling he foresaw for himself.

Gandhi believed that when facing a trial of this magnitude, you must gather around you all the resources of your spiritual tradition—and indeed, of any other spiritual traditions that might provide sustenance. He implored his followers: Bathe in spiritual experience, in spirituality of the highest sort. Feed the soul. Remember Krishna's exhortation: "Fill your mind with me; love me; serve me; worship me always. Seeking me in your heart, you will at last be united with me."

It must be said at the very outset that in regard to spiritual practice, Gandhi was profoundly pluralistic. He looked for spiritual power and wisdom wherever he could find it. He believed in communal prayer, in fasting, chanting, hymn-sings, sermonizing, and worship. He was devoted not only to the scriptures of his native Hinduism—especially, of course, the Bhagavad Gita—but to many parts of the Christian Bible, especially the Sermon on the Mount and the Beatitudes. He was devoted, too, to the spiritual and political writing of Leo Tolstoy—an ardent advocate of pacifism and nonviolent resistance to oppression. In the midst of his despair, Gandhi intentionally marinated himself in many of the world's wisdom traditions.

And by the way, retreat into spiritual community was not new for Gandhi. Indeed, throughout his adult life, he had insisted on creating and living within a spiritual community. In South Africa he had created two lasting spiritual communities: the Phoenix Settlement and Tolstoy Farm. Especially in times of difficulty, he sought out—and created—places of retreat, recollection, quiet. Most importantly, he believed that he *could only live his dharma fully if sustained by a group of other seekers, and by the wisdom of the ages.* He believed that his dharma would flow out of his immersion in these spiritual resources—much as Martin Luther King Jr., himself inspired by Gandhi, would later insist upon gathering around him, and, indeed, creating everywhere he went, what he called "the beloved community."

We learn from Gandhi's autobiography that he understood all too well the spiritual peril of his situation—and of India's moment. Gandhi was confronting a Gordian knot of such complexity that it was guaranteed to overwhelm the mind. The complexity of the task would tie an ordinary mortal mind up in knots. Gandhi believed that only God could solve a problem such as India. Therefore, he saw the disorienting dilemma as an opportunity for deep soul work: for surrender to the wisdom of God.

This is Gandhi's first lesson for us: When confronting the disorienting dilemma, see the moment as an opportunity to dive more deeply into your spiritual practice, your heritage, your deepest spiritual resources—into those resources you know, and perhaps those you do not yet know. Tune in to the hunger in your soul. Feel it. Feed it. Understand the dilemma itself to be a problem that must be solved in the soul, just as Krishna taught. The world—and your own ego—will try to entice you into immediate and impulsive action. Resist that urge. First, look inward.

9

A disorienting dilemma immediately presents the self with two major problems. We might call these "disturbance" and "disorganization."

First, the mind is "disturbed." The mind is upset. The yoga scriptures would say, "We have lost the balance of the mind." We have lost what the Eastern traditions call "equanimity." In yoga, the word for equanimity is *upeksha*—which might be roughly translated to mean "balance." Yogis say that the mind, in times of deep stress, is "heated up." Agitated. Uncalm. Disturbed. Certainly not at peace. And, as Krishna has taught in the Gita, when the mind is disturbed, it cannot see clearly—it cannot make wise choices. As Krishna said, in these moments we are "lacking the factor of discernment."

And the second major problem is this: when overtaken by the disorienting dilemma, the mind becomes "disorganized." The mind has lost its usual sense of organization. In fact, the human "self" is nothing other than a way of organizing our thoughts, feelings, sensations, actions—a way of organizing our sense of meaning and purpose. When this internal self-organization confronts a massive anomaly, it can leave us feeling unglued. The world has lost its order and meaning. There is a sense of the self falling apart.

After one of my own biggest disorienting dilemmas—the sudden and untimely death of my best friend when I was just thirty years old—I often felt like I was falling apart. And it scared me. Would I really come unglued? Could I go crazy? Was that a possibility? Depending on the extent of the trauma, this sense of falling apart can range from mild discomfort all the way to terror, existential angst, and annihilation anxiety—the most severe form of human anxiety.

So, when undone by a devastating dilemma, we desperately seek out environments and people who will help us to do two things: regain the *balance* of the mind, and *reorganize* ourselves internally.

10

The great Austrian psychoanalytic writer and teacher, Heinz Kohut, studied this state of "falling apart" in depth. He called it "fragmentation." In the face of the disorienting dilemma, "the stability of the self can be lost," he writes, "gradually or suddenly, and there may be rapid changes in function and manifestation, such as an altered sense of self, or a lost feeling of well-being. This can lead to the sense that the self is falling apart."

Just so. Under the sway of a devastating dilemma, one may have an alarming sense of coming undone. Think, perhaps, of the unfortunate pilot who has "lost the horizon"—his touchstone and lifeline. The horizon is the very core of the organization of his flying skills. Without the horizon, the pilot cannot tell what is up or what is down. This leads to an immediate sense of disorganization and panic. Have you ever pondered—as I have—the last moments of the life of John F. Kennedy Jr., who himself lost the horizon while piloting his small plane and crashed to his death? Have you tried to imagine what it must have felt like to him as he lost the horizon and felt his high-powered plane go entirely out of control? For several terrifying minutes, he would have felt himself soul-shakingly disoriented. And then, of course, he plunged into the sea. This is disorganization of the most disastrous kind.

This experience of disorganization and fragmentation can happen in whole societies, as I have said. A *culture itself* can lose the horizon—like the loss of social organization and meaning that happened to the Lakota Sioux tribe in 19th-century America when they were brutally displaced from their lands. Or the loss of the "horizon" in Irish society during the "great troubles" of the early 1900s. Irish bard William Butler Yeats, who understood the depth of this disorganization, wrote perhaps the classic poem about the disorganization of a society:

Turning and turning in the widening gyre
The falcon cannot hear the falconer;
Things fall apart; the centre cannot hold;
Mere anarchy is loosed upon the world,
The blood-dimmed tide is loosed, and everywhere
The ceremony of innocence is drowned;
The best lack all conviction, while the worst
Are full of passionate intensity.

Fragmentation—coming apart—is terrifying. We panic. We do anything we can to recapture the horizon. We do everything we can to find the ground again under our feet. We often find "the ground" in the great wisdom traditions of the world. Why? In part because they provide us with highly organized, internally cohesive, and non-fragmented views of reality. And then, with the calm that comes from an alignment with this deeply organized view, we become momentarily organized again. We *introject*—or take in—the deep sense of order and cohesion these traditions provide.

11

If you pay attention, you will notice that much of the great spiritual writing of the world's wisdom traditions begins with a hero or heroine who has fallen apart, as Arjuna has. In John Bunyan's spiritual classic, *Pilgrim's Progress*, for example, our protagonist—named Christian—finds himself at the outset of the tale in the "City of Destruction," surrounded by chaos and disorder. As he gradually reorders his life, he finally comes to the "Celestial City," where a deeper spiritual order reigns.

We can see why conversions to the spiritual life often happen at times of profound reorganization of the self: because these times offer both a peril and a possibility. The protagonist is broken open. And that means that he or she is *most available to learn something new.* And this is what the Gita points us toward: an opportunity for a possible reorganization of the mind around a higher, more complete, and more nuanced vision of reality.

Why did Gandhi flee to the ashram? Simple: to find a protected psychic space within which to heal. To calm down. To regain the balance of the mind. And also to reestablish the organization of the self. Or possibly to find a new and more effective self-organization. As you will see, a central theme of this book is *the reorganization of the self that often happens in the midst of difficulty*—the reorganization of the self around a higher, more cohesive, interiorly consistent view and way of life. And, of course, the reorganization of the social structure in the case of social breakdown.

In many cases—in the best of cases—this reorganization leads the self to a more mature state, which is manifested in *a higher degree of order and complexity.* Self-organization, when it matures, always moves us toward greater complexity. This internal organization is very like what is happening in the incubating egg. It is safe it its shell, and within that protected space it is continually reorganizing itself at a much higher level. More complexity means more life.

12

What, then, can we say about the particular qualities of the "protected psychic space" that the Sabarmati Ashram offered to Mr. Gandhi and his followers? Heinz Kohut and those of his peers who were interested in the experience of "fragmentation" developed helpful theories about the precise qualities of protected psychic space required for self-reorganization. Chief among Kohut's peers in this inquiry was the English psychoanalyst Donald Winnicott.

Dr. Winnicott taught us that *all human maturation* depends upon the special elements of this protected psychic space—and he really meant *all* human maturation, from our earliest development as infants all the way through our development into old age. How so? Well, as Winnicott points out, in the first instance, our earliest development proceeds within a kind of invisible, subtle "external womb" created by what Winnicott dubbed "the good enough parent." This good enough parent herself becomes a kind of container—a human eggshell, if you will—for the emotional, physical, and mental development of the child.

What happens in this protected psychic space? Something magical. In the presence of the parent, or the "containing other," the infant feels literally "held together" by the safe holding environment that surrounds her. The bits and pieces of her own inner experience are momentarily *unified* in this container. This holding facilitates a sense of *being whole.* And now a small miracle occurs: over time, the baby begins to feel—as a consequence of loving and handling and holding—that this body is *herself.* These very moments of physical and psychological holding are the cradle of the *real self.* And we'll see as we go along how very important this is.

At every major developmental crossroads, we need some version of this same protected space. This reliable experience of containment—this protected psychic space—is not optional. It is absolutely required every time we experience an inner developmental urge to flesh out more of our inner possibility. But as we age and grow, this can happen in increasingly subtle, and even symbolic form.

Gandhi understood this as few others have. And so, voilà: Sabarmati Ashram.

Kohut and Winnicott and others have made a deep study of the necessary experience of containment. They found that something else happens, too, within this protected psychic space—something Gandhi may not have understood. Within the safe relational container created for you, you begin to connect with *your own internal experience*—your own naturally arising impulses, desires, aversions, emotions, body states. The loving gaze and the attuned gesture of your spiritual friends in community, for example, reassure you that these internal states are okay. It's okay to feel the fragmentation, the sense of falling apart. It's okay to be for a while "the one who does not know." The one who can barely cope. There is room for you in the world. There is room for you (and this is crucial) *just exactly as you are*. Within this protected psychic space, you are able to feel a deeper and deeper connection with your mysterious inner world. You begin to connect with your idiosyncratic genius. You begin to *sense* who you really are. You begin to prepare for being your own authentic self in the world. Every authentic step forward into the external world requires deep roots in the inner world. The outer always reflects the inner.

13

Part of Gandhi's genius was that he understood that a life lived in service to spiritual growth requires an oscillation back and forth between retreat—protected psychic space—and advance. Between action and contemplation. Gandhi's life moved back and forth between retreat to the ashram and advance into the public square—and into the activism for which we primarily know him.

Most people today will tell you that Gandhi's life was about his political activism. However, this is absolutely *not* what he thought it was about. We will see that Gandhi's whole life was about his pilgrimage to God—his interior journey to the Divine Source. For him, any effective action he could take in the world must flow from this deepest source. He wrote in his autobiography, "What I want to achieve . . . is self-realization, to see God face to face, to attain Moksha [roughly translated: salvation—oneness with God and freedom from later incarnations.] I live and move and have my being in pursuit of this goal. All that I do by way of speaking and writing, and all my ventures in the political field are directed to this same end."

Gandhi believed that all of his powers came from God—from his search for God. God came first. Everything else was afterthought. Gandhi's search for God was earnest, and lifelong. At the beginning of his autobiography, he wrote: "I have not yet found Him, but I am seeking after Him."

Much of this view he learned from studying the Bhagavad Gita. Action must flow out of one's relationship with God, with Divine Source. Only this kind of action facilitates true dharma.

Gandhi's great lesson is that in order to become human beings of wise action, we must also become mystics. The mystic seeks the deeper knowledge. The mystic seeks that which is beneath. That which is buried. That which is clouded. That which is, in Krishna's words, "enveloped in smoke."

It's easy for us to forget that in his own time, people were shocked by Gandhi's deep-seated spirituality—even religiosity. Indeed, many were frustrated or infuriated by it. Many thought that in this regard Gandhi was old-fashioned and was betraying the urgent action needed in order to gain independence for India. Indeed, Gandhi's own assassin, speaking contemptuously of Gandhi at his much-publicized murder trial, declared: "He preferred such old superstitious beliefs as the power of the soul, the inner voice, the fast, the prayer and the purity of the mind."

14

Gandhi began to work through his disorienting dilemma by seeking refuge in spiritual community. And what was this spiritual community like—this community that Gandhi worked so hard to create wherever he went?

Sabarmati Ashram, in Gujarat Province in India, was not a church per se. Gandhi was wary of the doctrines and dogmas of established religion. He was not a fan of rites and rituals. "Ritual is the husk of true religion," he would say (along with the author of the ancient Chinese book of wisdom, the Tao de Ching). He did not believe that one needed "the priestly intercessor"—in Hinduism, this would be the Brahmin priest—in order to have a relationship with God. He believed that all souls can go directly to God. So he regularly eschewed religious hierarchies. But his own experience taught him that this reaching toward God must be a *communal endeavor.* He believed that the defining characteristic of human life is our profound interconnectedness and interdependence.

There was a very predictable—orderly—ebb and flow to the spiritual life of Sabarmati Ashram. The heart of Gandhi's ashram was the daily meeting for prayer and meditation. These communal meetings combined three elements: they very often started with readings from the world's scriptures; they continued with Gandhi's sermon; and they ended with the singing of hymns, instrumental music, and often ecstatic chanting.

In structuring his ashram life, Gandhi promoted two traditional Hindu practices: *svadhyaya* and *bhajan.* Svadhyaya means scriptural study and the prayer and meditation that often accompany it. At Sabarmati, this would include the study of the Bhagavad Gita and the Ramayana (another classic Hindu text) of course, but also the study of scriptures of all religions (and especially the Bible) in the same spirit. Gandhi would regularly study Tolstoy's *The Kingdom of God Is Within You* and other works, as well as the New Testament and the poetry of Kabir and Rumi. He exhorted his friends to dig deeply into these spiritual treasures.

The meetings for worship ended with communal singing and chanting. A bhajan is a hymn sung in unison by the faithful, often the composition of a famous poet-saint of the tradition—but Gandhi widened its meaning to include hymns from other religions. There were many Christian hymns that Gandhi loved to sing, including "Dear Lord and Father of Mankind," whose words were written by John Greenleaf Whittier:

Dear Lord and Father of mankind,
forgive our foolish ways;
reclothe us in our rightful mind,
in purer lives thy service find,
in deeper reverence, praise. . . .

Drop thy still dews of quietness,
till all our strivings cease;
take from our souls the strain and stress,
and let our ordered lives confess
the beauty of thy peace.

Breathe through the heats of our desire
thy coolness and thy balm;
let sense be dumb, let flesh retire;
speak through the earthquake, wind, and fire,
O still, small voice of calm!

As you might imagine, Gandhi's constant prayer in that year after arriving home was for guidance: What should my next step be? And in making this decision, he waited to be led by "the still, small voice of calm" referred to in the hymn.

15

By the end of his year-long retreat, and the consolidation of Sabarmati Ashram, Gandhi had developed the view that would launch him onto the world stage and simultaneously provide the spiritual basis for the ongoing pilgrimage of his soul. Over the course of that year on retreat, the central facets of Gandhi's mature credo became refined. If we look closely at his spiritual credo, we can see that it reflects the wisdom of the Bhagavad Gita in every way.

First, and most importantly for Gandhi, there was this view: *all human beings are made in the image and likeness of God.* All human beings! This is, of course, the central view of yoga philosophy. All individual souls participate in divinity. In the Hindu tradition this is put succinctly: *atman*, the individual soul, and *brahman*, the Divine soul, are one and the same.

Second, *all human beings are equal members of one human family.* Equal members! Gandhi was relentlessly inclusive. He infuriated his own Hindu co-religionists by bringing so-called untouchables (people of the "lowest" caste) into the ashram. He insisted at all times on acknowledging the interconnection and mutuality of the human family. Women, men, Muslims, Hindus, Christians—all were given equal status.

Third, *Truth is one, paths are many.* As I have said, Gandhi, like many Hindu religionists, was profoundly pluralistic. He believed in the Hindu doctrine of *sanatana dharma*, the Eternal Truth, and he believed that the Eternal Truth could be seen reflected in almost all religions.

Fourth, Gandhi was *wary of doctrine and dogma.* The Eastern contemplative traditions, indeed, are all wary of what is sometimes called "the affliction of *ditthi*," or "clinging to views and beliefs." In Gandhi's mind the only views to which one could cling are the eternal absolute value of each human soul and the ultimate power of Truth.

Next, Gandhi placed an extremely *high value on serving the common good.* Indeed, he saw selfless service—or *karma* yoga, for which the Bhagavad Gita is the central scripture—as the path to God. "Take yourself to zero," was one of the central mottos of his life. Consider the common good first, not your own self. This is the true path to self-fulfillment. In this, he was aligned with Krishna's teaching, as we shall see.

Finally, Gandhi believed fervently that *only love can overcome hate.* The Buddha had said this two thousand years earlier: "Love can overcome hate," he taught, "but hate can never overcome love." Gandhi believed that if one consistently acts with love, he will slowly but surely bend the moral arc of the Universe.

16

After a year or so at Sabarmati Ashram, Mohandas Gandhi emerged from his fruitful retreat and rejoined public life—though much of his life would always remain centered on his Sabarmati community. He had gradually begun to work through his doubts and dilemmas, and acknowledged to himself and to the world that it was indeed his calling—his dharma—to become the spiritual head of the independence movement in India. He knew, too, that in fully expressing his sacred duty, he must follow the guidance of the Bhagavad Gita at every turn. After his year at Sabarmati, Gandhi had undergone a quiet internal reorganization that brought with it new energy, new purpose, new resolve, new understanding.

An outward and visible sign of this internal reorganization was this: Gandhi had begun to let go of his anger and ill will toward the British, and toward his own countrymen for what he perceived as their sloth and torpor. He was resolved to act out of love and goodwill—emphasizing nonviolent noncooperation with the British Raj as the preferred technique for gaining Indian liberation.

In the years after his retreat, Gandhi refined his strategy for resistance to British rule in India. Beginning with his work in South Africa, he had called this strategy *satyagraha*, which literally means "clinging to the truth." It was utterly novel as a political strategy: instead of fanning hatred with hatred, Gandhi insisted upon returning love for hatred, and even on returning respect for contempt. Gandhi's strategy has since been referred to, quite accurately I think, as Soul Force. Henry David Thoreau had earlier called this same phenomenon "the force of truth in action." Gandhi himself would later refer to it as "the moral equivalent of war."

In the years leading up to the fateful and explosive year of 1928 (about which, more in the next chapter), Gandhi and his devotees would lead countless acts of nonviolent noncooperation based on *satyagraha*. The British found themselves absolutely confounded by these loving offensives. In a mere ten years, *satyagraha*, Soul Force, slowly eroded the power of British colonialism in India in a way no violent protests had ever done. We will see precisely how Soul Force works in later chapters of this book.

17

I have begun our inquiry with this snapshot from the life of Mahatma Gandhi for two reasons. First, because Gandhi has been the world's most ardent and skillful student of the Gita—and our most important purpose here is understanding the lessons of the Gita. And second, because, as we shall see, Gandhi's understanding of the importance of retreat in relationship to action is revealed in the background of every single life we will study going forward. We will see how Gandhi's advice plays out in all of the stories to come in this book. In the aftermath of some disorienting dilemma, each individual in this book will take refuge in some form of the beloved community, and in an in-depth spiritual search. Each individual will undergo *an internal reorganization* that will compel him or her onto the world stage with an altogether new sense of energy and purpose, with a powerful and enlivened new sense of dharma. And that dharma will inevitably not only serve the spiritual development of the individual but also serve *the good of the whole.*

CHAPTER 2

MOHANDAS K. GANDHI II

Now, Listen for the Inner Voice

It is the still small voice that the soul heeds, not the deafening blasts of doom.

— William Dean Howells

"Gandhiji, please. I implore you. The people of India implore you. We *must* act."

Gandhi and Rabindranath Tagore (whom we met in Chapter 1) were sitting in the garden of Sabarmati Ashram under a large white canopy, having tea. They were surrounded by ashram workers carrying baskets of recently harvested potatoes into one of the wooden outbuildings.

Tagore was uncharacteristically shaken. There was urgency in his voice. And this voice of his was no small thing. As I have said, Rabindranath Tagore was one of India's greatest poets. He was also a writer and a composer—and at that time, a recent Nobel laureate. He was an imposing figure: moderately tall, with a long white beard and a shock of fluffy white hair. He dressed in loosely flowing gowns that seemed to enhance his sense of otherworldly power.

Gandhi was unrattled.

"Yes, yes, dear friend, and we *will* act." Gandhi poured another small cup of tea for Tagore. "Oh, we will act. But we will act when the time is *right*.

"Now relax for a moment," said Gandhi. "Let's drink some tea. Would you like some goat's milk in your tea? Very good. Very nutritious."

The men sat in silence for a few moments. Finally, Gandhi got up and walked a few yards out into the nearby field of potatoes, which were just ripening under the Gujarat sun. Gandhi was dressed in the garb he would wear for the rest of his life: a simple loincloth made of homespun cloth that Gandhi had woven himself. His torso and skinny legs were bare. He had homemade rope sandals on his feet.

"Gandhiji, please. With all respect. What are you doing up here when people are rioting in the streets of Delhi?"

Gandhi stood for a moment in silence, with his back to Tagore. Then he turned slowly. His face was serious.

"I'm praying."

2

What was going on here? We need some background in order to understand the import of this, our second snapshot of the life of Mahatma Gandhi.

We have moved our story forward by a little more than ten years. Our lens will now zoom in on Mr. Gandhi in the years 1928 and 1929. By 1928, Gandhi and his colleagues in resistance had been at work for almost a decade, challenging the grip of British imperial rule on the subcontinent of India. They had been remarkably successful in their campaigns of nonviolent noncooperation. The British hold was loosening. The call for independence from the British was now bubbling over in the cities and villages of India. The masses' expectations had been raised, and they could no longer be held in check. Gandhi, Nehru, and the other leaders of the Indian independence movement now truly felt like Arjuna standing on the edge of a great battlefield. Mother India itself was their Kurukshetra, the Bhagavad Gita's battlefield on the plain of Kuru.

Throughout the critical year of 1928, strikes and demonstrations flared up around the country, and newspapers in every city took up the cry. But though the colonized Indians were on the move, the British were determined to slow-walk this process. The situation seemed paralyzed. In December, the Indian National Congress—the party of Gandhi and Nehru—held its annual meeting in Calcutta. Its leaders were ready to take a step forward. They passed a bold resolution: If the British government did not grant India dominion status (so-called home rule) in a year's time, by December 31, 1929, then the Indian National Congress would declare *swaraj*—literally "self-rule," or independence. After the Congress declared independence, it would then launch a massive campaign of nonviolent noncooperation with the British colonial power.

The fateful month of December 1929 did finally arrive, of course, but the British, though under severe pressure from the INC, had come no closer to granting India dominion status. The INC was ready to move, and had a plan: in Lahore, Jawaharlal Nehru would unfurl an immense tricolor independence flag at the stroke of midnight on December 31. The Indian National Congress would keep its promise of declaring independence on that last night of 1929.

And this is precisely what happened. "A happy new year and an era of independence," Nehru did indeed shout that night at INC headquarters as the crowds cheered. His message was broadcast by radio to every village in India. The wheels had been set in motion for the threatened declaration of swaraj. When the signal was given, the people of India would rise up in a campaign of massive civil disobedience unlike anything the world had ever seen. But there was one problem: no one knew precisely what that act of civil disobedience would be.

Of course, everyone looked to Gandhi for the answer. As spiritual head of the independence movement, the decision would be his.

3

Gandhi, meanwhile, was at Sabarmati Ashram, praying, meditating, and spinning cotton into thread. The masses found this endlessly frustrating. Just when action seemed called for, Gandhi would inevitably go into retreat. So, on January 18, 1930, Rabindranath Tagore implored him. "What will it be?" he asked Gandhi. "What action shall we take?" He was dismayed to find that Gandhi still did not know. Gandhi patiently remained in his retreat, praying and meditating while the entire country was boiling over. What, precisely, was Gandhi doing?

He was, as he himself said, "listening intently for the inner voice." Throughout his career as an organizer and leader in the Indian independence movement, as before in South Africa, Gandhi would often keep the anxious masses waiting as he listened for guidance. He would simply wait with exquisite patience until the "still small voice" spoke.

Gandhi himself had written, "The only tyrant I accept in this world is the still small voice within. To that voice above all others, I am compelled to listen."

4

What, then, was this still small voice upon which Gandhi relied so profoundly?

The primacy of this inner voice is central to the view of Hindu spirituality, as it is also to the views of Christianity, of Islam, of Judaism—indeed of all major wisdom traditions. The view is simply this: if all human beings are made in the image and likeness of God, then somewhere in our very core—in our soul, or atman, the Hindu tradition would say—we are already one with God, and therefore with the Divine Voice, and the Divine Mind. Different traditions call this Divine Mind by different names, of course: enlightened mind, *buddhi*, Awake Mind, the Mind of God, Buddha mind, or the mind of Muhammed, or Yaweh. But they all have a very similar view of its presence. "Let the same mind be in you that was in Christ Jesus," writes St. Paul. "Seek only the Inner Light," declare the Quakers.

Though the names of this "awake" mind differ, the one view that all these traditions hold in common is that *this inner voice of wisdom must be cultivated in silence and stillness.* The ancient yoga tradition, with which Gandhi would have been very familiar, had put it succinctly in its most exalted scripture, the 2nd-century Yogasutra: "When the mind becomes still and quiet, all wisdom is effortlessly self-revealing." In other words, wisdom is the true nature of the mind, but it usually reveals itself in silence, in stillness, and in its own time.

The Christian tradition teaches the same thing. "It is the still small voice that the soul heeds, not the deafening blasts of doom," wrote the popular 19th-century English preacher William Dean Howells, referring to the biblical story of God's revelation to the prophet Elijah.

Remarkably, human beings of all religious stripes—or none—say the same thing. Franz Kafka, for example, the 20th-century Czech novelist who fused realism and the fantastic, grasped the truth of this. He wrote, "You do not need to leave your room. Remain sitting at your table and listen. Do not even listen, simply wait, be quiet, still and solitary. The world will freely offer itself to you to be unmasked, it has no choice, it will roll in ecstasy at your feet."

5

In the Eastern contemplative traditions, where practitioners have been experimenting with the wisdom of "Awake Mind" for millennia, there is a highly refined understanding of its characteristics. In the yoga tradition, for example, this wisdom function of Awake Mind is called the Witness—*drashtri*, in Sanskrit: literally, "pure awareness."

In the mystical traditions of the world, the function of *knowing* is the holy grail. Early mystic traditions in ancient Greece were known as "gnostic" traditions, from the Greek word *gnosis*, which means "to know." "Knowing the very essence of things" allows us to know what really matters, to know "how things really work," and eventually to know how to act. Krishna tells the doubting Arjuna that this mind—"the mind that knows"—is immortal, and remains when the body is gone.

In Chapter 2 of the Bhagavad Gita, Krishna exhorts Arjuna to

> *Realize that which pervades the universe and is indestructible; no power can affect this unchanging, imperishable reality. (Gita 2:17)*

Of course, Arjuna, being Arjuna, pushes back. He whines. He does not yet understand.

"Well, tell me more then, because I'm not getting it." Arjuna is always the skeptic.

6

And Krishna does, indeed, flesh out the view. He teaches that because this mystic knowing is our true nature, the capacity to see and to know the essence of things already exists in us. It is not created by anything we do, and it cannot be destroyed. Krishna calls this power of knowing and of seeing, this wisdom function, "the great Unborn, the uncreated, the undying"—the True Self. He declares:

> *The body is mortal, but he who dwells in the body is immortal and immeasurable . . . . Unborn, eternal, immutable, immemorial . . . (Gita 2:18, 2:20)*

7

At the outset of the Gita, Arjuna has made the mistake we all inevitably make: he has confused the knowing function—awareness itself—with the physical body, and particularly with the brain. Krishna straightens him out.

Krishna teaches Arjuna that it is very common to confuse the brain and the physical body—even in its more subtle aspects—with the awakened mind. In fact, he says, the mind is not in the brain, as we commonly suppose. The mind is not *in* the body at all. Rather, *the brain and the body are in the mind.* The mind contains all.

Our friend Emily Dickinson understood this, as all mystics do. "The Brain is wider than the Sky," she begins one of her now famous poems. (Note that when she writes "Brain," she means what we have been referring to as "mind.")

The Brain - is wider than the Sky -
For - put them side by side -
The one the other will contain
With ease - and You - beside -

The Brain is deeper than the sea -
For - hold them - Blue to Blue -
The one the other will absorb -
As Sponges - Buckets - do -

The Brain is just the weight of God -
For - Heft them - Pound for Pound -
And they will differ - if they do -
As Syllable from Sound -

8

The dilemma, of course, which Gandhi and his tradition fully realized, is this: the sublime knowing about which we are talking only happens in the deepest part of the mind. It does not happen in the surface mind, the so-called ordinary discursive mind, or what we might call the ego. It happens in a part of the mind that we in the West can only call the soul. The East has mapped this out with great precision. And enlightened Western theologians have for hundreds of years held the same view. William Law, a great Christian adept, wrote:

> Though God is everywhere present, yet He is only present to thee in the deepest and most central part of thy soul. The natural senses cannot possess God or unite thee to Him; nay, thy inward faculties of understanding, will and memory can only reach after God, but cannot be the place of his habitation in thee. But there is a root or depth of thee from whence all these faculties come forth, as lines from a centre, or as branches from the body of the tree. This depth is called the centre, the fund or bottom of the soul. This depth is the unity, the eternity—I had almost said the infinity—of thy soul; for it is so infinite that nothing can satisfy it or give it rest but the infinity of God.

Most traditions believe that *attunement to the Mind of God*, to the inner voice, to our own knowing, to what Law calls "the center" or "the soul" is a lifelong project. It requires a training program to facilitate deep attunement to the Divine Mind—a training program that is believed in the East to last through many lives.

Writes Meister Eckhart, the great medieval mystic:

> The seed of God is in us. Given an intelligent and hard-working farmer, it will thrive and grow up to God, whose seed it is; and accordingly its fruits will be God-nature. Pear seeds grow into pear trees, nut seeds into nut trees, and God seeds into God.

Our job? To create the right conditions for the God seed to grow.

9

This view is not unique to the yoga and Hindu traditions. The central view of all the world's great wisdom traditions is this notion: To get close to the Mind of God, *we must live in the world in a certain way.* What way? We must live with an authentic aspiration toward moral purity. Gandhi subscribed wholeheartedly to this classic but often unpopular view. He wrote: "The higher the moral purity of one's life, the greater the probability that it is God's voice that is being heard." "Blessed are the pure in heart," says the Christian scripture called the Beatitudes—one of Gandhi's favorite Christian scriptures—"for they shall see God." By the way, all of these scriptures also teach this: It is the *aspiration and the wholehearted effort* toward purity that counts. Not perfection.

10

When I was a young graduate student living in Boston, I had, for several years, a relationship with a local Episcopal monastery situated just on the banks of the Charles River within the beating heart of Harvard University. I often visited the monastery on weekends, and sometimes did long retreats there. I found the dark, solemn Romanesque sanctuary to be a refuge and a balm. Several times a day, the monks chanted the psalms in the ancient Gregorian mode. I was entranced.

Once, during a retreat at the monastery, I happened into a room where the monks were having a meeting of some kind. They were huddled around a blackboard, where I read a phrase written in white chalk: "A spiritual life is a disciplined life." My friend, a monk named Bede, who was huddled with the other monks, saw me hovering at the door and motioned to me to come in and take a seat. A visiting scholar was talking about the "meaning of order" in the community. Why was the day so highly structured? What spiritual purpose did this serve? What was all the daily discipline really for?

I remember journaling that evening about the phrase I saw on the chalkboard: "A spiritual life is a disciplined life." I realized that I had been touched by the disciplined life of the monastery. I thrived on the order, the predictability, the rhythm. I realized, too, that it was, at least in part, that very sense of sacred order that made me feel safe and at ease in the monastery and allowed me a deep sense of being at home there. It was like being enfolded in some big, solid, loving arms. At the same time, the structure of the day allowed me to make methodical daily progress in my self-inquiry—in my knowledge of spiritual tools.

All religious traditions agree on this fact. Each tradition has at its core some form, some practice, in which the deepest adherents—novices, trainees—can immerse themselves in the kind of lifestyle that is most generative of spiritual depth. And as it turns out, these lifestyle prescriptions are very similar. Gandhi's ashram and my monastery were almost identical in the basics. They both prescribed a certain amount of quiet, of contemplation. They always featured spiritual exercises to train the attention—some form of meditation and deep prayer. They always featured singing and chanting, scripture study, and the study of the deepest thoughts of the masters—indeed, all of the things that Gandhi enthusiastically sponsored in his ashram.

11

It must be said, too, that in seeking Truth, all great wisdom traditions rely on the same "still small voice" that Gandhi sought. But they all do so only in the context of three other essential factors. These three are important. In Western religious traditions, they are often referred to as Revelation, Tradition, and Emulation. These very same three factors are emphasized in the Hindu tradition as well. Gandhi's own Indian tradition calls them *sruti* (Revelation), *smriti* (Tradition), and *acara* (Emulation of the Worthies). The still small voice, the fourth factor, in Hinduism, is sometimes called "conscience," or *atmatusti*.

It's interesting, isn't it, that these four pillars seem to be universal?

- *Revelation*. In most established traditions, revelation comes in the form of "canonical"—or widely approved—scriptures. So in the Christian tradition, for example, the canonical Old and New Testaments are seen as the very revelation of God; in the Jewish tradition, the Torah is God's revelation to humankind; in the Muslim tradition, the Koran, and so forth. The Bhagavad Gita is one of the central scriptures of revelation in the Hindu tradition.[1]
- *Tradition*. The second pillar, called Tradition, always refers to *the sum total of accepted spiritual practice* in a given religion. Over time, the great wisdom traditions slowly discern the rites and practices and doctrines that they have found to be most useful in creating a union with the Mind of God. These are taught with varying amounts of discipline to every generation of aspirants.
- *Exemplars*. Third, of course, every wisdom tradition has its own roster of saints—of women and men whose lives they believe are worthy of emulation. This "emulation of the worthies" is seen as an indispensable guide to behavior and practice, and a continuing inspiration to live the prescribed spiritual life.

1 Not all corners of the Hindu world accept the Gita as *sruti*, or "revelation." Most do. However, some see it as "tradition."

- And finally, of course, *Conscience.* This refers to the "still small voice" as we hear it in our own hearts and minds and souls.

Gandhi respected all four of these pillars of wisdom, but generally held that in difficult times—when a creative and inspired response was required—one must privilege *conscience.* One must privilege direct communion with the Mind of God: Inspiration. Divine hunches. Signs. Inner promptings. And for these, of course, one must get quiet. Very quiet.

It's important to note, by the way, that Gandhi added a fifth factor to this list, one that is unfortunately not often included in the great wisdom traditions. He declared that he "refused to be bound by any interpretation of scripture, tradition, or the lives of the saints that was repugnant to reason or moral sense."

In the Bhagavad Gita, in fact, Krishna himself privileges "conscience." He teaches only one actual *practice* to Arjuna—only one technique to cultivate union with Divine Mind. This is meditation.

> *When meditation is mastered, O Arjuna, the mind is unwavering like the flame of a lamp in a windless place. In the still mind, in the depths of meditation, the Self reveals itself. (Gita 6:19–20)*

Gandhi—serious student of the Gita that he was—would take up the question of meditation in depth. In fact, he created for himself an entirely new form of meditation: spinning cotton into thread on an old-fashioned spinning wheel. He organized his ashram around this practice. Adherents found that, just as Gandhi said, this practice had all the central ingredients of meditation: simplicity of method and the provision of a one-pointed focus for the mind. Spinning, like other forms of meditation, provides a rhythmic, repetitive movement that draws the mind into a state of absorption, creating a kind of seclusion from the roiling thoughts of greed and hatred—widely believed to be the major obstacles to awakening.

In long sessions of spinning, Gandhi found that his mind settled and he could once again attune to the Mind of God. His adherents, likewise, discovered this magic. Perhaps his closest follower, the well-known Indian poet Sarojini Naidu, took up the craft, and was transformed by it. "You sit in your room and you spin and you spin," she wrote, "but the long, long thoughts you think as you twist the long, long threads reach out across the world."

12

So, in January of 1929, Gandhi and his community sat and prayed and meditated and spun and worked in the gardens and chanted and lived their disciplined spiritual lives—Gandhi himself pondering and praying about India's dilemma day and night.

India waited with bated breath. Gandhi tells us later in his autobiography, "I could tell [the people] nothing [about the act of civil disobedience we should follow], as I myself knew nothing about it."

Finally, the answer came to him, as in a dream. Up from the depths of his mind came the solution. Gandhi himself describes it: "But like a flash it came, and as you know it was enough to shake the country from one end to the other." Gandhi tells us later that he was as surprised as anyone by his epiphany.

What would the proper act of civil disobedience be? What did the still small voice say to Gandhi? Just this: The country would rise up in resistance to the oppressive British "salt laws"—the laws that gave a monopoly on the sale of salt to the British imperial government. Under these oppressive laws, India's own salt could be mined exclusively by the British and then sold back to its rightful owners—Indian citizens. Gandhi's epiphany was this: the first pan-Indian act of civil disobedience would be a great march to the sea to make salt, in direct and explicit contravention of the law.

Huh? This was the brilliant revolutionary act? Making salt?

At first, Gandhi's companions found this answer baffling. They didn't get it. But of course, it was brilliant. And Gandhi was firm. "Next to air and water," he exhorted, "salt is perhaps the greatest necessity of life." And here was the problem: Indians could not consume any salt at all that was not sold to them by the British. Although

India itself had massive deposits of salt on the subcontinent, the British had now enabled themselves to *sell Indians their own salt back to them.* Gandhi had always felt that this was an outrage.

"There is no article like salt (outside water) by taxing which the State can reach even the starving millions, the sick, the maimed, and the utterly helpless. The tax constitutes the most inhuman poll tax that the ingenuity of man can devise." Gandhi was right. There was perhaps no more universal symbol of colonialism. Wrote Gandhi: "The salt tax oppresses all alike, Hindus, Muslims, etc. It hits the poor man hardest, whatever be his religious persuasion."

Gandhi was pleased and relieved to have found the solution: "It is the formula of which I have been in search these long and weary months," he said. And it had emerged out of the depths of a quiet, illumined, peaceful mind.

13

Gandhi had learned that the still small voice of Awake Mind was highly creative, innovative, and wildly unpredictable. Gandhi himself often had no idea what creative solutions would emerge from his inner guidance—or *when* they would emerge. It is positively thrilling to read his life story and to observe from afar the wildly creative way that Awake Mind works.

Because he relied on this inner voice of wisdom, "Gandhi was the most bewildering opponent any nation ever faced," wrote his disciple Eknath Easwaran. "Every move he made was spontaneous. Every year that passed found him more youthful, more radical, more experimental. British administrators were baffled and exasperated by this little man who withdrew when they would have attacked, attacked when they would have withdrawn, and seemed to be getting stronger day by day."

Gandhi's actions were always fresh, surprising, befuddling—and almost always frustrating to his British peers. The British secret police, trying to fathom the way Gandhi functioned, wrote about him in a secret memo: "the workings of his conscience . . . his ethical and intellectual attitude . . . baffles the ordinary processes of thought." "No one knew what Gandhi was going to do next," wrote Easwaran, "for his actions were prompted not by calculations of what seemed politically expedient, but by a deep intuition which, as we have seen, often came to him only at the eleventh hour."

14

And how did Gandhi's flash of genius—the march to the sea—work out?

Brilliantly.

To protest the salt laws, Gandhi would lead thousands of followers in an epic, weeks-long march from the Sabarmati Ashram at Ahmedabad to the small coastal town of Dandi, on the Arabian Sea. Upon arrival the massive throng camped overnight on the beach. Then, on the morning of April 6, 1930, Gandhi emerged from a simple bungalow in Dandi. Four thousand people awaited him. Observers from around the world were there. The news cameras were there en masse. Gandhi's political allies were there: churchmen, politicians, swamis. And thousands of ordinary Indian citizens.

Gandhi waded into the water. He reached down and scooped up a handful of sand rich with salt. "With this salt I am shaking the foundations of the empire," he declared.

By making salt, Mahatma Gandhi was breaking the salt laws and signaling the people of India to immediately embark on massive acts of civil disobedience. Wrote Nehru, "When Gandhi gave the signal, it seemed as though a spring had been suddenly released. Salt-making was spreading like prairie fire."

The first massive act of noncooperation had begun.

The rest is history. This was the beginning of the end of the British Raj in India.

15

Over the course of his life, Gandhi received the wisdom of the Divine in flashes, hunches, intuition, and sometimes in a clear, even audible voice. In the Farewell section of his autobiography, Gandhi says that he has seen "flashes of truth," which he equates with God.

"Truth is the highest attribute of God," he was fond of saying. Nevertheless, most of us are capable of perceiving only shards of Truth. In summing up his experience of this Truth, Gandhi would write: "The little fleeting glimpses, therefore, that I have been able to have of Truth can hardly convey an idea of the indescribable lustre of Truth, a million times more intense than that of the sun we daily see with our eyes. In fact, what I have caught is only the faintest glimmer of that mighty effulgence."

At every crossroads moment of his life, Gandhi prayed, chanted mantra, meditated, and spun. Gandhi claimed in his autobiography that "[God's] voice has been increasingly audible as the years have rolled by. He has never forsaken me, even in my darkest hour."

Who or what is God for Mr. Gandhi? Gandhi described God as an indefinable, mysterious power that pervades everything and that can be felt but not seen. As an unseen power, it defies proof because it transcends the senses. For him, as we have seen, God *was* Truth. God's voice could be heard as the still small voice within. That was where his guidance came from. That was his steering mechanism. But much of his life had to be dedicated to *cultivating* this inward hearing.

While outrage and shock move most people into action, they moved Gandhi into meditation. When most people thought action was the answer, Gandhi went into retreat. The guy was profoundly counterintuitive. Those who lived and studied with Gandhi knew that at any point he might withdraw into prayer, meditation, and solitude. He might disappear for months at a time. He might sit and spin thread from cotton for hours on end. He had, in the midst of a life already devoted to struggle, developed a profoundly meditative mind. He had developed the mind of the Seer. The Knower.

All the great wisdom traditions have understood, with Gandhi, that the cultivation of attunement to God's voice is really the primary task of life. In the Jewish mystical tradition, it is said that "A man who struggles long to pray and study Torah will be able to discover the sparks of divine light in all of creation, in each solitary bush and grain and woman and man." A spiritual life is a disciplined life, and the fruit of this discipline is the gradual capacity to see God everywhere and in every created thing.

Continues the Jewish teaching, "when [the seeker] cleaves strenuously to God for many years, he will be able to release the sparks, to unwrap and lift these particular shreds of holiness, and return them to God. This is the human task: to direct and channel the sparks' return."

Bhagwan Shree Rajneesh (who, despite his bizarre behavior toward the end of his life, was author of a ten-volume set of brilliant expositions on yoga philosophy) struggled to articulate the position of the yoga traditions. "God *is*," he wrote. "There is no question of God's *being*."

> The question is, we cannot see Him. We don't have eyes. All the meditations and the prayers and the purifications only help you, make you capable of seeing. Once you can see, you will be surprised—it has always been there. Day in, day out, year in, year out, it was showering on you, but you were not sensitive enough to catch hold of it, you were not empty enough to be filled by it. You were too much full of your own ego.

16

Yogis have understood for at least two millennia that "the Witness" cultivated by Gandhi—the Seer, the Knower, Awake Mind—has certain immutable characteristics. These characteristics of Awake Mind are laid out systematically throughout the Bhagavad Gita. I will list them here, and we will slowly unpack this list through the coming chapters. (If this all seems a tad too metaphysical in your first introduction to it, you are in good company. Arjuna thought the very same thing. He was a spiritual skeptic of epic proportions, and he made no effort to hide his skepticism from his friend Krishna. So stay with me here. In the coming chapters, we will be grounding these metaphysical statements in real events and real lives.)

- Awake Mind stands still at the center of the whirlwind of life and is not shaken by "the vicissitudes"—not shaken by the so-called pairs of opposites: gain and loss, pain and pleasure, praise and blame, fame and ill repute.

- This Mind sees clearly into the very structure of reality—apprehending how all things work. The Buddha, on the night of his enlightenment declared, "Oh builder of the house, I have seen you. I know how the house is built." In other words, I see exactly how the human self is built, is structured. I see how human perception, motivation, and volition are conditioned.
- Awake Mind sees not only the present but the past and future. "The Seer," declares the scriptures, "has a panoramic vision of the entire field of mind and matter." Awake Mind transcends the ordinary space/time continuum.
- This Mind can directly know the subtle interior life of all beings, all objects. The Witness directly "knows" the very essence of all created things.
- This Mind perceives the inherent interconnectedness of all things and sees that no event is unrelated to any other. This mind understands the laws of cause and effect and sees how they are active in every situation.
- Awake Mind perceives all the potential events in the Universe in each aspect of the Universe. In other words, this wisdom function sees the holographic quality of phenomenal reality. The Witness sees that in every instance, *the part is in the whole, and the whole is in the part*, and understands that we can therefore know the universal through the particular.

Most of us—perhaps like Arjuna in his initial confrontation with Krishna—will read through this list and find some of it incomprehensible. We will be skeptical of its contents. This is good. We *should* doubt. We should push back. However, we shall see through the course of this book how very real these powers are, and how they play out all the time even in our own daily lives. And one day we might see, right along with the great skeptic Franz Kafka, that occasionally in the very depths of our inner silence, "the world will freely offer itself to [us] to be unmasked."

LESSON TWO

PEER CAREFULLY INTO THE CHAOS FOR THE SURE SIGNS OF DHARMA

Krishna and Arjuna are still in their hastily improvised camp at the edge of the field of Kurukshetra. Their horse is bedded down for the night. They're sitting by a small campfire they've started with sticks of fragrant neem wood. For the last several hours, they've been deep in conversation. In the distance they can hear the call of the conch shell, which signals the end of the first watch of the night.

"Midnight," says Arjuna.

The sky is black and pocked with stars. The breeze has quieted, but an evening chill has settled in. The men have each wrapped themselves in woolen shawls—gray linen and wool military shawls into which the gold insignia of the Pandava family is woven.

As they've shared their thoughts and feelings over the past couple of hours, Arjuna has felt increasingly relaxed and comforted. He's breathing normally again—at times reaching his arms and torso closer to the fire like a big, lazy cat in her morning stretch.

"Can I tell you a story?" Krishna asks Arjuna.

Arjuna's response is immediate. "A perfect time of night for a story!"

Within the kingdom of Kuru, Krishna is a renowned storyteller, and his stories always contain kernels of wisdom, for which Arjuna is hungry just now. The young warrior pulls his woolen shawl more closely around his shoulders.

"Okay, then," Krishna launches in. "This story concerns the mighty Indra. You already know that he was the greatest god of our ancient mothers and fathers."

Arjuna nods his head and smiles. "The thunderbolt god." (Arjuna prides himself on his knowledge of the ancients, their stories and doctrines.)

Krishna continues: "Well, as you know, Indra lived on the sacred mountain, Mount Meru. And it was said that from his perch high up on the mountain, Indra had cast a vast net over the entire Universe." With this, Krishna makes a sweeping gesture toward the sky, which is now partially illumined by a half moon.

"At the vertex of each warp and woof strand of this universal net, there is a jewel," says Krishna. He looks directly at Arjuna to make this next point clear. "Each jewel, Arjuna, is *an individual soul.* And it is that soul's purpose to hold together his or her particular part of the net."

Arjuna nods. "Of course I know the story. Every soul has a duty to uphold."

Krishna stands up now, and begins to pace back and forth beside the chariot, as if inspired to movement by his own words.

"Each one of us is one of those jewels, holding together the Universal Web of Life. We each have a sacred duty in this life, my friend, to hold together *our* part of the web. We each have a dharma.

"Always look to your dharma when you are undone," says Krishna. "Look to your dharma to save you!"

And then Krishna says, in no uncertain terms:

You must fulfill all of your sacred duties. (Gita 3:8)

"Dharma is the force that holds life together, Arjuna. The very purpose of this life is to find and live out your own calling. What *exactly* is your duty in this life? What precise part of the web of life are you holding up?"

2

After a moment, Krishna sits down again on the log next to his friend. He looks over at Arjuna's dark frame, illumined by the campfire. Arjuna's brow has furrowed. For a moment, Arjuna had almost forgotten about the dilemma he faces.

"But Krishna. That's just the point. That's where I'm stuck. Haven't you been listening? I don't *know* what my calling is in this situation."

Arjuna lays it all at Krishna's feet. "In the midst of this insanity, I'm so confused. I thought I knew what my dharma is, but now I'm not sure. Up is down. Down is up. Am I to fight, or not to fight?"

Arjuna looks up at Krishna: "How do I know for sure what I am called to *do*?"

Krishna has warmed to the topic of dharma, and goes on at some length. "Okay, Arjuna, here is where we begin." Krishna explains to Arjuna that he must begin with the recognition that we each have idiosyncratic gifts and talents—inner possibilities.

"There is a particular mix of gifts that only *you* have, you know," he says to Arjuna. "Only you. You are unique in all the world. And so is your particular calling. There is a special seed buried *within you* that wants to sprout."

Krishna picks up a bundle of new firewood and throws it into the fire. "We each have a responsibility to this seed of possibility—to our own gifts, our own possibilities, our own particular genius."

Krishna turns back to his friend and addresses him with passion in his voice: "To pursue your dharma fully will require every ounce of ingenuity that you have. All of your courage. You must call all of your gifts to the surface, Arjuna. Your very soul must rise up. You must bring everything to this. It is the *most* important thing in life."

"But Krishna. You will help me. Won't you?"

"I will help you. But know this: no one can rescue you, Arjuna. You must listen inside for the answers to your questions. You must learn to discern the inner voice."

3

The two men are quiet for a long moment, listening to the crackling and popping of the fire.

"Arjuna," says Krishna finally. "I know how confused you feel. And it's true: we *are* in a perilous moment. But there is some good in this. Difficult moments bring us to the edge of the cliff. They force us to understand who we really are.

"Standing as we are at the edge of the cliff, we are forced into a bigger view of the world, a view that encompasses more of reality—a view that stretches our sense of who we could be in the world."

Arjuna sighs.

"You must search through the chaos, Arjuna, to find signs of dharma. Search for signs of an open door. Search for the gift at the heart of the pain. Search for glimpses of your future. You will find these signs in hunches, in dreams, in inner and outer visions. Listen, look, feel.

"You must find the precise place where you are called to intervene in the world's sorrow. There is a small door open somewhere—open only to you in particular. It is the 'narrow door' that the ancients speak of, and you must go through it."

Arjuna gets up now, wearily, and stretches his back and legs. He looks at the black sky, now even more alive with stars. He smells the fragrance of the campfire on him, the pungent smell of neem wood.

"Krishna, I'm going to take a walk over to the river to get a drink and clear my mind."

And with that, Arjuna walks off through the grove of trees and toward the now engorged Saraswati River, which flows at the very edge of the great field of Kuru. Krishna settles back in by the fire, wraps himself more tightly in his shawl, closes his eyes, and begins to meditate.

How will Arjuna find clarity about his calling in the midst of these troubled times? What kinds of signs, hunches, omens, should he look for?

This will be our inquiry in Lesson Two.

CHAPTER 3

HENRY DAVID THOREAU

Look First in Your Own Backyard

The best place for each is where he already stands.

— HENRY DAVID THOREAU

"Oh for God's sake, Henry, just pay the damned fine." Sam Staples was at the end of his rope.

Henry's deep blue eyes looked back at Staples for a long moment. His expression was calm and earnest. "No, sir. I cannot pay it. I will not pay it."

Staples rolled his eyes and let out a long sigh. This is just what he should have expected from Henry. "Well then, I'll pay it for you. And that's the end of it."

"No, Sam." Henry's face betrayed some slight alarm. "On no account."

Both men stood together quietly for a moment. Staples was really not sure what to do. He shook his head back and forth several more times, as if trying to clear his brain of this muddle. He let out a sigh.

"Well then, Henry. Let's go. It's jail for you."

2

Henry David Thoreau had not expected to end his day in the local hoosegow. How, indeed, had it come to this? The afternoon had begun in routine enough fashion. It had been late in the afternoon on a sunny Thursday in July of 1846 when Thoreau decided to walk into the village of Concord, Massachusetts, from his cabin at nearby Walden Pond. His mission: to pick up a pair of shoes that had been mended by the town cobbler. Instead, along the way, Thoreau crossed paths with his friend Sam Staples, the town tax collector. Both men knew that Thoreau had not paid a cent of his poll tax since 1842. It was a small amount. But not quite negligible.

For years, Staples had been nagging Thoreau about the tax. Now he was coming to the end of his tenure as tax collector, and he needed to clear the books, lest his own personal account be debited for uncollected sums.

"Okay, then, Sam. To jail it is." Thoreau did not hesitate.

And why did Thoreau refuse to pay this minimal tax? For this important reason: he considered it his small protest against a government that was acting horrendously—and specifically as a protest against the government's explicit acceptance of slavery, its ghastly treatment of Native Americans, and its role in the exploding war with Mexico. Thoreau wrote at the time, "How does it become a man to behave towards the American government today? I answer, that he cannot without disgrace be associated with it."

3

Thoreau and his sometime jailer strolled into town, chatting amiably along the way about the summer's crops and the recent lack of rainfall. The Middlesex County Jail toward which they were headed was no small thing: it was a three-story granite building, with three-foot-thick walls and heavily barred windows—a small, fortress-like structure that had been rebuilt and fortified since the Revolutionary War, just seventy years earlier. It routinely housed thieves and murderers. Now it would house one of Concord's first citizens.

It was late in the evening by the time Henry got settled into his freshly whitewashed cell on the second floor. He spent the later hours of the evening chatting with his disheveled cellmate, who calmly explained to him—quite unconvincingly—that he had "accidentally burned down a barn" and was awaiting trial in the comfort of the clean and orderly cell. After his new roommate went to sleep, Henry lingered at the cell's double-barred windows, watching the bustle in the tavern next door and listening to the voices echoing in the street. Thoreau was fascinated. He later wrote that "it was a closer view of my native town than I had ever had . . . It was like travelling into a far country, such as I had never expected to behold . . . It seemed to me that I never had heard the town-clock strike before, nor the evening sounds of the village."

A popular legend has it that Thoreau's famous mentor, Ralph Waldo Emerson, happened to walk past the jail that night and spotted Thoreau at the barred window on the second floor. "Henry," he exclaimed, "why are you in jail?" To which Thoreau replied, "Mr. Emerson! Why are you not in jail?" It is very unlikely that this exchange actually happened. But it underlines the very point of Thoreau's imprisonment. Why, Thoreau wondered, wasn't *everyone* who disagreed with the government's policy on slavery and on the Mexican-American War also here in jail with him?

Thoreau lingered late into the night at the window and pondered his situation. He would say later in life that this night in jail woke him up to "the reality of the State" in which he lived. And it forced him to think about his actual relationship with the government of the town, the state, and the country.

As it turned out, Thoreau did not stay long behind bars. Later that night, Henry's Aunt Maria—mortified for her nephew, and wearing a veil so no one would recognize her—approached Sam Staples at his home and paid Henry's tax. When Thoreau found out the next morning, he was furious. "I'm staying," he insisted as Sam Staples attempted to usher him out. He wanted his act of "resistance to civil government" to be noticed, and to count.

Nonetheless, after a hearty breakfast, Thoreau left the jail and continued with his previously arranged plan for the morning: to lead a huckleberry-gathering party with women and children at nearby

Fairhaven Hill. He later commented that among the huckleberry bushes "the State was nowhere to be seen."

4

As Thoreau walked the several miles to his huckleberry party that morning, he was troubled. What did his night in jail really signify? What had he intended by this almost-accidental act of "resistance to civil government"? What price, indeed, was he willing to pay to resist collaborating in any way with a government that sanctioned slavery and war—both of which he heartily opposed? What, indeed, *is* the citizen's duty to an erring State?

As he ambled through the woods and up to Fairhaven Hill, Thoreau's brow was knit. One look would tell the passerby that Henry Thoreau was unsettled. His face, as everyone in town knew, was utterly transparent. One could see straight through to the man's feelings. Almost two centuries later, Thoreau's face is well known to us through the many sepia-toned photographs of him that survive. It is, indeed, a fascinating face. Even when he lived—and before he became a household name—his face mesmerized people. Henry's friend Ellery Channing said of it:

> [Thoreau's] face, once seen, could not be forgotten . . . The features were quite marked . . . the nose aquiline or very Roman, like one of the portraits of Caesar (more like a beak, as was said); large overhanging brows above the deepest set blue eyes that could be seen, in certain lights, and in others gray—eyes expressive of all shades of feeling, but never weak or near-sighted; the forehead not unusually broad or high, full of concentrated energy and purpose; the mouth with prominent lips, pursed up with meaning and thought when silent, and giving out when open with the most varied and unusual instructive sayings.

In his short life, Henry David Thoreau had already become a well-known character in the town of Concord and its surroundings—and increasingly, too, in Boston. He was known principally for his brilliant lectures on philosophy and nature. In his lectures, as in his daily life, he was outspoken, colorful, and blunt—sometimes to the point of being rude. Young Henry insisted on speaking the truth as he saw it. Indeed, he understood his very life as one dedicated to Truth. "Rather than love, than money, than fame, give me Truth," he declared.

Thoreau-the-Truth-Seeker was not universally loved. He was seen by many in his hometown as a "ne'er-do-well" and "an idler." Here, after all, was a brilliant Harvard graduate who could never hold a job. Here was a classics scholar who preferred to spend his time in the woods with the local hunters and fishermen who eked out a living at the margins of society. Here was a man who openly mocked the puffery of the village elite—even though his family was arguably one of them. Here, egad, was a man who refused to go to church. Here was an eccentric man who managed to be at the very center of village life and completely on its periphery at the same time. Many of his contemporaries looked at him as merely "a bad copy of his mentor, Emerson." "He is considered to resemble Emerson," one local had it, "but I do not think he does. Mr. Emerson is a God by the side of him."

As the twenty-nine-year-old Thoreau ambled through the woods that morning, fresh from jail, he would have been a wonderful sight. He was short and lean—standing just five foot seven inches; he was rough hewn, with an unkempt mane of hair; he smelled strongly of woodsmoke; and he would have been dressed shabbily (as one of his friends observed) in "a straw hat, stout shoes and strong gray trousers."

If Henry David Thoreau was sometimes difficult to actually like, he was nonetheless respected by many in the village. He was wonderful with children: Generous. Thoughtful. Creative. He was known to be a genius with words—a visionary, and an intellectual who had a masterful command of world literature as well as contemporary science. He often spoke at the local Concord Lyceum on matters of national and international concern to his fellow Concordians. Even those who disliked him listened begrudgingly.

The fact that Thoreau had spent a night in jail would have been no small deal in the village. The gossip quickly got around town, and Henry soon found himself the subject of heated controversy: "it was a brave act of conscience"; "no, it was an unseemly way to protest." Ralph Waldo Emerson was not a fan of what he thought of as Thoreau's "jailhouse stunt," and to their mutual friends Emerson simply shook his head with dismay. But many others wanted to hear more from Thoreau himself. What did he mean by this action?

Thoreau would talk about his single night in jail for the rest of his life. It woke him up, he said. And he would make great use of it. It would bear fruit in one of the most influential documents of 19th-century America: Thoreau's monumental essay "Civil Disobedience," which has influenced generations of thinkers and activists down to this very day. Thoreau's questions to himself that day in July of 1846 were very similar to Arjuna's, and to Gandhi's: What fights are we duty bound to take on? What is our dharma in the face of injustice and oppression? What laws should govern our actions? Did paying one's tax really make one complicit with the State in its ongoing support of slavery and violence?

Young Mr. Thoreau had reached a crossroads moment. He had now been caught up in one of the most important disorienting dilemmas of his life. Indeed, his life would never be the same. And, as we shall see, Thoreau—like Gandhi—consulted the Bhagavad Gita to determine what actions he should take going forward.

5

In order to understand Thoreau's particular dilemma, we must have a basic understanding of the conflicts that roiled the young American democracy in the decade of the 1840s. These conflicts can be summed up in one word: slavery. This was the central conflict that kept Thoreau's country almost constantly at war with itself. And now, in Thoreau's little New England town, as everywhere else in America, the question of slavery was pushed to its very breaking point by the eruption of war with Mexico.

In 1845, just as Thoreau was beginning his two-year retreat at Walden Pond, an epic drama was playing itself out in Austin, Texas. Texan legislators were approving the immediate annexation of the Texas territory to the United States. This territory included not just what we know today as Texas but a vast amount of land reaching north to Colorado and west to California. Of course, Mexico had considered all of this to be Mexican territory, and was determined to go to war with the United States to preserve its sovereignty. The conflict sparked a bloody war that would last from 1846 to 1848. Most scholars see this war as providing the final shove toward civil war in the United States, because of its implications for slavery. The newly annexed state of Texas would be a slave state, vastly expanding the reach of slavery in America.

Thoreau and his abolitionist friends in Concord were outraged by the Texas annexation. Thoreau, who had always been opposed to slavery, had been further radicalized in this regard by his mother and sisters, who were fervent abolitionists, and founding members of the Concord Female Anti-Slavery Society—begun in 1837, and one of the first of its kind in the United States. (In the coming two decades, this particular antislavery society would become the model for similar societies all across the North.)

So the approaching war with Mexico stirred the pot in Concord Village, as it had all across the North. As the annexation of Texas drew nearer, one of Thoreau's best friends, Wendell Phillips—a Boston Unitarian minister of widespread influence—mounted the podium of the Concord Lyceum one evening to warn of the danger. He pointed out that admitting a new slave state would give pro-slavery forces a permanent majority in Congress. This would permanently end any hope for the abolition of slavery through legal means.

Thoreau, in his journals, tells us that he was greatly moved by Phillips's speech that evening at the Lyceum. Thoreau saw the Reverend Phillips as one brave man standing against the storm of do-nothingism that prevailed in the Northeast in the face of the evil of slavery. He was moved by Phillips's call to action. Notes one of Thoreau's biographers, "Thoreau didn't want to merely *hear* Phillips, waving his approval from the sidelines as the great leader passed by. He wanted to *be* Phillips, to stand alone before the million with just such dignity courage, and integrity, to be—in words he would soon write—'a majority of one.'" After Phillips's speech, Thoreau became obsessed with the question of "right action" in the face of a malign State.

"To do right" became Thoreau's largest project in life. And in order to "do right" he had to be led by his own conscience—not by the prevailing winds of fashion. In his view, slavery was not only a cause but also a symptom of everything that was staining the soul of America. Says one biographer: "In his view, slavery was not a single cause whose cure would solve everything; rather, it was one symptom of a larger sickness preying on a universe of beings." Thoreau was determined to call out this sickness. To name it. And to act against it to the limits of his ability.

6

As I have said, after his night in jail, Henry went off on an adventure picking huckleberries. Apparently, his berry picking was successful, for he arrived home with his hands stained blue and carrying enough buckets of berries to take home to his mother for pies. After a visit to his mother's house, Henry walked back in the twilight to Walden Pond, to the one-room cabin where he had now been living and writing for almost a year. Henry lit a couple of candles and looked on the bookshelf for the one book he knew would help him resolve his thoughts about right action. There on his shelf sat a prized possession: a now dirt-smudged copy of the "Bhagvat-Geeta," loaned to him by Ralph Waldo Emerson himself.

The Bhagavad Gita was not then well known in the United States. It had been translated into English by Sir Charles Wilkins in 1784, but copies were not yet widely available in New England. Emerson insisted that Thoreau read it. Thoreau was mesmerized by this ancient tract from the very first. He was awed by the majesty of its philosophy, and declared that it brought him closer to "the Divine" than anything he read in the Bible. "The oldest . . . Hindoo philosopher raised a corner of the veil from the statue of divinity," he would later write in *Walden*, "and still the trembling robe remains raised, and I gaze upon as fresh a glory as he did . . ."

Day after day, Henry dove into the text of the Gita, searching for answers. He had already come to believe that the Gita was the world's most incisive treatise on *action*. So what did his very own action of "civil resistance to unjustly used authority" mean in the larger perspective of this ancient text?

Thoreau—like Arjuna—wanted to know from Krishna, "How would a wise man act in my situation?" Arjuna poses exactly this question to Krishna in one of the most oft-cited stanzas of the Gita. Arjuna asks:

Tell me of those who live established in wisdom, ever aware of the Self, O Krishna. How do they talk? How sit? How move about? (Gita 2:54)

Thoreau must have been enthralled, then, with the very long description Krishna gives about the way in which a person of wisdom carries himself in the world. Mahatma Gandhi would later say that this long sermon (Gita 2:55–72) is the very heart of the text. He believed that had nothing else survived of the ancient tract, this sermon would be enough to guide one through an entire lifetime. Krishna begins his sermon thus:

They live in wisdom who see themselves in all, and all in them . . . (Gita 2:55)

His sermon ends with the words Gandhi found most stirring:

They are forever free who renounce all selfish desires and break away from the ego-cage of "I," "me," and "mine" to be united with the Lord. This is the supreme state. Attain to this, and pass from death to immortality. (Gita 2:71–72)

7

Henry David Thoreau was smitten with Indian literature in general, and not only by the Bhagavad Gita. He read deeply into the ancient Vedas (a thousand years older than the Gita), The Laws of Manu, the great Indian drama named *Shakuntala*, and the few Upanishads that he could get his hands on. His imagination was caught up with the philosophy of yoga that he found in these tracts. In fact, he tells us in *Walden* that he saw his two years and two months at Walden Pond as a very explicit attempt to live life "as a yogi." In an 1849 letter to his friend Harrison Blake, Thoreau writes, "Depend upon it that rude and careless as I am, I would practice the yoga faithfully. To some extent, and at rare intervals, even I am a yogin." He often commented that the "sacred Ganges River flows into Walden Pond," and he owed his intellectual genesis to the "divine mixing" of both. Particularly during his time at Walden Pond, Thoreau began to see these Indian yoga tracts as his "scriptures for life."

What was it, precisely, that attracted him to this ancient literature? Most importantly, he found there an antidote to what he thought of as the stranglehold of Puritanism on American thinking. The Transcendentalism that he and his Concord friends espoused pushed back against Puritanism in every way. Transcendentalism was based on a belief in the innate goodness of the human being and of nature itself. As it turned out, these ancient Indian documents echoed this view exactly. And Thoreau found that these treatises portrayed a fundamentally different view of wisdom from the mainstream Western view—and one that more closely mirrored his own. For the yoga tradition, as for Thoreau, knowledge by itself—so prized in the West—was not necessarily wisdom. No. "Real wisdom" was much more practical than that. It was all about how one led one's life. Real wisdom must be seen in one's daily life—one's actions, one's daily pursuits. The real question was not *what did one know*, but *how was one living?* Was one living life to the fullest? "There are nowadays professors of philosophy, but not philosophers," Thoreau would later write in *Walden*. "To be a philosopher is not merely to have subtle thoughts, nor even to found a school, but so to love wisdom as to live according to its dictates, a life of simplicity, magnanimity, and trust. It is to solve some of the problems of life, not only theoretically, but practically."

A life of simplicity, magnanimity, and trust. This is what Thoreau wanted for himself. He would later write that "the mass of men lead lives of quiet desperation." The men and women he saw around him in Concord seemed constantly distracted by what he saw to be mundane and unworthy pursuits and obsessions. And he was determined to get beyond that in his own life. He wanted to simplify his life. To pare it down to its most essential elements. He tells us in Walden:

> I went to the woods because I wished to live deliberately, to front only the essential facts of life, and see if I could not learn what it had to teach, and not, when I came to die, discover that I had not lived. I did not wish to live what was not

> life, living is so dear; nor did I wish to practice resignation, unless it was quite necessary. I wanted to live deep and suck out all the marrow of life, to live so sturdily and Spartan-like as to put to rout all that was not life, to cut a broad swath and shave close, to drive life into a corner, and reduce it to its lowest terms . . .

Through his in-depth reading of yogic literature, Thoreau connected with an ancient society of human beings who had been *willing to go to any lengths* to find the Truth. Through these treatises, he was introduced to an entire culture devoted to living an optimal human life—just as he was. Nothing could thrill him more.

8

So Thoreau read, read, read. And, as always, he wrote in his journal to help him understand and digest what he read. It was at Walden that Thoreau read The Laws of Manu, an essential Hindu text dating from approximately the same period as the Gita. And he found that this somewhat legalistic and highly detailed text filled in the background of the story of the Gita for him in important ways. It was in The Laws of Manu that Thoreau found for himself a chunk of true gold: he found the ancient Indian teachings on the laws of karma, or "the laws of action."

The world thinks of Thoreau as a man of contemplation. But that is not how he saw himself. He saw himself decidedly as a man of action. An entire section of The Laws of Manu was devoted to the question of *right action*. It raised the very theodicy issue that we mentioned in the Prologue—that is to say, the question of Divine justice and its relationship to action. Thoreau saw that all of Krishna's teachings about action in the Bhagavad Gita are based on the "laws of karma" that were so clearly laid out in other ancient texts. The Sanskrit word *karma*, indeed, means "action." Here was a treasure trove of wisdom about action, and Henry Thoreau made a project of understanding this wisdom.

What precisely are the laws of karma, or the laws of action? In their simplest form, just this: Every "effect" in the Universe has a "cause," and every "cause" has an "effect." In other words, absolutely nothing in the Universe is random. The world unfolds in an orderly and predictable fashion according to certain laws. "A" leads to "B." "B" leads to "C." "C" leads to "D." Thoreau was a scientist at heart. He agreed with the yogis: on its face, nothing can be random. He dug deeper.

The mechanics of the laws of karma were worked out in great detail in the early culture of the yogis, and had been understood for at least 600 years before the writing of the Bhagavad Gita. Yogis practicing deep forms of meditation saw that certain so-called unwholesome actions have a predictable effect on the world. These unwholesome actions affect both the *actor* and the *acted upon*, and this effect shows up both in the moment and over the long term. In the actor, the performance of such actions inclines the mind of said actor to suffering and difficulty. In the acted upon, they lead to conflict, difficulty, and ill will.

What, then, did these yogis mean by "unwholesome actions"? The scriptures are very clear about this: unwholesome actions are actions motivated by greed, hatred, and delusion.

Yogis observed the opposite as well. They observed that certain so-called wholesome actions have a decidedly *salutary* effect on the world. In the actor himself, these wholesome actions create happiness and well-being. And in the acted upon, they promote gratitude, generosity, and loving-kindness. And what are wholesome actions? Again, the texts are crystal clear: wholesome actions are actions motivated by generosity, love, and wisdom.

Thoreau was intrigued to find that in the yoga tradition, when discussing action, adepts continually refer to *actions of body, speech, and mind*. Of course, in the West we don't usually think of the mind as an actor, but in the yoga tradition, *thoughts* are believed to be the most important aspect of action. Indeed, the laws of karma taught that it is the *mental volition* behind an act that determines its effect on the field of life. Further, they taught that the roots of volition are buried deep in the mind. So *actions are believed to be the outward and visible effects of deep mental volitions and intentions*. Mind, then, is in fact the first actor.

The Buddha—himself a yogi who, during his youth in the 4th century BCE, had studied all of the then-latest yogic wisdom (including the very wisdom tradition that Thoreau would later read at Walden Pond)—put this teaching most eloquently. "Mind precedes all phenomena," taught the Buddha.

Mind matters most
Everything is mind-made
If with an impure mind you speak or act, then
Suffering follows you as the cartwheel follows the foot
Of a draft animal.
If with a pure mind you speak or act
Then happiness follows you
As a shadow that never departs.

This brings us back to "cause and effect." It follows, teach the laws of karma, that if there is a precise understanding of what *causes* suffering, then our practice in this lifetime should be all about *attenuating those particular causes*. If, on the other hand, there is a precise understanding of the actions that *cause* happiness and well-being, then we should *cultivate those actions*, thereby bringing about wholesome effects.

In the West, the laws of karma are sometimes thought of as a manifestation of a kind of dysfunctional Eastern fatalism. Nothing could be further from the truth. The laws of karma embody the possibility of free will in every way. Indeed, early yogis called the laws of karma the "light of the world." Why? Because they allow us to understand exactly how we create suffering for ourselves, and by pinpointing the cause, they create the possibility that we might free ourselves from that suffering through our very own actions. Consequently, we can become masters of our own fate by becoming masters of our actions.

So the yoga tradition asks practitioners to look closely at their own actions and the volitions that motivate them. By proceeding in this way, yogis dedicated themselves to living the quintessential "examined life."

9

Thoreau, of course, was also living the "examined life." And he was most interested in what these laws of karma meant for his daily life, and for his own actions and the consequences of his actions. What seeds were planted by his trip to jail? Thoreau wondered. Seeds of happiness for himself and others? Or seeds of ill will and unhappiness? How would his act bear fruit in the future?

The laws of karma tell us that every action we take has an effect on "the entire field of mind and matter." Every action we take *matters absolutely.* Our every action begins a chain of events that leads both the individual and society toward either happiness and fulfillment or toward unhappiness and suffering. Every action, no matter how small, ripples through the Universe and is the cause of a subsequent series of actions. A to B to C to D. No exceptions.

This teaching contains within it an oft-overlooked implication: there can be no justification for performing an unwholesome action simply because it may eventually lead to what the actor might consider a "good end." Absolutely not! The ends can never justify the means. In fact, in the view of the yoga traditions, the means *are* the ends. The means—the quality of the action itself, right in the here and now—is everything.

Do you see? Because every action has a mystic effect on the entire field, there can be no rationalization for "unwholesome" acts—whatever their purported aims.

Of course, this view is no more popular in today's cultural milieu than it was in Thoreau's. Like Thoreau, we live in a political and economic culture that justifies all sorts of unwholesome actions simply because they appear to be effective means to certain wished-for ends. (In Thoreau's day, the most stunning examples of this error in thinking were the many rationalizations for the ongoing support of slavery. For example, the Northern states justified their support for slavery with the pernicious view that slavery provided the true engine of economic prosperity for both the North and the South, and as such, it provided livelihoods for thousands of people. Or this equally perfidious view: slavery could never be ended without a war, which, the argument went, would be demonstrably worse than slavery itself. So, the ends justify the means.)

But Thoreau understood the fallacy. "We have not yet understood that the Universe simply does not work that way," he insisted. Unwholesome *means* inexorably yield unwholesome *ends*. Period.

Parenthetically, there is no more persuasive proponent of this view—the view that the means *are* the ends—than our friend Mr. Gandhi. Speaking of means and ends, Gandhi wrote: "By detachment I mean that you must not worry whether the desired result follows from your action or not, as long as your motive is pure, [and] your means [are] correct. Really, it means that things will come right in the end if you take care of the means and leave the rest to [God]." We shall look much more closely at Gandhi's thinking about the question of means and ends in the final chapter of this book.

10

After his night in jail, Henry Thoreau dedicated himself to getting to the bottom of the question of his duty as a citizen of the United States of America. What duty did he have to *act* in the face of injustice and oppression? What actions on his part might lead to happiness and well-being for the *whole* citizenry?

Thoreau followed his own time-tested routine when wrestling with such thorny questions. He would state the questions as succinctly as he could. Then he would ponder them. Make notes in his journal. And read, read, read. He would read what great minds had written and spoken about the question. And eventually, having begun to digest the issue, he would put his thoughts together in the form of a talk. He would very often start with a talk at Concord's own small Lyceum, which was hosted variously at local churches and halls. And eventually, he would move on to a larger venue—perhaps closer to Boston.

Early on in his process of putting together a talk, Thoreau would sometimes try it out on a small group of friends gathered outside his cabin door at Walden. He would gather together a group of two to fifteen souls to listen to him declaim. On these occasions, Thoreau would speak from the door of his one-room cabin as his friends and neighbors spread out on the slope going down to the pond. The talks were often controversial. (Thoreau thoroughly enjoyed shocking people.) They were always colorful. They were full of allusions to nature.

Above all, we must observe that once Thoreau had formulated something that he needed to *say*, he insisted on being heard—live and in person. He simply had to bring forth what was within him. It was a central aspect of his calling. Versions of these talks—formal and informal—can still be found, and they are solid gold to read.

I often wonder if Thoreau knew Walt Whitman's poem about "speaking out," the great poem in which Whitman compares himself to the hawk overhead who insists on being heard. "The spotted hawk swoops by and accuses me," writes Whitman, ". . . he complains of my gab and my loitering." (Many people in Concord accused Thoreau of the very same thing: being a "gab" and a "loiterer.") But Whitman—like the hawk, like Thoreau—was not to be tamed:

I too am not a bit tamed—I too am untranslatable;
I sound my barbaric yawp over the roofs of the world.

Thoreau's barbaric yawp was routinely heard all around Concord Village.

11

Henry David Thoreau was now preoccupied with his great dilemma. What is the individual's duty to the state? What is his duty to his own conscience? In the years just before the Civil War, of course, this was America's dilemma too. And, in fact, it is America's dilemma even now, almost two hundred years after Thoreau lived. How does one act in a situation in which one's own government is obviously doing the wrong thing? Thoreau, from his cabin at Walden, would take this on for all of us—the way a monk in his monastery prays for the good of the whole; the way my monk friends back in Cambridge lived quietly in the monastery and reached out and touched the whole world with their prayers. Thoreau's writing and his speaking *were* his form of prayer. Thoreau, in fact, sometimes thought of himself as a monk. He acknowledged that because he was not married, had no children to care for, and no real job—like a monk—it would be his job to think these things through for all of us. He could risk going to jail. He could risk speaking out. And so, he must.

By the time Henry Thoreau got halfway through his retreat at Walden Pond, he was already well on his way to an understanding of his own dharma. Words were Thoreau's craft. Words were his métier. Words were his dharma. Words gave him his power to act. He would be "a poet, a writer, a man of letters," he declared out loud, at a time when poetry was hardly considered a real vocation. And, of course, Thoreau went well beyond that. He wrote: "I am a mystic, a Transcendentalist, and a natural philosopher to boot." He understood that his dharma was just exactly as wild and crazy and unorthodox as he was in every way.

Because it was at the very heart of his dharma, Henry David Thoreau took the craft of writing seriously. He was highly disciplined. He held the same view that my Harvard Square monks did: a spiritual life is a disciplined life. Writing was his calling, and he would bring everything he had to it. His retreat at Walden Pond was an outward and visible sign of this. At Walden he would retreat to the woods to refine his craft. He saw his dharma as getting to the very bottom of things through his writing. Big things. Indeed, at Walden, he was investigating nothing less than the meaning of life. He would not be deterred by the size of the project.

Thoreau wrestled with his night in jail for a very long time. In fact, it would take an entire eighteen months for Thoreau's mind and heart to integrate his experience. But finally, on January 26, 1848, Thoreau announced that he would step up to the podium of the Concord Lyceum to explain, at long last, why he had gone to jail rather than pay his poll tax. The town was abuzz: Henry had a new lecture. This one was called "The Relation of the Individual to the State."

12

It was a freezing cold afternoon when Thoreau finally did mount the podium of the Lyceum—the same podium that Wendell Phillips had mounted two years earlier (when Thoreau had decided that he wanted to *be* Wendell Phillips). Lamps were burning around the old hall, and there were roaring fires in the two black-piped stoves at the back of the room. The smell of damp wool and woodsmoke saturated the air. The windows along both sides of the hall were almost completely frosted over.

And yet. Here they were. En masse. The villagers of Concord. The town had come together to hear Henry explain himself on the matter of jail. As usual, he did not disappoint. Thoreau was on fire that afternoon.

By way of introduction, Henry emphasized that he took his obligations as a citizen seriously. As a citizen, he said, he had not only a *right*, but a *moral obligation* to speak out. He began his talk boldly:

"I cannot for an instant recognize that political organization as *my* government which is the *slave's* government also," he said. Townspeople knew they were in for something important. They settled in. A hush came over the crowd.

Thoreau then launched into the body of his talk. He began by mentioning three abuses of "the State" that he found particularly unacceptable: first, the state sponsorship of slavery; second, the unwonted and reckless war in Mexico; and third, the state-sponsored robbery of the lands of Native Americans. He made it clear that he saw in each of these a form of state-sponsored violence. And he saw in each of them a violation of his personal moral code. But he would insist that each instance must also be a violation of the *ethical conscience of the larger community*. He implored his neighbors to see what was happening in their name and under their very noses. He had no time for sweeping these things under the rug.

Then Henry laid down a challenge to his neighbors: the State's action requires each of us to withdraw from the State in some meaningful way. He said, "If the injustice is of such a nature that it requires you to be the agent of injustice to another, then, I say, break the law. Let your life be a counter friction to stop the machine. What I have to do is to see, at any rate, that I do not lend myself to the wrong which I condemn."

This sparked some commotion in the audience, and some murmuring. Would Thoreau go too far?

Henry continued: our motivation cannot be convenience, safety, and merely the exigencies of the moment. He pinpointed the error in this way of thinking. Yes, it's true that the ultimate social good is "a smooth-running social machine," such as one often experienced in rural Concord. But when the smooth-running machine of civil government causes injustice, the citizen's moral duty is not submission but resistance. "Put a spoke in the wheel!" said Henry.

Here, Thoreau gave a vivid analogy. "If I have unjustly wrested a plank from a drowning man, I must restore it to him though I drown myself . . . He that would save his life, in such case, shall lose it. This people must cease to hold slaves, and to make war on Mexico, though it cost them their existence as a people."

Thoreau went on to insist that by "resistance" he meant not just self-defense, defense of one's fellow citizens, or even of one's own nation, but *defense of all those lives entangled with our own.* This meant slaves, upon whose labor even "free" Massachusetts depended economically; this meant Mexicans, the declared enemies of the state; and this meant Native Americans, in some quarters the declared enemies of civilization itself.

Now Thoreau barreled into the heart of his argument. He wanted to get the crowd to understand the *mystic power of right action.* He had himself already come to understand this—to understand, as the Gita taught him, that when we act based on generosity, loving-kindness, truth, and defense of the right, our actions have mystic power. They change the entire field around us. But how could young Thoreau move his neighbors toward this understanding as well—when the insight had taken him years to achieve?

"I know this well," said Thoreau. His voice was now raised to a fever pitch, "that if one thousand, if one hundred, if ten men whom I could name—if ten honest men only—ay, if one HONEST man, in this State of Massachusetts, ceasing to hold slaves, were actually to withdraw from this co-partnership, and be locked up in the county jail therefor, it would be the abolition of slavery in America. For it matters not how small the beginning may seem to be: what is once well done is done forever."

For it matters not how small the beginning may seem to be: what is once well done is done forever.

What you do *matters utterly.* What you do in every moment of your life matters utterly. A "right action" done well becomes immortal. It is done forever. In Thoreau's view, a right action, a just action, exists beyond time.

Thoreau came to believe that any "right action" that is well done—that is done with all of our energy, commitment, and intelligence—

changes the field around it. He wrote: "It is not so important that many should be good as you, as that there be some absolute goodness somewhere; for that will leaven the whole lump."

Your own action, no matter how small, will leaven the entire lump.

The crowd sat in silence. It was after 4 p.m., and the sun had gone down. The room grew colder, even as Thoreau grew hotter and more intense. The murmuring had died down as Thoreau's talk came to a close. Applause was sparse, though some of Henry's friends congratulated him with a handshake after the talk. The crowd ushered themselves out of the hall and into their carriages in almost complete silence. They had been confronted with the full force of Henry David Thoreau. They were not sure if they liked it.

13

Thoreau had brought everything he had to this talk. And what was its fruit? Well, at first, it seemed to have borne little fruit at all. Indeed, this brilliant lecture initially appeared to have died on the vine. On May 14, 1849, Thoreau's talk was published as an essay in a small New England journal under the title "Resistance to Civil Government." There, alas, it had a minuscule readership. And then, Thoreau's "barbaric yawp" about civic duty and right action vanished almost immediately into obscurity.

But it would not die. What is once well done is done forever. When the essay was republished in 1866, four years after Thoreau's death, under the new title, "Civil Disobedience," it coined a phrase, started a movement, and eventually earned itself and Thoreau international fame. The essay—barely noticed in his own lifetime—became one of Thoreau's most lasting contributions to the world.

The message, eventually, would reverberate around the world. In America it would become the template for what civil rights icon John Lewis came to call "good trouble." In India it would become the manual for "the moral equivalent of war" waged by Mahatma Gandhi in his successful campaign to free India from the British Empire. And on and on.

14

Through acting on his own dharma—his genius as a thinker and wordsmith—Thoreau would make an epic cautionary tale out of his single night in jail. Mahatma Gandhi, Nelson Mandela, and Martin Luther King Jr. would read and reread his words as they sat in their own jail cells after their own acts of civil disobedience—inspired by Thoreau.

Indeed, Thoreau's essay would completely reframe the experience of jail for many generations of activists. "Under a government which imprisons any unjustly," Thoreau wrote in "Civil Disobedience," "the true place for a just man is also a prison." Gandhi found great encouragement in reading Thoreau's words: "The proper place to-day, the only place which Massachusetts has provided for her freer and less desponding spirits, is in her prisons, to be put out and locked out of the State by her own act, as they have already put themselves out by their principles. It is there that the fugitive slave, and the Mexican prisoner on parole, and the Indian come to plead the wrongs of his race, should find them on that separate, but more free and honorable ground, where the State places those who are not *with* her, but *against* her—the only house in a slave State in which a free man can abide with honor."

Thoreau then provides the *coup de grace*. "A minority is powerless while it conforms to the majority; it is not even a minority then; but it is *irresistible* when it clogs by its whole weight. If the alternative is to keep all just men in prison, or give up war and slavery, the State will not hesitate which to choose. If a thousand men were not to pay their tax-bills this year, that would not be a violent and bloody measure, as it would be to pay them, and enable the State to commit violence and shed innocent blood. This is, in fact, the definition of a peaceable revolution, if any such is possible."

Gandhi, of course, understood Thoreau's idea perfectly. It is estimated that Gandhi spent a total of at least seven years of his life behind prison walls. He thought of prison as "sacred space," where he did some of his best writing and praying. Gandhi himself wrote from prison in a way that amplifies Thoreau's argument. Gandhi writes: "I believe that if one man gains spiritually, the whole world gains with him, and, if one man falls, the whole world falls to that extent. I do not help opponents without at the same time helping myself and my coworkers."

Gandhi continues: "All of us are one. When you inflict suffering on others you are bringing suffering on yourself. When you weaken others, you are weakening yourselves, weakening the whole nation."

Thoreau understood that doing the "wrong thing," on the other hand, has "a wounding effect" on both the individual and society. He wrote: "Is there not a sort of blood shed when the conscience is wounded? Through this wound a man's real manhood and immortality flow out, and he bleeds to an everlasting death." (We can see, can't we, that Thoreau privileges "conscience" above all things, just as Gandhi did.)

Therefore, as I said at the end of Chapter 2, "the whole is in the part, and the part is in the whole." We are all joined utterly. And we share in the consequences of one another's actions. It is well to recall here Krishna's teaching about Indra's web. Remember: each jewel in Indra's net represents both itself as a particular jewel and, at the same time, the entire web. So any change in one gem would be reflected in the whole. Indeed, the individual gem is the whole. In the words of Indologist Sir Charles Eliot, "Every object in the world is not merely itself but involves every other object and in fact IS everything else."

This view must utterly reframe our ideas about action.

15

"Cast your whole vote," wrote Thoreau, "not a strip of paper merely, but your whole influence." In other words: bring the full weight of your soul to your duty.

We will see that every truly dharmic act lives at the intersection of several components. A dharmic act is like a jewel with many facets—a jewel that exists both *in* time and *out of time*.

Krishna teaches that when one's idiosyncratic gift is put unreservedly in the service of one's individual soul *as well as* the common good, this action is the quintessence of dharma—and it has a particularly powerful mystic effect. It is happening now, and it is also happening forever, because it is aligned with our Immortal True Nature.

We sometimes call certain acts "immortal," don't we? Lincoln's signing of the Emancipation Proclamation was an "immortal act." Why is that? It was an act done well. It is done forever. It is immortal.

16

In order to see what this means for our own lives, we might put this in the form of a question. How does *your* idiosyncratic genius serve both your own soul and the common good most effectively right now—in this particular moment in time? It is at this intersection that you will find dharma of the most robust, world-changing kind.

Thoreau could not possibly have been more correct in his understanding of the mystic power of right action. Indeed, he could hardly have known how powerful his own small act of civil disobedience would be. The essay that resulted from his night in jail would inspire a host of important world actors. Danish resisters used it in their fight against the Nazi invaders during World War II. Martin Luther King Jr. depended upon it in his battle against racial segregation in our own South. And anti–Vietnam War protesters used it to force Lyndon Johnson to abandon plans for a second term of his presidency and to force Richard Nixon to bring that war to an end. Thoreau's night in jail became immortal.

Henry David Thoreau did it all from his own backyard. From the little village of Concord, Massachusetts. Thoreau is said to have once quipped, "I have travelled extensively in Concord." Indeed he had.

17

In the final chapters of the Bhagavad Gita, Krishna teaches Arjuna that the energy of dharma is a real, palpable force in the world. It is invisible, yes—sometimes subtle, always mysterious—but it is more real than rain. And it is an active force throughout our every breathing moment.

Simply look to your own small actions to change the world. If they are right, if they are aligned with truth, they will change the world. Just look in your own backyard for your opportunity. "The best place for each is where he stands," wrote Thoreau. Because the whole world is right there. Your own deeds, as small as they may seem to you, will reverberate through the entire field. We think we have to do great things. No! No! No! What we must do over and over again are "small things well-done."

Most of us do not realize how much our lives have been touched by Henry David Thoreau. We do not know how much the world we live in has been formed by his powerful dharma actions—actions whose effect reach out to us from almost 200 years ago. We all stand on Thoreau's shoulders. Our friend Walt Whitman, however, was one human being who actually did understand—in real time—the mystic effect that both he and Thoreau would have on the world. Of himself and his own dharmic actions, Whitman wrote:

I bequeath myself to the dirt to grow from the grass I love,
If you want me again look for me under your boot-soles.

You will hardly know who I am, or what I mean;
But I shall be good health to you nevertheless,
And filter and fibre your blood.

Failing to fetch me at first keep encouraged,
Missing me one place search another,
I stop somewhere waiting for you.

CHAPTER 4

HARRIET BEECHER STOWE

Look for the Gift in the Wound

Deep unspeakable suffering may well be called a baptism, a regeneration, the initiation into a new state.

— George Eliot, *Adam Bede*

Even before it began, the people of Boston knew that January 1, 1863, would be a New Year's Day unlike any other. The United States had for two years been plunged into a horrific civil war—provoked, as Henry David Thoreau had anticipated—by the issue of slavery. Now President Abraham Lincoln had promised that on this first day of 1863—deep into a war that was going badly for the Union—he would sign the much-anticipated Emancipation Proclamation. With this proclamation he would declare that all slaves in any state still in rebellion against the United States "shall be then, thenceforward, and forever free."

In anticipation of the signing, crowds had begun to gather early in the day—not just in Boston, of course, but all across the North. Public spaces everywhere were overrun with expectant citizens awaiting news. There was some unanticipated suspense in the moment, however. In spite of his promise, many believed that it was by no means certain that Lincoln would sign, especially since the recent defeat of the Union Army at Fredericksburg had changed the national political calculus.

The hours dragged by. No word came. Hearts sank. Crowds began to wane.

Finally, the news broke. Around 10 P.M. runners from the telegraph office in Boston arrived breathlessly in front of the gathered crowds. Lincoln had signed. Enslaved persons in the rebellious Southern states had been freed.

Upon hearing the news, the large crowd packed into the Boston Music Hall erupted in almost frantic joy. And as the rejoicing hit its peak in that particular temple of American culture, a slow chant began to emerge spontaneously from the crowd. "Harriet Beecher Stowe!!! Harriet Beecher Stowe!!!"

Harriet Beecher Stowe was indeed there in the Hall that night—along with many of Boston's literary greats, including Emerson, Longfellow, Whittier, Fuller, and much of the local abolitionist community. And as Stowe slowly made her way to the front of the Hall, the crowd quieted. Here she was: the author and abolitionist whose work had turned the tide in the North against slavery. Here she was: a small, middle-aged woman, unprepossessing in appearance. Here she was. Rumpled. Bonnet askew. Tears streaming down her lined face. Most people had never laid eyes on her.

Stowe strode slowly toward the podium. She was quietly self-assured. Modest. Upon getting a glimpse of her, the crowd began the chant again, even louder than before. The audience in the Music Hall that night understood that this slight woman, as much as any single individual in the land, had helped bring freedom to the enslaved South. She had done it with her pen, with her passionate, informed prose. She had recounted the suffering of slavery in such a riveting fashion that Northerners almost overnight joined the antislavery movement.

Harriet Beecher Stowe's novel *Uncle Tom's Cabin*—the cause for her notoriety that evening—had become the best-selling book of the century, second only to the Bible. It so vividly depicted the suffering of slavery that the degradations of this institution became unbearably real for hundreds of thousands of readers. And it sparked them to take action. The book itself had been an act of moral courage. The woman, a phenomenon. How do we explain her?

Harriet Beecher Stowe's novel was, in fact, the fruit of a devastating and disorienting personal loss that she suffered at the age of thirty-eight. In the process of resolving her own life-altering dilemma, she turned her wound into light for millions of people. She transmuted her own personal suffering into a new literary form. She looked for, and found, a gift in the very heart of her own wound. This will be the subject of our next inquiry into the discernment of dharma in difficult times: look for the gift in the wound.

2

As an eighteen-year-old undergraduate at Amherst College, I was always puzzled by a larger-than-life bronze statue of a man that stood just at the entry to the campus. Who was this guy? Most Amherst students at the time, I'm sure, could not have told you, even though we all passed him ten times a day as we walked to and from classes. But there he stood through the seasons, strangely invisible—like wallpaper. The words beneath the statue said, simply, "Henry Ward Beecher. Class of 1834." At that time, I was a hayseed from Ohio, recently transplanted to this old New England college. I had little sense of the history of this place, its early 19th-century origins, its heroes. I had no idea what Beecher represented to Amherst and to the United States of America. (How often have you walked past a monument or a statue—utterly oblivious of its meaning?) But as I read the story of the abolitionists later in life, I became fascinated by this Henry Ward Beecher guy who came from one of America's preeminent abolitionist families. And I inevitably bumped into the even more interesting tale of Henry Ward Beecher's younger sister, Harriet.

3

Harriet Elisabeth Beecher was born in Litchfield, Connecticut, in June of 1811. She was the sixth of eleven children of the then famous Calvinist preacher Lyman Beecher. She grew up steeped in a severe form of Christianity, which would produce, in Harriet's generation, a plethora of fiery abolitionists and brilliant preachers, including her aforementioned brother, Henry.

By her late teens, Harriet had grown into a quietly impressive woman. She was, of course, a devout Christian. But she was not pious. She was not stuffy. She was, rather, a creature of authentic and well-studied faith. Throughout her life, she would show herself to be remarkably pluralistic in religious matters, much as Gandhi was. Her upbringing had produced in her a sincere interest in truth. And again like Gandhi, an interest in soul and something very like what Gandhi would have called Soul Force.

Biographer Nancy Koester gives us a good description of Harriet. "[She] possessed character and wit in abundance," writes Koester, "though no one described her as beautiful. She was small in stature with sparkling grey blue eyes. Her nose was long and her cheekbones high, but dark curls framed her face, softening her features."

By her early twenties, Harriet Beecher had already become an interesting combination of religious mystic and activist. She had the sensibility of a visionary. In a letter she wrote to her brother Thomas, Harriet confided that she saw "a deep immortal longing" in human beings—a longing to find a true and worthy calling in the world. This very longing would haunt her life.

4

Until the age of twenty-one, Harriet lived a sheltered life in small-town Connecticut. There, she could entertain her high aspirations without much risk of challenge. This would all change. At twenty-one years of age, Harriet would be thrust into the very heart of America's biggest conflict: slavery. In 1832, she moved to Cincinnati, Ohio, to join her father, who had become the president of Lane Theological Seminary there.

Cincinnati in those years was a rough-and-tumble frontier town. Perched as it was right on the Ohio River, it had inevitably become an important hub for trade and shipping. But the river was notable for something else. It was the dividing line between Ohio, a free state, and Kentucky, a slave state. As you might imagine, then, in the decades leading up to the Civil War, self-emancipated slaves, desperately heading north, would routinely cross the river right at Cincinnati. Slave catchers scoured the town for them. As a result, the city was always full of self-emancipated slaves and the bounty hunters who followed them across the river. Violence rumbled just under the surface of Cincinnati's life. In the 1830s it regularly erupted in the form of riots—often between its many Irish immigrants and African Americans, who competed for jobs on the canals and railroads.

In Cincinnati the ghastly reality of slavery was right in Harriet's face on a daily basis. Boats carrying slaves to be sold in the South often lay over in Cincinnati. Harriet observed them closely and was shocked at what she saw. On the upper deck of these boats, she wrote, "were happy mothers, wives and husbands, brothers and sisters rejoicing in secure family affection, and on the deck below, miserable shattered fragments of black families, wives torn from husbands, children without mothers and mothers without children . . ." Stowe knew that the slaves on the lower deck were bound for the hell of captivity "down river" in the Deep South, where they would likely never be heard from again.

5

In the summer of 1833, Harriet, with a friend, made her first excursion to a slave-owning plantation across the river in Kentucky. This visit made a strong impression on her, and she would later use it as the model for the Shelby plantation in *Uncle Tom's Cabin.* (In those years, Harriet was constantly gathering material for what she hoped would someday be a fulsome "writing-life." She harbored a secret hunch that her true calling was writing, but she just had not yet been able to make it happen.) The friend who accompanied her on this excursion noted that throughout the visit to the plantation, Harriet said little, but that "her eyes were big," and she was clearly taking it all in. We know now that the scenes she observed never left her.

Cincinnati in those years simmered with stories of slaves' harrowing escapes across the Ohio River. One of these stories made a powerful impression on Harriet and would become a central story in *Uncle Tom's Cabin.* Once, when her father had taken her on a visit to the home of the Reverend John Rankin—one of her father's fellow clergymen—Rankin told a story that Harriet would never forget. The good Reverend lived in a home situated high on the bluffs overlooking the Ohio River. At night he had the custom of setting up a signal light that might guide self-emancipated slaves to the safety of his home. When they arrived, wet and shivering, he would hide them in one of his outbuildings until it was safe for them to move farther north.

Harriet was riveted by one of these tales of escape, told with such emotion by the Reverend Rankin. Later, Rankin would write a memoir in which he tells this very story in detail. Here it is in his own words:

> A Kentucky slave mother having been harshly treated by her mistress, took her child in her arms and in the night started for Canada. She came to the house of an old Scotsman who lived on the Ohio River. She asked him what was best for her to do. My house being on top of a high hill, he pointed to it and said, "A good man lives in that house. Go to it and you will be safe." The river was frozen over and a thaw had come so the water was running over the ice, which was just ready to break up. She waded across and went to my house, went into the kitchen, made a fire and dried herself. Then she waked up two of my boys and they conveyed her to another depot that same night. The lakes being frozen over she could not get to Canada till spring. She passed the winter at Greenfield. Her husband, who was also a slave, followed her there."

This story haunted Harriet's imagination. As we will see, it would later become transformed into the story of "Eliza" in *Uncle Tom's Cabin.*

6

At the age of twenty-three, Harriet met Reverend Calvin Ellis Stowe, a widower who was a professor of biblical literature at Lane Seminary. The two married at the seminary on January 6, 1836. Calvin Stowe was an ardent critic of slavery, and he and his new wife would go on to support Cincinnati's active Underground Railroad in every way that they could.

I remember, as a boy growing up in central Ohio, visiting a house that had been a way station on the Underground Railroad. It was a cavernous brick building dating from the 1830s. I couldn't have been more than six years old when my mother took me to this house, which was owned by a close friend of hers. I remember Mom holding my hand as she led me down two flights of stairs into a dark cellar, lit only by a kerosene lantern that gave off small puffs of black smoke and an acrid smell. There, with the help of our hostess, we found a secret door carved into a wall. Upon opening it, we entered into a very small room dug out of the pure rock and earth. It was damp and cold. I couldn't quite make out the unique combination of smells that hit me like a wave. Roots of trees had penetrated the room and twisted around themselves. It was impossible for me to believe: Runaway slaves hid here? I asked Mom. How could they even breathe? I remember being just a little claustrophobic myself, holding Mom's hand tighter, and being relieved when we left and climbed the rickety stairs back to safety. At the top of the stairs, I took a deep breath.

The memory of this secret room has stayed with me throughout my adult life.

That was my first small whiff of the harrowing reality of slavery. My maternal grandmother would later recount to me that my own family had participated in the very same Underground Railroad in their homes in upstate New York.

7

By the year 1847, Calvin and Harriet Stowe had delivered five children together. The Stowes' sixth child was born in January of 1848. They named him Samuel Charles and called him "Charley."

By Harriet's own account, Charley was a special delight to her. He was, she wrote, "a beautiful, loving, gladsome baby . . . full of life, strength and hope." For the first time, Harriet had no trouble nursing her baby. It had been her happiest pregnancy and delivery. There was clearly a special bond between Harriet and little Charley.

I've heard other mothers describe this special bond—often with their last and youngest child. Harriet later described how she would "hold [Charley] to my bosom and feel the loneliness and sorrow pass out of me with the touch of his little warm hands." I remember some of those very feelings when I held my niece, Catherine, as a baby. It was as if merely holding her altered my body's chemistry. I couldn't get enough of her—of that feeling. It's clear, in all that Harriet wrote later, that baby Charley had brought her special joy and comfort.

8

As you might already have guessed, tragedy loomed. In early 1849, several cases of cholera broke out in Cincinnati, and by late spring the disease had become epidemic. Cholera: a dreaded word. Cholera was then and still is today a particularly grisly disease. Doctors during Stowe's lifetime had no idea what caused it, nor was there any known cure. To catch the disease was an automatic death sentence. And what a terrible death it was. Patients suffering cholera were wracked by convulsions and quickly lost all of the fluids in their bodies. Families gathered around a cholera deathbed watched helplessly as their loved one writhed in pain. Nearly a hundred people died like this every day during the epidemic in Cincinnati. Panic spread quickly. Soon, word got out along the Ohio River. Signs went up along the riverbanks approaching the city. *Epidemic! Pass on by!* Henceforth, riverboats refused to stop at Cincinnati.

By July, eighteen-month-old Charley had begun to get sick, and it soon became clear that it was, indeed, the curse of cholera. Harriet realized it was a death sentence, of course, and nursed Charley as best she could. But in fact, all she could do was watch helplessly while her child was racked by unbearable suffering.

On July 26, Harriet broke the devastating news by letter to her husband, Calvin—who was traveling and not able to get home in time to say goodbye to his son. "At last it is over," she wrote, "and our dear little one is gone from us." Harriet wrote the letter upstairs in her room, while Charley lay in the parlor below, as she wrote: "shrouded, pale, and cold." It was the custom in those years to pose deceased children for death photos. Such a photo exists of Charley. It is hard to look at. Posed as he is in these photos, he looks like he is sleeping. His blonde hair is neatly combed. Is it possible he is dead?

9

It is a truth universally acknowledged that the death of a child is the most devastating loss a parent can sustain. It is often called the ultimate tragedy, and it leads to what some psychologists have classified as a special form of grief: "long-term, high-intensity grief." There is a great deal written about this. Says one writer, in an understated fashion: "Along with the usual stages of grief, there are many complicating issues that can make parental bereavement particularly difficult to resolve." She continues: "During the early days of grieving, most parents experience excruciating pain, alternating with numbness—a dichotomy that may persist for months or longer. Many parents . . . report that they feel that they can only 'exist' and every motion or need beyond that seems nearly impossible . . . All bereaved parents lose a part of themselves."

As it turns out, at the very time I was writing this chapter on Harriet Beecher Stowe, I lost my thirty-five-year-old nephew, Henry, in a tragic car crash in South Carolina. Henry was the son of my twin sister, Sandy, and her husband, Val. The phone call from my devastated niece (the aforementioned baby Catherine, now grown, and Henry's only sibling) came to me late at night. It is burned into memory. Henry had been in a car crash in Charleston. Catherine recounted the story in a voice shaking with emotion. Henry was in intensive care. On life support. Then, the dreaded, "You should come."

I scrambled to pack, and to cancel all my plans up North, and arrived in South Carolina on the next plane. I waited with my older brother, Randy, at Sandy's home in Columbia. Sometime after midnight, Sandy and Val and Catherine arrived home from their vigil at the hospital. They were dazed—staring at one another and at my brother and me with vacant disbelief. Our silence acknowledged the obvious: there were no words. They had made the decision that night to take Henry off life support. He would die within hours.

The next day I went with the family to the funeral home. No one wanted to identify the body. The sight would be too gruesome. Ghastly. Unthinkable. At the thought of it, Catherine ran down the hall in a fit of screaming and sobbing. All of us were in uncontrollable tears as we together wrote the obituary of this handsome, charming thirty-five-year-old boy. He left behind an eight-year-old daughter, Ella Grace.

What followed was, I suppose, predictable. There was a huge outpouring of grief. School friends of Henry's were shocked, unbelieving—and showed up by the dozens; there were hundreds of people in the receiving line at the calling hours; there was a solemn service, with remembrances of Henry; there were rooms draped in massive floral arrangements; there was hushed conversation. Soothing music was piped in, and unobtrusive men in black suits managed the flow of the crowd and brought bottles of cold water.

Then, in the days after the funeral, came the real stuff. I watched as the entire family—myself included—descended into a level of disintegration and disorganization I had never before experienced. As I've said, Henry was the son of my twin sister, Sandy. I watched helplessly as Sandy went through months of searing, tearing grief. At times she would have blackouts and could not remember whole parts of days. More than once she literally fell to the floor because her legs would not hold her up. We all struggled together to make sense of the tragedy, and to hold one another up. But for many months, we felt like drowning people, just barely staying afloat. We each struggled to make meaning of this senseless and gruesome death. How do we understand this? How does it change our view of the world? Of the laws of nature? Of God? Of the apparent random violence of life.

For many months it felt to us as if we were on a journey with only a few of us on board. It is a fact that a grisly death like Henry's—and at such a young age—is just too terrible for most people to even imagine. The mind reels, and will not process it. Friends don't call because they simply don't know what to say. People avoid the subject. After two weeks of fraught activity, there is deafening silence.

This is precisely how it must have been for Harriet Beecher Stowe. How could it have been otherwise?

10

Different parents have different abilities to cope, of course. One father dealing with the death of a child reported that his faith in life in general had been shattered. He had long believed that if you lived your life as a good person, striving to make a positive contribution to the world, life would turn out well. The death of his son robbed him of that belief. This reaction is not uncommon; losing a child feels like the ultimate violation of the rules of life.

Says one researcher: "The search for meaning in a child's death is especially important to parents. An understanding of how a death fits into the scheme of life is difficult and often unattainable. Faith is a source of comfort for some parents, but others with religious beliefs report feeling betrayed by God. Religious confusion is normal, as is questioning many things that you may have believed to be certain."

Most people do not understand that, especially for the mother, there is a very real struggle simply to survive—to want to go on. Several years ago I went to speak and teach at Sandy Hook Elementary School in Newtown, Connecticut, the site of America's largest shooting of young children. One of the parents of a slain child—a parent who had been a leader in the struggle to survive the massacre—had just committed suicide. He simply could not go on. The community was rocked again. I saw it in the faces of the crowd as I was speaking that day.

Says one author: "Surviving the death and loss of a child takes a dedication to life. As a parent, you gave birth to life as a promise to the future. Now you must make a new commitment to living, as hard or impossible as it may seem right now. You will survive this; however, the experience may change you."

11

After one of the two losses that upended her life, Emily Dickinson wrote something incisive about her own grief process.

I measure every Grief I meet
With narrow, probing, eyes -
I wonder if It weighs like Mine -
Or has an Easier size -
I wonder if They bore it long -
Or did it just begin -
I could not tell the Date of Mine -
It feels so old a pain -

"I measure every grief I meet . . ." I went through this after Henry died. All of a sudden I had a kind of newly installed radar for the suffering of loss. I saw it everywhere. Until this point in my adult life, of course, I had heard many, many stories of child death. I had heard the stories, yes. But I now realize that until you've actually been there yourself, these stories simply roll off you.

More than once, Sandy—like Emily Dickinson, like the father from Connecticut—thought of suicide.

I wonder if it hurts to live -
And if They have to try -
And whether - could They choose between -
It would not be - to die -

Having experienced the death of a beloved child is like having been to a new land. One begins to feel a deep communion with others who have been there. It is something you see in the eyes. It is the initiation into a new country. Writes novelist George Eliot (aka Mary Ann Evans), who experienced her own dreadful loss, "Deep unspeakable suffering may well be called a baptism, a regeneration, the initiation into a new state."

12

Henry's death gave me a new understanding of Harriet Beecher Stowe's situation. In the aftermath of Charley's death, Harriet, too, must have surveyed every grief she saw. I am sure that in Cincinnati she saw grief and loss all around her, and began to identify with it and relate to it in a way she never had. She tells us that she would lie awake night after night, listening to the wind, "thinking of [her] summer child who died of cholera."

How did Harriet get through this? Well, we know that she turned to her faith. She sought refuge. She immersed herself in her religious life, just as I did after my best friend, John, died when I was thirty. Harriet wrote to her husband, Calvin: "I am strong in spirit, and God who has been with me in so many straits will not forsake me now. I know Him well; He is my Father, and though I may be a blind and erring child, He will help me for all that . . . we shall not sink, my dear Husband."

We shall not sink!

How could Harriet make peace with her loss? She later wrote that there were circumstances of "such bitterness in the manner of Charley's death" that she didn't think she could ever be reconciled to it *unless his death allowed her to do some great good to others.* And now a new note enters in: she also wrote that losing Charley made her understand "what a slave woman felt when her child was taken away from her at the auction block." It had allowed her to empathize with slave women whose children had been violently ripped away from them. She felt how they lost a part of themselves.

Harriet's heart was ripped open. This allowed her to empathize with others whose hearts had been similarly broken. And she noticed that this gave birth within her to an altogether new feeling of compassion—a deep feeling of sympathy for the suffering of others. Indeed, more than a feeling of sympathy, she describes it as a feeling of "unity" with others.

What was this new experience of compassion? Eastern texts describe this quality of compassion at great length. In yoga texts it is called *karuna* and is seen as a state that naturally arises when the *open heart comes near to suffering.* It is sometimes described as "a quivering of the heart with the heart of a suffering other." At its core is an experience of seeing deeply into another's suffering and reverberating with the loss, understanding its dimensions—in a sense, joining with the suffering other. Karuna prompts one to deeply wish to bring comfort, balm, healing, and holding to the suffering other.

In the contemplative traditions, the mind state of compassion is seen as a particularly strong quality—a quality that raises energy deep within the soul, energy that might be used for good. One noted teacher observes, "[Karuna] is the strength that arises out of seeing the true nature of suffering in the world. It allows us to bear witness to that suffering, whether it is in ourselves or others, without fear."

So, for Harriet, it turned out that there was a surprising gift in the wound of Charley's death. It was the gift of compassion. A new form of deep connection with the suffering of others began to spontaneously arise within her.

Krishna teaches Arjuna that this state of compassion is one of the highest states known to humankind. He says:

> *When a person responds to the joys and sorrows of others as if they were his own, he has attained the highest state of spiritual union. (Gita 6:32)*

Krishna here points to a liberating insight: to acknowledge the truth of suffering allows us to feel our intrinsic unity with others, to feel our shared humanness. One classic Buddhist text offers the following meditation on karuna:

> Strive at first to meditate upon the sameness of yourself and others. In joy and sorrow all are equal; thus be guardian of all, as of yourself.

At the same time, this stance is not easy. It requires the courage to look unflinchingly at the reality of death.

Writes American Buddhist teacher Sharon Salzberg: "The goal of our spiritual practice is to be able to understand, to be able to look without illusion at what is natural in this life, at what is actually happening for others and for ourselves. This *willingness to see what is true* is the first step in developing compassion."

Harriet Beecher Stowe is a case study in the development of compassion. She prayed that "the crushing of my own heart might enable me to work out some great good to others." She declared that "God hath chosen the weak things of this world" as instruments of his power. Harriet—moderately affluent, privileged, well set up in life, supposedly one of the lucky ones—had now become one of those weak things.

13

For the better part of a year after Henry's death, I spoke at least once a day with Sandy. After a few months, I told her about Stowe, whom I was just then researching. I told her about the death of Charley. About the way it had opened Stowe up to the true suffering of slavery. About how Stowe had actually seen and understood this newly aroused compassion to be a gift buried in the very heart of her loss. About how it had moved her to action.

This points to a facet of compassion too seldom commented upon. In Eastern texts, compassion is very often linked to action. At its best, it was compassion that motivated Gandhi. He discovered that compassion can lead to very forceful action without any anger or aversion in it. Writes Salzberg: "[Compassion] allows us to name injustice without hesitation, and to act strongly, with all the skill at our disposal."

Sandy and I talked at length about the meaning of Henry's death. What would the gift be? we wondered. Some of the gifts were immediately apparent. Henry's death brought us closer together as a family. Indeed, I had not spoken daily in a sustained way with my twin sister for decades. The sharing of this tragedy took us on a journey together. We both began to see that the shredding pain of grief can create deep connection. And we began to create meaning by dedicating our future philanthropy as a family to an illness from which Henry had suffered—and once again, this unified us.

I've said: Look for the gift in the wound. But very often in order to find that gift, we must actively look for it, seek it out, pursue it. One gift of Henry's death for me is a deeper understanding of Harriet Beecher Stowe. I had read all the biographies before writing about her life. But now I understood Harriet's dilemma in an entirely new way.

14

In the months that followed Charley's death, Stowe saw one slim window, as she would put it, "open to heaven." It was this: For many years, she had longed to write. Indeed, as I have said, she saw writing as her true calling. And of course she *had* written short pieces, and even, at one point, a book. She had written some articles for a variety of magazines, and essays for her family. But she had never been able to come into full ownership of writing as her *vocation*. All the while, even when doing small writing projects early in her career, she felt conflicted about the calling. She felt that her children deserved her undivided attention. She felt guilty about the time that writing would inevitably take away from her family. And, besides, as she often commented, she had no "room" in which to write—no dedicated space.

After Charley's death, Harriet tells us that she felt "old." Used up. And she was aware that she had not yet accomplished her mission in life. "Why, look at it," she exclaimed to her husband. "Life is half gone. What have we done?" She brought this to God in her prayer life: "I have not finished the work Thou hast given me to do. My heart is not yet wholly renewed . . ." She had not yet been saved by her dharma, and she knew it.

In previous years, Harriet had not found the time to write. And she was not sure that she had found her subject. But now it was staring her in the face. She would take her compassion for the suffering of the slave mother—and the slave father, and family—and transform it into a story that would awaken the conscience and the heart of a nation.

As the vocation began to rise up in her, she declared to her husband, "I must have a room!" I must have a room in which to write. Harriet began to exhibit the sense of urgency that is characteristic of dharma. When dharma rises up, there is very little that can stop it. It brings with it an enlarged perspective. "Now by the grace of God," Harriet wrote, "I am resolved to come home and live for God, it is time to prepare to die—the lamp has not long to burn—the hour is flying—all things are sliding away and eternity is coming." "Practice as if your hair were on fire," said the Buddha.

15

Harriet Beecher Stowe began to find her voice.

She slowly developed a sense that she could indeed transform her loss into something helpful. And now, her family—seeing the possibilities as well—supported her in every way it could. Harriet received a letter from her sister Isabella that she read aloud to the family. Isabella wrote, "Now Hattie, if I could use a pen as you can, I would write something that would make this whole nation feel what an accursed thing slavery is." Harriet had a powerful reaction to this letter. Calvin Stowe remembered the moment years later. He wrote: ". . . [She] rose from her chair, crushed the letter in her hand" and declared "I *will* write something. I will if I live." Calvin now supported her writing in every way. "You must be a literary woman," he exclaimed. "[You must] spend the rest of your life with your pen." Here was a powerful sense of vocation—seen not only by Harriet but by those around her.

At about this time, Harriet left Cincinnati and moved with her family to Brunswick, Maine, where her husband would teach at Bowdoin College. But no matter. In Maine, the inspiration kept coming. Harriet was now distinctly aware of an inner voice that would lead her. She claimed to have had a vision of a dying slave during a communion service at Brunswick's First Parish Church—a vision that inspired her to write his story. "Having experienced losing someone so close to me, I can sympathize with all the poor, powerless slaves at the unjust auctions. You will always be in my heart Samuel Charles Stowe."

16

As a woman about to unload her thoughts on the issue of slavery, though, Harriet was in a unique bind. In mid-19th-century America, women were expected to remain silent on so-called "public" issues like abolition. Women who spoke out were routinely ostracized from society. But Harriet would not be dissuaded. She decided that she was willing to suffer the consequences of fully living out her dharma. She was, as she said, "willing to sacrifice her womanhood . . ." to become a warrior "in a righteous cause." She would find her voice. The consequences be damned.

We can begin to feel Harriet's growing resolve. On March 9, 1850, Stowe wrote to Gamaliel Bailey, editor of the weekly antislavery journal *The National Era*, that she planned to write a story about the horror of slavery: "I feel now that the time has come when even a woman or a child who can speak a word for freedom and humanity *is bound to speak*. The Carthagenian women in the last peril of their state cut off their hair for bowstrings to give to the defenders of their country; and such peril and shame as now hangs over this country is worse than Roman slavery, and I hope every woman who can write will not be silent . . ."

In 1851 Harriet told her brother Henry—who had already become a powerful voice for abolition—that she was doing something too. "I have begun a story, trying to set forth the sufferings and wrongs of the slave." This was a defining moment for Harriet. It sealed her resolve to fight with everything she had.

17

The story poured out of Harriet Beecher Stowe. It was not so much "composed by her [as] imposed upon her." She wrote in the Introduction to the 1879 edition of *Uncle Tom's Cabin* that "scenes, incidents, conversations [poured into my] mind with a vividness and importunity that would not be denied. The book insisted upon getting itself into being." She later said of her novel, "God wrote it."

Krishna teaches Arjuna repeatedly that when his consciousness is unified with God, he is "not the Doer of his actions." Those actions proceed from the Divine within.

> *Those who follow the path of service, who have completely purified themselves and conquered their senses and self-will, see the Self in all creatures and are untouched by any action they perform. Those who know this truth, whose consciousness is unified, think always, "I am not the doer." (Gita 5:7–8)*

As she plunged into the writing, Harriet felt for the first time in her life that she was in complete alignment with God's will for her. This is a typical feeling of one who has found her dharma. Harriet's whole life had been a preparation for this. A neighbor in Brunswick described Harriet's almost manic behavior during the writing of *Uncle Tom's Cabin*. "As soon as she had swallowed her breakfast," said this neighbor, "she would hurry down to the village and write, write, write till the dinner bell sounded. Then [she would] hurry home, eat, and

[go] right back and write till tea time." This same neighbor described her utter lack of concern for appearances, with "her frizzy hair tossing in an unkempt disheveled mass up on her neck and shoulders, and her clothes hanging loosely about her form, as if they got there by accident." Harriet was a woman possessed.

Uncle Tom's Cabin was completed in 1851, and the world would never be the same.

18

Shortly after completing the book in June 1851, when Harriet was just forty years old, the first installment of her *Uncle Tom's Cabin* was published in serial form in the aforementioned *The National Era*. She originally used the subtitle "The Man That Was a Thing" but soon changed it to "Life Among the Lowly."

Installments were then published weekly from June 5, 1851, through April 1, 1852. For the newspaper serialization of her novel, Stowe was paid $400. *Uncle Tom's Cabin* was published in book form on March 20, 1852, by John P. Jewett with an initial print run of 5,000 copies. Each of its two volumes included three illustrations and a title page designed by Hammatt Billings. In less than a year, the book sold an unprecedented 300,000 copies.

19

A central part of the plot of the novel was drawn directly from Stowe's own experience—that very story told to her by Reverend Rankin on the cliff overlooking the Ohio River. "Eliza," in Stowe's story, is a beautiful young enslaved woman who is facing disaster. She discovers accidentally, as a result of eavesdropping on a conversation, that she is about to be sold into "the fancy trade"—prostitution—while her young son, Harry, is about to be sold away from her "down river" into the Deep South. She knows that this means she will never see him again.

Upon hearing news of her fate, Eliza resolves to steal away with Harry in the night. She packs up some few belongings and sets out into the bitter cold, wintry night—carrying the child in her arms for as long as she possibly can. At a critical point in the journey, Eliza and Harry come to the Ohio River—the very boundary between the slave state of Kentucky and the free state of Ohio. They approach the ferry, but are told by the ferryman that the cakes of careening ice on the river make a passage by boat absolutely impossible. Eliza is almost undone at this moment. She hears the voices of the slave catchers in hot pursuit and, out of desperation, grabs her child and leaps onto an ice cake. She jumps as quickly as she can from one ice cake to the next—miraculously finding her way in the pitch black across the river.

Eliza and Harry arrive thoroughly soaked and freezing cold on the far bank of the Ohio River. Somehow, she finds her way from the river to a nearby Quaker settlement, which is famous among her kin for harboring self-emancipated slaves. At the village she encounters the Halliday family, who warm and feed the mother and child, and house them until Eliza's husband, George, is able to join them several nights later. Eventually the Hallidays guide Eliza, Harry, and George through all the hazards of the trip farther north—all the way to the Canadian border, and safety.

20

In her writing, Stowe does something remarkable. She creates vivid female characters, many of whom have been touched by the loss of a child—as most people had been in 19th-century America. The fictional character of Eliza herself had lost two infants before giving birth to her son Harry—the son she now carries across the river to safety. As she crosses the river, Eliza shouts out, "This child is all that I have." Stowe counts on women readers to identify with Eliza in this. "Stronger than all," she writes in this section of the book, "was maternal love, wrought into a paroxysm of frenzy by the near approach of a fearful danger."

In Stowe's hands, grief connects her and her characters to the community, to the common good, and the common suffering. It creates a bridge. "Stowe asks the reader to use suffering as a means to reform the heart and to prepare it for compassionate action," writes Stowe scholar Retawnya Provenzano. "[She] often assumes this shared experience of loss among mothers. Her presentations of maternal responses to child death seek to access and intensify feelings within the reader to break down any barrier between the bereaved and the observer. Likewise, in the novel we witness this collapse of distance and obstructions between mothers based on their shared grief. This sense of connection supports Stowe's object of building bridges between the races."

Harriet Beecher Stowe recognizes the upending of everything by death. "She witnesses loss as something that cannot be entirely comprehended, and then she intentionally participates in that upending and incomprehension in order to refashion her world." Critic Ann-Janine Morey argues that Stowe's female characters "have a spiritual gift that no one wants to hear, and they are alone, 'shuddering in the midst of mirth and festival with the weight of a terrible wisdom.'" Many of Stowe's women understand the nearness of death, and they make no attempt to hide or repress this awareness. Instead, "this secret knowledge leads to the perception of the suffering of others and then to compassionate action."

21

When *Uncle Tom's Cabin* was put onstage at the National Theater in New York, it was said that there was "not one dry eye" when Eliza reached the other side of the river. Stowe presents the reader with the very real and palpable presence of suffering.

Writes one scholar: "Written in tears, the book participates in a sentimental aesthetic scorned by most intellectuals and the academy in the twentieth and twenty first centuries, but highly valued by readers in the nineteenth. It is intended to evoke tears." And it did. It evoked tears across the globe, for it was written in tears. Any writer knows the old meme: no tears in the writer, no tears in the reader.

But more than that. Stowe insisted on holding close the suffering of child loss, and transforming the grief into a balm for others. She describes herself as one of "those whose sorrows all spring up into joys for others, whose earthly hopes, laid in the grave with many tears, are the seed from which spring healing flowers and balm for the desolate and the distressed."

22

Propelled by Stowe's grief and her prophetic voice, *Uncle Tom's Cabin* took the world by storm. Realizing the power of Stowe's vivid prose, supporters of slavery rose up everywhere to denounce the book. It was banned across the South.

Over the years, many have criticized Stowe for making Tom (the book's other main character) altogether too passive—the archetype of the long-suffering Christian man. Those who criticize Stowe for Tom's resigned and religious attitude should look more closely into Stowe's life and work. What most readers today do not know is that with *Uncle Tom's Cabin*, Harriet Beecher Stowe was only just getting started. The fire had been lit. In the writing of her novel, she had discovered that slavery was even worse than she had thought. After *Tom*, she went on to write two much more radical books. One, *A Key to Uncle Tom's Cabin*, brought together massive amounts of real data and research on the effects of slavery. Its impact was, if anything, even more devastating than the original novel.

Stowe's *Key* was a powerful antislavery document in its own right, and it was a devastating read. In it, she systematically produced documents that corroborated the stories she told in *Tom*. Stowe quoted directly from the important slavery narratives of Josiah Henson, Henry Bibb, and Frederick Douglass. In one section she drew on legal cases that produced, in graphic detail, treatment of slaves that was more real and more horrific than anything she had yet documented. Much of this was to answer her critics in both the North and the South. Frederick Douglass would declare that Stowe's new book would "unlock the prison-house for the deliverance of millions who are now pining in chains . . ." He understood that Stowe's *Key* was far more radical than *Tom*. "There has not been an exposure of slavery so terrible as *[A] Key to Uncle Tom's Cabin*," he said.

In her next novel, entitled *Dred*, Stowe anticipates the violence of the Civil War. "Tom suffered in patience," writes Nancy Koester, referring to the original character of Uncle Tom, "but Dred wants revenge and plots a slave revolt . . . [and in writing him, Stowe] gives black agency and rage larger place . . ." By this point in her career, Stowe clearly had little hope that slavery could be ended through peaceful means. *Dred* introduces a Black revolutionary character who can truly be seen as both an heir to the American Revolution and a precursor of the civil rights warrior of subsequent American history.

23

By the fall of 1860, Harriet Beecher Stowe was burning with indignation and righteous anger, not only at slavery but also at her very own Christian church, which had stood by so idly and watched the degradations of slavery increase. She wrote that she felt "a mighty force, which we call the spirit of the age, burning like an oven," against injustice and cruelty. At around this time, Stowe wrote a fiery poem entitled "The Holy War," which is full of imagery of a righteous Union Army riding forth as if from the Bible's Book of Revelation. She saw the fight against slavery as a righteous war for freedom and justice. Koester points out that Stowe's "millennial vision anticipated Julia Ward Howe's 'Battle Hymn of the Republic' which appeared in the *Atlantic Monthly* in February of 1862." Howe's hymn would perfectly sum up the abolitionists' ecstatic vision of God intervening in history to right the wrongs of centuries of slavery.

Mine eyes have seen the glory of the coming of the Lord;
He is trampling out the vintage where the grapes of
wrath are stored;
He hath loosed the fateful lightning of His terrible
swift sword;
His truth is marching on.

24

On the evening of December 2, 1862, Harriet and her daughter Hatty went to the White House to meet President Abraham Lincoln. As the story goes, Lincoln greeted Stowe warmly and then quipped, "So you are the little woman who made this big war." The story of the quip may well be apocryphal. But *had* it been made, there would have been much truth in it. As much as any single cause, Stowe's novels and writings had unified opinion in the North against slavery.

For the rest of her life, Harriet Beecher Stowe would live a life balanced between the two extremes of contemplation—which for her meant, primarily, writing and prayer—and action. She is remembered as one of a group of American abolitionists—a list that includes the likes of Frederick Douglass, Harriet Tubman, William Lloyd Garrison, Sojourner Truth, and Ann Phillips.

Did Stowe and Thoreau know one another? They lived concurrent lives. They were both powerful voices in the same arena. They certainly had many friends in common. But it's doubtful, strangely, that their paths ever crossed. First of all, it's unlikely that Harriet Beecher Stowe read *Walden*, which wasn't at all popular in its day. And it's even more unlikely that Thoreau read *Uncle Tom's Cabin*, since for the most part he didn't read novels—especially contemporary novels. But in his journal Thoreau wrote that he owned a figurine of Uncle Tom and Little Eva, the gift of one of the many self-emancipated slaves he had helped escape the clutches of the slave catcher.

After the Civil War, like many other abolitionists, Stowe turned her impressive intellect and energies to the fight for women's equality, and for women's suffrage. She became a fierce promoter of women's rights. She died at the age of eighty-five, on July 1, 1896.

25

"Sandy, see how wide the river is at this point," I said. I was pointing across to the West Virginia side of the river, and peering through binoculars at the settlements on that side. "It must be three quarters of a mile across, at least. Maybe a mile."

Sandy and I were standing on the banks of the Ohio River. It was a cool day in early October, and blue and gray thunderheads gathered darkly over the river in the distance. The trees on the other side of the river had already turned yellow and orange. The smell of damp leaves saturated the air. Sandy absentmindedly took the binoculars from me and looked through them into the far distance.

"I'd forgotten it was so wide," she said. "Did Grandma say that Dad used to actually swim across to West Virginia and back every day in the summer?"

"I know. Hard to believe," I said. My father, as a boy, must have been a very strong swimmer. And brave.

After I finished the manuscript for this book, Sandy and I had taken a trip to the Ohio River to see where Harriet Beecher Stowe had lived and worked. As it turned out, of course, Cincinnati was not so very far from my father's boyhood home, which was perched above the Ohio River upriver from Cincinnati. Sandy and I spent a day exploring the neighborhood in which my father had grown up.

Dad's family had lived in a simple brick home overlooking the Ohio River—on the Ohio side, and opposite West Virginia, not Kentucky. The home was mostly in shambles at the time of our visit. The front porch, so often seen in family photos, had been removed. But the wide granite stoop remained, with the name "COPE" deeply etched into its side. We sat on the stoop and stared out over the river.

"Steve, can you even imagine the slaves who crossed that river, chased by hounds and slave catchers? In winter. On ice cakes." Having studied Stowe's life, Sandy and I had now gotten a new sense of the river, its meaning, its history, its ghosts.

Sandy and I talked at length about Henry and how much he would have enjoyed this adventure with us—looking through the local museums and historic homes to find traces of the Cope family. Visiting the cemetery where many of the family were buried, including our grandmother, who had herself died an early and tragic death.

The trip had all the qualities of a sacred pilgrimage. I told Sandy about the notion that those of us who have been through child death have a secret knowledge—what Stowe might have called "a terrible wisdom." And I wondered aloud whether we might not transmute that into a secret strength.

I had with me a copy of the page proofs of this book, and I read to her the stunning insight that Stowe's female characters "have a spiritual gift that no one wants to hear, and they are alone, 'shuddering in the midst of mirth and festival with the weight of a terrible wisdom.'" I read to her from the manuscript: "Many of Stowe's women understand the nearness of death, and they make no attempt to hide or repress this awareness. Instead, this secret knowledge leads to the perception of the suffering of others and then to compassionate action."

For some reason, I thought of George Eliot—who was, of course, a woman (Mary Ann Evans)—and a woman who had clearly been wounded by loss and tragedy. In her novel *Adam Bede*, Mary Ann Evans wrote about loss in a way that no one can who has not suffered through it. But she—like Stowe—wants to transmute it into a secret strength. "It would be a poor result of our anguish and our wrestling," she wrote, "if we won nothing but our old selves at the end of it . . . let us rather be thankful that our sorrow lives in us as an indestructible force."

"Our sorrow lives on in us as an indestructible force." I repeated the words out loud.

Sandy and I stood with our arms around one another and looked out on the river that "Eliza" had crossed. We had a good cry. Most of all, we cried with Stowe and Charley and Calvin and the multitudes of slave mothers whose children had been ripped away. We cried for Henry. We cried for our grandmother, who had sat and rocked my father on this very front porch—and whom we had barely known. We cried because we were happy to have one another. We knew we had been changed by unthinkable loss. But would it become an indestructible force within us? Perhaps this very book is a part of that force.

LESSON THREE

UNDERSTAND THAT TRUE PERSONAL FULFILLMENT AND THE COMMON GOOD ALWAYS ARISE TOGETHER

"Time to wake up, my friend."

Arjuna has fallen asleep with his head on Krishna's shoulder. For about an hour, he has dropped into a blissful sleep in the safe presence of his Divine friend. Krishna has wrapped them both together in his shawl.

Arjuna rouses himself slowly. He takes a long, deep breath and lets it out with a sigh, and then takes a stretch toward the now waning fire.

As he wakes up, Arjuna realizes that he and Krishna have talked the entire night away. But had it really been only one night? Arjuna feels as though it may have been an entire eon that he and his friend had been together next to the fire.

"Krishna, the sun will rise in an hour or so. We should go!" Arjuna stood up hastily.

"No, Arjuna. We still have time. Sit back here by me." Krishna's voice is calm, soothing—authoritative.

Arjuna hesitates for a moment. Then he returns to sit next to Krishna, reluctant to let go of the sweetness of their time together.

"Arjuna, I have something important to say.

"Very shortly you must make your decision. And in making your decision about how to act, you must remember this: It's not just *your* fate that you hold in your hands. There are hundreds of others who are crossing through this difficult moment with you."

Arjuna nods his head slowly, and he thinks about his Pandava kin, his friends and his teachers, who are even now gathering just several hundred yards away.

"Your friends rely on you doing *your* dharma wisely, so that they can do theirs.

"Most importantly, remember this: The mark of true dharma is that it fulfills the destiny of your soul on Earth. But at the same time, it must also promote the good of the world.

"Your own fulfillment could never be for you alone." Krishna is serious about this. He says:

> *Strive constantly to serve the welfare of the world; by devotion to selfless work one attains the supreme goal of*

life. Do your work with the welfare of others always in mind. (Gita 3:19–20)

"Arjuna, our dharma takes us right to the very spot where we can be most useful. It takes us to the precise intersection between our own fulfillment and the common good. There, we will always find our highest dharma.

"Arjuna, know that when you act from that very point of intersection, your actions have a hidden, mystic effect on the whole web of life."

As the sun peeks over the horizon, the whole field of Kuru seems lit up as if from within. Anticipation hangs in the very air.

As we approach the next part of our inquiry, remember that Arjuna was called to fight in the greatest battle of the age. It is no accident that our conflicted friend found himself at the very center of the most important social, moral, and political dilemma of his age. Why? Because dharma inevitably takes us there. Our dharma takes us to the very spot where we can be most useful. Our dharma demands that in some small way we struggle with the dilemmas that are "etched in rock" on the whole of society. In the tale of the Gita, Lord Krishna is the aspect of God who fosters and preserves the Universe against the forces constantly working to destroy and corrupt it. Krishna teaches that we must always work not only for the sake of our own soul, but for the welfare of all beings.

CHAPTER 5

CHARLES RUSSELL LOWELL

Trust in the Mystic Power of Duty

To every [human being] there is appointed a certain ministry and service, a path described of duty, a work to perform, and a race to run, an office in the economy of Providence, for usefulness is a necessary property of goodness.

— Anna Jackson Lowell

It's hard for us to imagine it today, but it is a fact that Abraham Lincoln—now honored as one of American democracy's most important leaders—was almost defeated in his 1864 bid to be reelected president of the United Sates. Indeed, Lincoln himself doubted that he would win the 1864 election.

By 1864, the Civil War had already ground on for four brutal years—much longer than most in the North had anticipated. Many decisive battles had been lost. The Union Army was exhausted. More men had died of disease than bullets. Many in the North just wanted the suffering to end, and they cast about for a candidate who would, above all, pledge to end it quickly.

The political situation leading up to the election was dire. Lincoln—who ran again on the Republican ticket, of course—was opposed on the Democratic side by the dashing former commander of the Union Army, General George B. McClellan. McClellan was the choice of the Democratic Party's wing called the "Peace Democrats," who wanted an end to the war at any cost, and were quite willing to concede the issue of slavery to the South. "Just let them have their slavery, and let this whole catastrophe end." This view was remarkably pervasive. McClellan and his Peace Democrats had experienced an enormous wave of Northern support leading up to the election in November of 1864.

To many Northerners the cause seemed lost.

2

Events would intervene, however. The election's seemingly inexorable march to doom was transformed almost overnight by a series of last-minute Union victories, including General Sherman's taking of Atlanta in September 1864. But perhaps no victory was more important in shaping the immediate result of the 1864 election than the stunning Union victory at Cedar Creek, Virginia, which came just days before the election.

The Battle of Cedar Creek helped turn the tide of the Civil War. Yet strangely, the details of this important story are all too little known today.

3

Here is a snapshot of the Cedar Creek story.

Throughout the war, Confederate forces had continually harassed and threatened Washington, DC—the capital of the Union. Confederate strongholds in the Shenandoah Valley of Virginia allowed rebel forces remarkably easy access to what was then called Washington City. By late in 1864, the wily Southern general Jubal Early decided that the time was ripe to wipe out the Union Army's forces in the Shenandoah Valley once and for all. He believed he could effect this with a surprise attack across the strategically important Virginia river known as Cedar Creek. On the morning of October 19, he began the offensive. Initially General Early had devastating success. But when he failed to continue his attack, Union forces determined to take the advantage. They would counterattack.

Late in the afternoon of October 19, a young Union cavalry officer rallied his men to attack the now stationary General Early. This young officer was the twenty-nine-year-old Colonel Charles Russell Lowell, who had in his four years of service to the Union become a kind of legend in the Union Army.

It is this complex man who will be the subject of our next inquiry.

4

Charles Russell Lowell—Charlie—was twenty-five years old when he enlisted in the Union Army in 1860. He rose steadily through the ranks, gradually proving himself a brilliant leader and a master of cavalry strategy.

Charlie Lowell's rise to prominence on the battlefield was completely counterintuitive. He was a slight, physically unprepossessing, and often shabbily dressed young man—fresh faced and boyish, in spite of his attempts at a mustache. He had been all but killed by a struggle with tuberculosis in his early twenties, and for all intents and purposes had only one good lung. He was the son of prominent Boston Brahmin parents—devout abolitionists and freethinkers—and as such had any number of opportunities to make a successful professional life for himself. He was a brilliant student at Harvard College. But when war came, in 1860, he decided that it was his sacred duty to fight.

During his first few months in uniform, Charlie Lowell surprised everyone. As it turned out, Lowell's lean, wiry frame and agile, aggressive personality made him an almost perfect horseman, and much to everyone's surprise, a gifted leader. He had become well known during his three years on horseback, and would later be called one of several "boy generals" in the Union Army. (He would be made a brigadier general after the Battle of Cedar Creek.) During his two years of fighting a quasi-guerilla war in the Shenandoah Valley, Lowell had thirteen horses shot from beneath him, yet no bullet ever touched him. Bullets destroyed his horses, his uniform, even his sword and scabbard. But never him. As a result, an air of magic surrounded him. Men learned to trust him. Eventually, they would follow him anywhere.

One of Lowell's most important biographers, Carol Bundy, observed that Lowell "had a curious power over people. Certainly his charm, his naturally jubilant spirit, and his wit had been attractive. His photographic memory and impressive intellect had inspired, awed, and impressed. He was much trusted for his fairness, for being a moral anchor." Lowell's power over people, says one Harvard biographer, was such that he "drew their wills to him, as a lodestone attracts iron."

5

The Battle of Cedar Creek would assure Lowell's place in Civil War history.

On that day in October 1864, Lowell and his men made two charges upon General Jubal Early and the stalled Confederate army. In the first charge, Lowell was hit by a bullet high in the chest, knocking him from his horse. His troops were stunned. What? The impossible had happened. Their colonel had been hit. When his aides found the wounded Lowell, they feared the worst. He could barely speak. But in a whisper, he refused to leave the field. He was doubtful that his men would perform their best under a substitute leader, so he commanded them to strap him back into the saddle.

With sword drawn, the severely wounded Charles Russell Lowell—now literally tied to his horse—led the second charge as well. His officer's uniform marked him out as a high-value target for Confederate sharpshooters. And when he was hit a second time, the bullet passed from shoulder to shoulder, severing his spinal cord.

Lowell was carried to the rear of the field, where he was laid on a table next to his wounded comrade Captain Rufus Smith—a friend and trusted fellow officer. They were both closely attended over the coming hours by the regiment's eminent surgeon, Dr. Oscar DeWolf.

6

As it turned out, Lowell's cavalry charge was spectacularly successful. It broke the back of Early's army. (Union troops would soon raise the chant "Early came late!") The Union Army won the battle decisively, and that pitched struggle marked the end of the Confederate's invasion of the North. The Confederacy could no longer protect its strategic territory in Virginia. This, along with the taking of Atlanta by General Sherman, was the beginning of the end of the Confederacy. The North was jubilant, of course. Just days later, on November 8, Abraham Lincoln won the presidential election in a landslide.

The Battle of Cedar Creek had a powerful domino effect. It helped to decisively turn the tide of the war, and to assure the reelection of Abraham Lincoln and therefore the successful completion of the war—which would eventually mean the end of slavery in the United States of America. Even at the time, in the fog of war, most everyone understood, intuitively, what the victory meant. It marked a new beginning of America's communal attempt to atone for the stain of slavery. Yes, it was only the beginning. But it was a necessary beginning.

Meanwhile, both Colonel Lowell and Captain Smith were in the brigade field hospital, suffering grievously from their wounds. Smith had been shot through the stomach and had lain for quite some time on the battlefield untended. He was now, despite heavy doses of morphine, in enormous distress. Charlie Lowell comforted him, despite being seriously wounded himself.

In the days that followed, Lowell's actions on the field—his heroism—would be trumpeted in all the major papers of the Northeast. The public understood the role that the Cedar Creek victory would play in the outcome of the war.

Who was this compelling young man? How did he find and understand his own sacred duty? What motivated him to perform the many acts of self-sacrifice that he made for his cause? Was he a modern-day Arjuna? Is he an example of how Arjuna *might* have acted, had he indeed decided to fight in the battle of Kurukshetra?

7

In certain ways, Charlie Lowell was not exceptional. It is now well known that during the Civil War—from 1861 to 1865—the Union Army depended upon the leadership of a group of highly educated, earnest young men like Lowell. Many of these men were barely more than boys, but they were motivated by what we can only today call a sense of *sacred duty*. This same kind of devotion to sacred duty is not entirely absent today, but it would seem to be much more rare. Why should this be the case? We can learn a lot about this from Lowell's story.

Charlie Lowell was only one of dozens (more likely hundreds) of sons of Boston Brahmin families who fought in the war. Many of them were sons of prominent families who had been abolitionists in the decades leading up to the war. These young men had names that resonate even today: Henry Lee Higginson. Oliver Wendell Holmes. Frank Sanborn. George Putnam. Paul Revere. Robert Gould Shaw. (Rob Shaw, by the way, another Civil War hero, was Charlie Lowell's best friend and his future brother-in-law. Shaw would become the commander of the first African American corps of troops in the American army.)

This flock of earnest young men had been deeply touched by the teachings on character and duty by America's then most prominent philosopher, Ralph Waldo Emerson, who, as it happened, regularly held court at the Lowell home when Charlie was a boy. All of these men had been touched by the idealism of the Transcendentalists—including, especially, Emerson, Thoreau, and Margaret Fuller—and by the utopian experiment of Brook Farm, where some of them, indeed, had lived as children. They were idealists. They believed in progress. They believed that human beings should always aspire to be better. Thoreau had written, "I know of no more encouraging fact than the unquestionable ability of man to elevate his life by conscious endeavor."

Shaw, Bowdoin, Lowell, Sanborn, and the others were citizen warriors, scholar warriors. Having hung out at Harvard University during my graduate school days, I remember pictures of many of these young men around the Harvard campus—in the library, in student housing, in classrooms. Who were these guys, I wondered then, and why had I not learned more about them in college? They were so young. So handsome. To my mind, so noble. Soldiers Field—the great coliseum-like field where Harvard still plays Yale and Army in football—was dedicated to them. The magisterial Memorial Hall at Harvard was dedicated to them as well. And on and on.

At the highest spot on the Boston Common—just across from the gilded dome of the statehouse—stands a statue of Robert Gould Shaw. It was designed by the great sculptor Augustus St. Gaudens. There, in bronze, stands Shaw, at the front of his corps of African American troops, marching into battle—and, as it turned out, to his death. William James, speaking at the unveiling of this monument in 1897, said about St. Gaudens's depiction of Rob Shaw and his troops:

> There they march, warm-blooded champions of a better day for man. There on horseback among them, in his very habit as he lived, sits the blue-eyed child of fortune, upon whose happy youth every divinity had smiled . . .

I walked by this statue regularly during my student days in Cambridge and Boston. But, as with Henry Ward Beecher at Amherst College, I failed to understand its meaning. I had not yet encountered the true power of sacred duty.

How did these young men understand their duty? Why did they see this war, in particular, to be *their* sacred duty? None of them had any real military skill or training. For the most part, in fact, none of them had any particular talent for it. Most of them would be injured, killed, or grievously disabled by war's end. Did these men know of the notion of dharma? Did they know of Arjuna? (Some of them certainly would have. We know, for example, that Charlie Lowell himself read widely into Eastern literature while an undergraduate at Harvard, and had most likely read at least parts of the Bhagavad Gita.)

8

It doesn't take much digging to find the answer to our question about the relationship of these young men to sacred duty. Lowell and his idealist friends were enraged by the horrors of slavery and were indignant at the failure of American society to care for the poor and underprivileged. They were fed up with the generation of their parents, who had so clearly *not* been able to right the wrongs that they saw as obvious—the same parents who had not, in their view, been able to keep the American experiment in freedom moving forward. These young men were intent on action. As with Emerson and Thoreau, they were idealists of a practical bent. For the most part, as I have said, they had enviable opportunities to achieve success in business and had immediate entrée into the old boys' network. But no. They would focus on atoning for the many sins of America. They would fight.

Many of these men grew up in families whose chief concern was civic duty. They learned early on that a good life was "a life lived for the well-being of the whole." Charlie's family, for example, had long opposed slavery. They were active in the Boston Vigilance Committee, which worked for the relief of self-emancipated slaves—providing funds, shelter, clothing, and medical assistance. At least one of the Lowell family's houses was used as a way station for fugitives from slavery.

As I dug deeper into the history of this group of young men, it was not all that hard for me to put myself in Charlie Lowell's shoes. I can relate directly to some aspects of his story. After all, my very own generation—we so-called Baby Boomers—also felt a calling to right institutional wrongs. In our very youth, we felt called to fight against racism and for civil rights—and many of us did. We were offended by the savagery and offenses of the Vietnam War. Like Lowell, during our college days, we also felt a sense of duty to our country, to our constitution, to our fragile experiment in freedom. We felt a duty to continue the struggle that men and women a hundred years earlier had in so many ways begun. In many cases, our families had fought—and in some cases died—for these principles.

And so, as undergraduates, we held intense "rap groups" late into the night in our college dorms. We struggled with our duty during the horrors of the bombing of Cambodia and the killings at Kent State in 1970. At Amherst College, as around the country, we protested in the streets and went on strike. We "captured" and occupied Converse Hall—the administration building. We called for a moratorium on classes. We marched. Something must be done! Carol Bundy comments on this: "Students during Lowell's years at Harvard," she wrote, "felt a 'slow-burning rage' that was not equaled among later generations of students until the late 1960s." That's it exactly: a slow-burning rage.

9

But Lowell and his generation of friends had even deeper motives. Bundy tells us:

> Charlie Lowell and his group of friends lived in a time that still touched the deepest roots and meaning of the American experiment. Many young men volunteered because they considered the American experiment in self-government an example for the world; now that it was imperiled, so were the principles of democratic self-rule. Would American democracy end in fratricidal slaughter, as the French Revolution had? Lowell and most if not all of his friends had a direct personal or familial connection to the American Revolution. Charlie's friend Paul Revere [for example] was the grandson and namesake of the silversmith and Revolutionary War hero.

Think of it. Most of Charlie Lowell's friends had immediate ancestors who had fought in the Revolutionary War—or who had participated in one of the many state or continental congresses. As children they would have grown up with mementos of these early struggles—even worked-over copies of state and federal constitutions. Their desire to defend the Constitution and its principles, and to preserve the Union, was intensely real and, as Bundy says, "imbued with almost hereditary, even proprietary feelings, perhaps even some of the irrational protectiveness one has for family—sentiments that these men might never have known they possessed had the war not come."

This group of young warriors understood the greater meaning of America. Charlie Lowell wrote to his friend Charlie Perkins that he would not have thought of taking up a soldier's life "were it not for a muddled and twisted idea that somehow or other this fight was going to be one in which decent men *ought* to engage for the sake of humanity." Lowell was talking not just of the cause of human rights in general, but specifically about slavery—which he and his friends rejected.

10

This begs the question: What about us? To what causes do we feel a sacred duty? Reading the life of Charlie Lowell has forced me to ask the question: What would I die for? My best friend, Brian, says he would gladly take a bullet for his son, Keane. Any parent would. I get that. So what do I have that's worth giving my life up for? Is sacrificing one's life even a good thing? Is war ever a good thing? Can violence ever be justified?

We will not be able to answer all of these questions in this chapter, of course. But in wrestling with the Bhagavad Gita, we must take on the biggest question of all: the question of sacred duty, and of the full sacrifice of ourselves in the service of the common good.

The authors of the Bhagavad Gita wanted us to put ourselves in Arjuna's shoes. And so they put this question in the starkest of terms. The tale is intentionally set on the night before a great battle that is universally seen to be a "just war." The writers quite strategically begin with Arjuna's terror in the face of his choice. Was this really *his* war to fight? Was this really his sacred duty? And they make Arjuna as full of doubt, neurosis, and fear as possible, so that we will identify.

11

We are now at the very heart of the Gita. What, precisely, do we mean by "sacred duty"?

One dictionary tells us that "duty" comes from the word *due*, which means "that which is owing," and from the Latin *debere*, or debt. It is "a commitment or an expectation to perform some action in general or if certain circumstances arise." But to whom do we owe this debt? What debt, for example, do we owe to our parents? The Buddha famously said, "You could carry your parents on your back for your entire life, and never repay the debt you owe them."

Cicero was an early Roman philosopher who became particularly interested in the question of duty and wrote an essay entitled "On Duty." He suggests that duties can come from four different sources:

1. Simply as a result of being a human being
2. As a result of one's particular place in life (one's family, one's country, one's job)
3. As a result of one's character
4. As a result of one's own moral expectations for oneself

I am partial to the first: "as a result of being a human being." If we are to be a fully alive human being—the *jivan mukti*, or "a soul awake in this lifetime" so often written about in yoga philosophy—then we have certain duties, do we not? Certain duties that derive simply from being a human being.

As Cicero points out, some duties are imposed from without. These include the specific duties imposed on us by law or culture, and they can vary considerably depending on jurisdiction, religion, and social norms. But the most important duties are called for from within—as Cicero would say, from within our humanness. My own view is this: sacred duty is the thing that if you *do not do it*, you will feel a profound sense of self-betrayal. The most important duties are not imposed from without, as in Arjuna's day. Charlie Lowell would say, after his mother, Anna Lowell: "What is your *highest form* of usefulness to the whole?" That, right there. That is your duty.

Remember, we have seen this view stated from the very beginning of our study of the Gita. We have seen the emphasis on the connection between one's individual calling and the common good. In the Gita, these are seen as inseparable. Krishna teaches that duty and humanity, indeed, were born together:

> *At the beginning, mankind and the obligation of selfless service were created together. (Gita 3:10)*

12

How is this notion of duty engendered within us? Charles Russell Lowell is a good case study, for he was brought up in a culture in which "duty to the whole" was highly regarded—indeed, actively cultivated, as it would have been in Arjuna's time.

Charlie Lowell's own home was a veritable training ground for civic duty. Anna Lowell, Charlie's mother, hosted voluble debates on religion, revolution, and slavery, and she regularly entertained the brightest and most progressive minds in Boston. The extended Lowell family would talk, talk, talk. (The Cambridge humor mills had it that "when the Lowells started talking, they could be heard a mile away in Harvard Square.") It was into this crucible of ideas and civic concern that young Charlie came of age. As I've said, Ralph Waldo Emerson was a regular at Anna Lowell's soirees. It's likely, too, that the Lowells knew Henry David Thoreau—and they most likely had read and studied his views on civil disobedience, on the war in Mexico, and the abolition of slavery. (Remember, Thoreau's essay on civil disobedience was published in 1849, the year before Charlie entered Harvard.) Because of Emerson's regular presence in their salons, Transcendentalism would have been one of the major topics of discussion at the Lowells', and they would have thoroughly digested its pros and cons.

When Charlie was just a boy, his mother fell on financial hard times, and in order to make ends meet, she set up a school in her home in Cambridge. She was a gifted teacher, and exposed her students to great literature from an early age. Her students, Charles among them, became devout readers. "Anna believed literature was there not simply to enjoy or edify but to stimulate, to challenge, and to inspire the reader to become and to do. Ideas were real; words had the power to change people." Anna Lowell was recognized for "arousing her pupils to intense action." This was the training ground for Charlie's views about civic duty.

And there was more. Charlie's uncle, the poet James Russell Lowell, belonged to the radical wing of the abolitionist movement. He had called for the abolition of slavery decades before almost anyone else. And Uncle James echoed in every way Anna Lowell's concern with "usefulness." He taught Charlie that "knowledge is power"—not because it made him superior in any way, but because "it enables us to benefit others and to pay our way honorably in life by being of use." There it is again: "usefulness" was everything in this family.

13

In the fall of 1850, Charles Russell Lowell went to Harvard College, as did most of his friends. At this moment in history, as we have seen in our study of Harriet Beecher Stowe, the issue of slavery was dividing the country. The widely hated Fugitive Slave Law had just been passed. This much-despised law required that the citizens of any state, free or slave, must assist a slave owner in the retrieval of his "property"—that is, the return of self-emancipated slaves to bondage. There was no statute of limitations on slaves' bondage to masters. A former slave could have been freed and living life in freedom in the North for decades. He or she was still considered someone else's property.

The Fugitive Slave Law directly impacted the Lowell family's life. Its passage put into jeopardy four to six hundred self-emancipated slaves in the city Boston. Immediately upon its passage, dozens of free Blacks fled the city. Slave catchers resurfaced around every corner. Boston's small African American community was rightfully panicked. At just this time, a girl attending Anna Lowell's school turned out to be the mixed-race child of a Southern white "owner." This teenaged girl was now in jeopardy of being "returned." Before she could be sent back to slavery, however, she committed suicide. This profoundly affected Charlie's family, and galvanized it to oppose the Fugitive Slave Law even more robustly. Young Charlie got deeply involved in the struggle, carrying messages back and forth between Anna and his uncles, and was thereby drawn into the gritty abolitionist network from a young age.

Charlie, seeing the hypocrisy of the Christian church around the issue of slavery—as both Thoreau and Stowe had—came to believe that organized religion was the cause of most human suffering and evil. He sought to replace the old religion with his own brand of mysticism. He was intrigued with the idea that there is a mystical pattern and order underlying perceived reality. In college Charlie read deeply into mystic literature. He read voraciously—the history of the Hindu gods, the life of the Buddha, the Bhagavad Gita, and tales of the Saxons. And then finally, of course, in 1852, Harriet Beecher

Stowe published her world-changing *Uncle Tom's Cabin,* and Charlie devoured it. Anna Lowell taught this book in her school and declared that it, "will do more to free us from slavery than all that has ever been done."

If we look closely, we can see that Charles Russell Lowell's family believed in an idea almost identical to dharma. Anna taught her children that "to every man there is appointed a certain ministry and service, a path described of duty, a work to perform, and a race to run, an office in the economy of Providence, for usefulness is a necessary property of goodness."

14

Charlie Lowell was widely viewed as the most outstanding student in his Harvard class, and as such, he was chosen to give the commencement address.

It was a hot day in mid-July when young Charles Lowell stood on the Quad before his class and the whole community of Harvard. Astonishingly, he was only nineteen years old and still looked more like a boy than a man. And yet what issued forth from his mouth was stunning. The title of the talk was "The Reverence Due from Old Age to Youth."

Charlie's talk that day was a cry for higher aspirations for American culture. For "fresher and purer ideals" and a spirit of real reform. He wove together wisdom from Hinduism and Islam and even from mathematics. No one who heard him that day would forget the speech. Lowell called for "daring acts." He called for his friends and his elders to dream of "impossibilities." "The world always advances," he said, "by impossibilities achieved." Much of this way of thinking came from his mother, Anna Lowell, who had prized young people. "Children are monarchs," she said, ". . . on them hangs the destiny of the New World."

For all his youth, Lowell was described as having a crystal-clear mind. Ralph Waldo Emerson, who was in the audience on that July day at Harvard, remarked on Charlie's address and his "generous discontent" with the conditions of society. "I hope he will never get over it," he remarked. (After hearing the speech, Emerson, we are told, "had decided there was a good crop of mystics at Harvard College.") "The speech was a cry against cynicism," writes Carol Bundy. "Finally, it was a sort of manifesto. This speech was [Lowell's] effort to define 'usefulness' for himself."

15

And then, of course, came war. On April 12, 1861, the confrontation in South Carolina began America's great civil war. Rebel artillery fired on the Union garrison at Fort Sumter, in Charleston harbor, as rebellious civilians watched and cheered from shore. The bombardment continued all day, until the fort was finally surrendered by Union Major Robert Anderson.

President Lincoln declared war on the rebellious states. Just two days later, on April 14, Lincoln called on the Northern states to immediately produce 75,000 troops for the Union Army. Charles Russell Lowell would now face his Arjuna moment. Was he called to fight this fight?

In Boston, Lincoln's call for enlistees was greeted with an overwhelming response—a response that surprised many. Writes Bundy, "decades of popular ambivalence about war appeared to end in an instant." Hundreds of men and boys immediately showed up at induction centers. Ralph Waldo Emerson described it as "an affair of instincts . . . we did not know we had them . . . and now a sentiment mightier than logic, wide as light, strong as gravity, reaches into the college, the bank, the farm house and the church. It is the day of the populace; they are wiser than their teachers. I will never again speak lightly of a crowd." Could we call this instinct "duty"?

For Charles Russell Lowell, his entire life had been a preparation for a response to this kind of call of duty. As it turned out, for him, duty had become—as Emerson said—a kind of instinct. An instinct, indeed, that he did not know he had until the situation arose.

But we are back to our central question: How do we know our duty when we see it? There are some kinds of duties that are surely instinctive, as Emerson said. We are sitting by the swimming pool on a lazy summer afternoon. A toddler accidentally falls into the pool. No one hesitates. Our duty is clear. We will do whatever it takes to save the baby. Many of the most human things we do, we do by this very instinct for duty. You hear it all the time. A plane crash-lands on the Potomac River in Washington, DC. Several bystanders jump into the freezing cold river to save lives. Later they say, to a person, "Anyone would have done it." They universally resist the cry of "hero." "No. It's just what human beings do for other human beings." There it is: Some duties we have, says Cicero, "simply as result of being human."

16

As I was writing this chapter, and was already consumed with questions about duty, it turned out that an immediate issue of duty arose. It was March of 2020. The world had been struck down almost overnight with one of the most virulent viruses known to humankind. We came to know it as COVID-19. We were told that it was a "novel coronavirus" that had perhaps escaped from a "wet market" in rural China. A pandemic quickly ensued, and shut down the entire world for a time. The world changed in shocking ways. Streets were empty and quiet. Whole cities hunkered down indoors. Within weeks, there were blue skies over Beijing for the first time in decades. Carbon emissions dropped overnight. The lights went off in the Eiffel Tower. Italians remained locked in their homes and shouted to one another, and to the quarantined world, from their balconies.

In New York City, infections escalated geometrically. The hospitals and their staffs were overwhelmed. Refrigerated morgue trucks began to line up next to hospitals. Deaths swelled quickly into the tens of thousands. By the time this manuscript was completed, in June of 2021, there were more than 600,000 dead in the United States alone. America was fighting a new kind of war.

During these months, we each asked ourselves: What is my duty now? How can I help? Okay, yes, I'll do whatever I must do for the common good: I'll wear a mask. Wash my hands. Social distance. Stay at home. Yes, of course, I'll do all of that, but more: Should I volunteer at the food bank? Help the elderly neighbors? Give money to the unemployed relative? What risks am I compelled to take in order to help? What is my duty here?

17

During the early days of the pandemic, I had a number of late-night calls from a friend of mine back in my home state of Ohio, concerning this very question of duty.

Toby Williams is a thirty-five-year-old nurse from a small town in Ohio—a suburb of Akron, Ohio, just a few miles from the town where I myself grew up. Toby is a gay African American man who had attended a number of my seminars at Kripalu over the previous five years. We had become good friends. We had bonded over all things Ohio, over our love of yoga, our dogs, and over being gay.

Toby called me several nights in a row from his home. He was wrestling with his conscience.

The COVID-19 pandemic had struck New York City particularly hard, and by early April of 2020, the New York City hospital system was overwhelmed. The evening news was full of stories of overflowing wards, refrigerated trucks full of bodies, lack of personal protective equipment (PPE), and a shortage of ventilators. The air was full of a new vocabulary: *pandemic*, *PPE*, *quarantine*, *social distancing*. President Donald Trump declared war on the pandemic (though his "war" was always too little, too late) and announced that he was now, egad, a "wartime president." Within weeks, the world was turned on its head.

On the phone, Toby sounded conflicted: "Steve, I feel that I simply have to go to New York and help. But I'm not sure it's my calling. What about Josh [his thirteen-year-old son]? Isn't he my first duty? I just don't fuckin' know what to do, man." This was an Arjuna moment. Conflicting sacred duties confounded Toby's mind, just as they had confounded Arjuna's on the night before the battle of Kurukshetra.

Toby was small of stature, lean and athletic, with a shock of hair arranged in some wonderfully funky new style. Toby was irreverent, fun, with a wicked sense of humor. He was, like me, a longtime yoga practitioner. At the time of the pandemic, he'd been divorced from his wife for seven years, and shared custody of his thirteen-year-old son with his ex-wife. I knew from my many workshops with Toby that he thought deeply about things.

The Ohio hospital in which Toby had worked for a decade had specialized in elective surgeries, and these were no longer being scheduled in the short term, so Toby was furloughed. The pandemic had not yet really hit Akron. Toby was sheltering at home with his boyfriend, Justin, his son, Josh, and their two dogs.

"I feel like it's my duty to go, man," said Toby.

"Tell me what you mean by that, Toby," I said.

"Okay, here's the thing: I'm trained in that very thing, in working with difficult patients. I know how to do it. I *can* do it. I prayed about it with my pastor. Weighed all the different factors. I just feel I gotta do it. I mean, I just do not feel right sitting on my ass here at home."

More of his story spilled out. Parts that I had not known.

Toby's mother and aunt were both nurses—RNs. "When people are in trouble, we help out, Steve. I mean, it's practically our family motto. Part of our code. It's what we do." Toby had had a difficult childhood. His mother's sister, Bess, had helped raise him while his mother was recovering from an addiction to prescribed medication. She had been in rehab off and on for almost two years—getting straight. But Aunt Bess was always there to help. Toby had always wanted to be like Bess.

So: Should he fight this fight?

Toby and I talked every day for two weeks. The crisis in New York City just kept getting worse. First Toby was a "yes," then a "no." What would it be like? How would Josh cope with his father being away, perhaps for months? Was it fair for Toby to ask his boyfriend, Justin, to shoulder the burdens at home? Why should Toby risk his own health and safety?

For a couple of weeks, Toby and I examined his doubts. In the yoga tradition, doubt is considered one of the five hindrances, and there is a very specific technique for working with it. It's simply this: when the mind is overwhelmed by doubt, first *name* it, then *investigate* it, lean into it, examine every issue, and endeavor to figure out "what's true."

"In a case like this, Toby," I said, "you gotta have absolute dedication to the truth. That's the only thing that can help you decide."

"Dude, what's truth?" said Toby. "I just don't know."

18

Several weeks into the crisis, Toby left Justin and Josh and headed to New York City to help. Upon arrival, he promised his handlers in New York only that he would stay for a month. This was the compromise he had made with himself and with Justin and Josh. Toby found himself assigned to the most difficult hospital in the city. He would be staying in a hotel with a bunch of other nurses and docs who had come from all over the country to help.

Throughout his first weeks in New York, Toby's doubts regularly flared again. One night he was musing about how he had ended up in New York. "Jesus, how did I get here?" he said to me in a phone call. "What the hell was I thinking? Steve, this shit is really dangerous. Six of my coworkers are sick already. I think I'd better come home."

"Well, what *were* you thinking, Toby?" I suggested we review his decision.

"I dunno, I just remember a sense of calling. It was on my conscience. What is conscience, anyway?" he asked. And then Toby began a kind of stream-of-consciousness answer to his own question. "An inner voice, an inner prompting of some kind. I had it before. In my marriage. I knew I was gay, and it wasn't right to tie Tanya to a gay man. But I was scared. Shit, it was enough being Black. Do I have to be gay too? Took me a long time to act. Hardest thing I've ever done. But it just wasn't right. This conscience thing weighs in. That inner voice thing that you must obey."

Toby and I sat in silence for a few long moments. I shared with him Gandhi's view of the matter: "The only tyrant I allow in my life is that still small voice inside."

"Wouldn't feel right about it if I left," he said finally, almost out of exhaustion. "I'll call you tomorrow night."

19

Upon hearing Lincoln's call for troops on April 14, Charlie Lowell sprung into action. Interestingly, there was no apparent ambivalence on his part. He never in any of his writings or letters shared serious doubt about his decision to fight in the war. Why? Lowell had been trained up to duty.

From the first, Charles Russell Lowell set about finding his place in the new order with characteristic resolve. On April 21, 1861, Charlie arrived in Washington and resolved to find a place in the U.S. Army. "A place in the economy of Providence," as his mother had said. He had his heart set on the cavalry.

Lowell was feisty enough (and connected enough) to obtain an interview with Simon Cameron, the secretary of war, himself. Something about this particular interview moved Secretary Cameron. The man Cameron saw before him was "a slight, rather shabby young man with boyish looks, curling locks, a somewhat pretty face, barely enough facial hair to shave."

"You, young man," Cameron boomed, "what do you know of a horse?"

Lowell would later tell this story to his fellow cavalry officers, who could only laugh at the paradox. As it turned out, Lowell knew plenty about horses. He had become an excellent horseman during the years just after Harvard when he was endeavoring—through concerted physical exercise—to cure himself of his lung disease. To everyone's surprise, Charles Russell Lowell received an officer's commission in a new cavalry unit in the rapidly forming Union Army.

20

We have seen that on the night before the great battle of Kurukshetra, Arjuna was terrified. In large part, as I have said, it seems he was terrified by the great moral dilemma before him. And part of his dilemma was this: As a warrior, he was only required to fight in a "just war." Was the fight against the Kaurava family a just fight?

It was a sign of wisdom that Arjuna was asking this question. Indeed, in the Hindu tradition, there are only a handful of instances in which a war can truly be considered "a just war." These all involve hostile and unrelenting challenges that threaten to undermine civilization itself. These situations are called *adharma* (meaning, literally, "anti-dharma"). They might include, for example, a wholesale slaughter of, or violent oppression of, a race—a violent oppression that has proved to be completely impervious to peaceful solutions. They might involve the widespread imprisonment, captivity, or enslavement of an entire population. Or they might involve an immediate threat to the life of one's family.

The battle of Kurukshetra was fought because the Kaurava family—Arjuna's cousins, remember—had illegally usurped the throne and were instituting an era of tyranny and extreme injustice. They were the very embodiment of adharma. But was war really necessary? Was that the only answer here?

Arjuna's family, the Pandavas, were the essence of dharma, and of righteousness, just as Lowell's family had been. But they hesitated for a long time before actually going to war. Indeed, the Pandavas resorted to war only after all their attempts at a peaceful solution with the Kauravas had failed. Indeed, the Pandavas bent over backward to make the negotiations work. It's important to state here that neither Krishna nor the Bhagavad Gita advocate violence in any way. But Krishna is squarely on the side of establishing dharma in the land, and in fact has taken human form precisely in order to help in its reestablishment. He declares:

> *Whenever dharma declines and the purpose of life is forgotten, I manifest myself on earth. I am born in every age to protect the good, to destroy evil, and to reestablish dharma. (Gita 4:7–8)*

Arjuna's cousins, the Kauravas, clearly represent adharma in the parable of the Gita. They were treacherous, selfish, jealous, evil, and consumed with hatred and power-lust. Arjuna's family, the Pandavas, of course, represent dharma in the tale, and they were always willing to tread the path of righteousness and uphold dharma. Thus, to reestablish dharma, the adharmic Kauravas had to be resisted, and regrettably, this would eventually mean violent resistance.

21

Any act of war in the Hindu tradition is wrapped around with severe restrictions. First of all, even in a just war, to harbor hate for one's enemies is still considered "poison." We are called upon to extend loving-kindness and compassion to our enemies, even when facing them on a battlefield.

"That's not possible," you may say. Still, this is the path of yoga that Arjuna trod.

This raises an important paradox. People sometimes seem to think that one is *obligated* to hate one's enemies. Some may say, "How can you speak well of someone who hates you?" The Hindu approach to this is that we can still choose not to hate people back. If you have to fight someone, then fight. But hate is optional, and you may choose otherwise. Fought without compassion for the enemy, war is always seen in the Hindu tradition as a criminal activity. Sometimes it is necessary to take life, maybe, but we never take life for granted.

22

Had Charlie Lowell and his peers thought about the morality of war? Was the American Civil War a "just war?" Yes, in fact, these young men had indeed thought deeply about this. Indeed, the question of "the just war" was a huge discussion that had been going on in America for the twenty years leading up to the Civil War. Early abolitionists, especially the most influential among them, were completely against violence of any kind. William Lloyd Garrison, Harriet Beecher Stowe, Sojourner Truth: they all dreaded war and did everything to avoid it. Abraham Lincoln held the same view. He refers to this in his Second Inaugural Address. "All dreaded [the coming of war] . . ." Lincoln declaimed, referring to *both* North and South, "all sought to avert it . . . . Both parties deprecated war, but one of them would *make* war rather than let the nation survive, and the other would *accept* war rather than let it perish, and the war came."

By 1861 it was clear that a war would be required. Even many of the most stalwart pacifists came to believe it was inevitable—including

Garrison and Stowe. But like the Pandavas, Lowell and his family and peers had wrapped war around with clear restrictions about how a just war must be fought.

Lowell and most of his peers believed that they were a civilized people who were morally responsible to God for their actions. Along with Henry David Thoreau, they believed in the mystic power of action. And this meant that they could not in any way abandon Christian principles in the course of the fighting. No matter how uncivilized the other side might be, they must adhere to their righteous standards—for the sake of their own souls.

23

Meanwhile, Toby was still in New York City, in the midst of his own war. He and I continued to talk regularly. One night in our talk, something interesting came up.

"I realized the other day why I'm *really* here, man. It's not only for the patients. It's for the other workers. To support them. I mean, Steve, this is my tribe. These are my people. I know what they go through. We form teams quickly in this business, and I know how to work in teams, and, honestly I really, really love that. Man, I do love it."

And then Toby described his experience of teamwork at the hospital: "That's what's happens at the hospital, man. Everyone pretty much knows what has to be done, even before being asked. I have this amazing experience there of being useful. Really needed. Effective. Essential."

Then he said something extraordinary. "Steve, I feel so held up by the others and by the team that it's almost like I'm not doing the work at all; it's not effortless, but there is someone else, some higher power doing it through me."

As it turned out, Toby stayed at his post in New York City for three entire months, and this is precisely why he stayed—in spite of his doubts. He began to get clear about precisely *to whom* and *to what* he felt a duty. He was acting for the good of the whole, yes, and not just for the patients, but for his fellow "soldiers" in the fight.

Toby was reflecting on his original decision to come to New York. "You know, I'd seen some of those nurses interviewed on TV. Those girls are gonna be in PTSD-land, I thought. I can tell, because they're so stressed they can't even talk about their feelings."

He continued: "I was right. When I got here, I noticed it right away. There was a shitload of drinking and smoking weed going on back at the hotel."

Toby had trained in part as a psych nurse, and this training came in handy in New York. He started a "share circle" back at the hotel every night after shift.

Toby laughed when we talked about this on the phone. He talked about the reflexology course he'd taken at Kripalu. "Oh, yeah, I used all of the reflexology stuff, man. Dude, we rubbed each other's feet every night. Helped us all to go to sleep."

He added this: "Steve, it's grueling. But there are at least a few moments every day that are worth their weight in gold. The squeeze of a dying woman's hand. The supportive touch of another nurse's hand on my shoulder. So much goodwill. So many little sacrifices people are making everywhere around us."

24

I talked with Toby at least once a week throughout the three months that he served in New York City. He was often exhausted. Stressed. Scared for himself. He routinely had second thoughts. His doubts were inevitable. But after a while, he started sending me texts about one or two things that happened every day that were bright spots of joy. He took to sending me texts and pictures from some little moment in the day. Often it was about someone else's sacrifice, which had moved him greatly.

Could it be that our duty to the good of the whole, to our fellow human beings, is an instinct? Does it have a mystical power that we simply do not understand?

25

Charlie Lowell and Captain Rufus Smith lay side by side on the surgery table in the field hospital, behind the lines of Cedar Creek.

According to firsthand accounts, Lowell's first instinct was to comfort Smith, his mortally wounded friend and colleague, who was suffering extremely—not just from pain, but also from the thought of the loss of his life with his family. Lowell was tender with his friend. He reminded Smith that he had been a pivotal actor in the victory of the day, and that as a result of their actions, Lincoln's reelection was assured.

Lowell spoke calmly to his comrade: "I have always been able to count on you; you were the bravest of the brave; now you must be strong, you must meet this as you have other trials. Be steady. I count on you."

Paradoxically, in encouraging his friend, Lowell found strength for himself. For Lowell it was "usefulness" to the last. Shortly after this, Rufus Smith died peacefully.

26

As it turns out, just prior to the Battle of Cedar Creek, Charles Russell Lowell had for the first time had premonitions of his own death. His last letter to his mother was dark. He sounded exhausted and depressed, utterly spent, and more fragile and emotional than his mother had previously heard him.

Leading up to Cedar Creek, it seems that Lowell sensed that his time had come. His cough had come back, and he once again suffered acutely from his lung disease. His breathing had worsened. He couldn't sleep. When the first bullet hit him, he certainly knew that he would die from the wound. But he understood the importance of his presence in leading his men. So he had himself tied onto his horse. He gave himself as a willing, living sacrifice.

As Charlie Lowell lay on the table next to Smith's now dead body, he fully realized that he himself was dying. In addition to comforting Smith in his last hours, he turned to the task of distributing his things. He wanted his close friend Lieutenant Colonel Caspar Crowninshield to have his pistol. "I was very fond of him," he said of Crowninshield (already referring to himself in the past tense).

In those final moments, Lowell felt acutely his duty to others—and primarily to his wife. Lowell broke down several times as he thought of his young wife, Effie, who was now with child and only a month from her delivery date. He barely managed to scrawl a brief handwritten note to her before his energy gave out. By 10 P.M. on the evening of October 19, his pulse and voice were weak.

Lowell drifted in and out of consciousness through the night, and early the next morning, his men filed by him one by one. Writes Carol Bundy, "All the energy had gone from him, and it was disarming to realize how little there was to him, lying on the dining table, propped up with pillows, his small, gaunt body barely evident beneath the blanket. Crowninshield and he spoke for some time, Lowell giving him last-minute directions. By way of parting, Lowell added, 'My only regret is that I cannot do something more for our cause.' Crowninshield was overcome."

Lowell remarked to Dr. DeWolf that he was not at all sure what he would find in the afterlife, but that he was ready, now, for death. "If there is another world after this I am prepared to meet it. If not, I am still willing to leave this one."

At nine o'clock, Charles Russell Lowell died.

Lowell's dignified death was not an anomaly. Eyewitness accounts are full of stories of men's brave deaths in Civil War hospitals. Walt Whitman—who was then serving as a nurse in the war's field hospitals (Whitman called himself "A Soldier's Missionary")—gives us many poignant accounts of these gentle, willing deaths. Whitman wrote to the mother of one Corporal Frank Irwin who had been wounded near Fort Fisher in Virginia:

> He was perfectly willing to die—he had become very weak and had suffer'd a good deal, and was perfectly resign'd, poor boy. I do not know his past life, but I feel as if it must have been good. At any rate what I saw of him here, under the most trying circumstances, with a painful wound, and among strangers, I can say that he behaved so brave, so composed, and so sweet and affectionate, it could not be surpass'd. And now like many other noble and good men, after serving his country as a soldier, he has yielded up his young life at the very outset in her service . . .

In the days that followed, Charlie Lowell's actions on the field, and his heroism, would be trumpeted in all the major papers of the Northeast. They understood the role that the Cedar Creek victory had played in the outcome of the war. "Lament for a True Knight," read one headline. And "A Noble Death," another.

27

The funeral for Charlie Lowell was held on the damp, chilly morning of October 28 at the Harvard College chapel. The outpouring of grief at this funeral became legendary. Boston's most famous figures were present, looking stunned and solemn. There were Longfellow, Emerson, and Oliver Wendell Holmes. There was Henry Lee Higginson, Lowell's oldest and most devoted friend, now permanently disabled himself. There were the overseers of Harvard University and members of the Harvard Corporation, dressed in ceremonial robes and broad collars. There were cartloads of flowers: orchids, camellias, miniature orange and lemon, geraniums, Cape jasmine. Eyewitnesses recount the magnificent drama of the floral display, but mostly they remark on the scent. Everyone commented on it. The air was perfumed.

The Reverend George Putnam, Unitarian minister of the First Church of Roxbury, gave the address. He wrestled to come to terms with the sacrifice of human beings in this war. His effort was noble:

> This mighty mother of us all, our country . . . steeps her soil in her children's most precious blood. She tears her brightest jewels from her own forehead, and flings them in the dust. She sends daily her swift messengers of grief and desolation from heart to heart, and from house to house, throughout her borders. She does all this; but she does it not in cruelty, but in love, that she may preserve her own glorious life, her own imperial sovereignty, and her benignant power to bless her children, and fold them under her brooding wings, to nourish and keep them, as she only can, in freedom, in honor, and in peace. And thus she pays the stupendous debt she owes to her afflicted people.

Turning to the coffin with outstretched arms, Reverend Putnam asked: "Are we paying too heavy a price for our country's freedom?"

What had been the price? Carol Bundy tells us: "A generation of men. A generation of mothers now sonless, sisters brotherless, wives husbandless, children fatherless."

Again, Putnam asked the question: "Too high a price?"

Turning back to the mourners, Putnam declared: "Here if ever we might be permitted to say so, but here, beside these precious remains, our full hearts answer—no—not too much—not too much."

28

The writers of the Bhagavad Gita make much of, and speak often of, sacrifice and its mystic power. When one's dharma is freely offered up to God and is enacted for the good of the whole, this sacrifice unifies the soul with the Divine. There are many ways to sacrifice, says the Gita, but there is no liberation, no awakening, without some kind of sacrifice.

> *Some offer wealth; others offer sense restraint and suffering. Some take vows and offer knowledge and study of the scriptures; and some make the offering of meditation. Some offer the forces of vitality . . . All these understand the meaning of service and will be cleansed of their impurities . . . . These offerings are born of work, and each guides mankind along a path to Brahman. Understanding this, you will attain liberation. (Gita 4:28–33)*

What is it in the nature of sacrifice for the good of the whole that gives it such a redemptive power? Human beings who are used up in the fire of dharma make a mystic contribution. We must admit that we do not understand the whole picture. But there is something about Lowell's conscious sacrifice that we understand to be the most noble of human acts. Indeed, a willing sacrifice for the good of the whole was at the very center of Lowell's family and their religious beliefs. Christ on the cross was apparent on the altar of the new Appleton

Chapel at Harvard on the day of Charlie's funeral. And perhaps that image of sacrifice now had special meaning for those assembled there.

I have struggled to understand what this sacrifice means. All serious examination of the meaning of the life of Charles Russell Lowell must come to terms with this. Carol Bundy, Lowell's oft-mentioned biographer, was, as it turns out, Charlie Lowell's great-great-great niece. She had found his battered sword, scabbard, and boots in the attic of her grandmother's home when her grandmother died. And feeling the emotional heft of these objects, Bundy felt compelled to dig deeper into Lowell's life. Who was this man? Who was this distant and much-revered uncle? Who was this war hero? She was fascinated. She got to the heart of the matter. Carol Bundy titled her book *The Nature of Sacrifice*. I challenge you to read it without soaking many of its pages in tears.

29

What was the fruit of Lowell's sacrifice? Well, there were the immediate effects, of course. Bundy gives us this: "Lowell had fallen at the head of his men, he had fallen leading the charge but the battle had been won. Without Lowell's decisive leadership, there would have been no army left for [Union General] Sheridan to rally after he made his famous ride from Winchester. The battle [of Cedar Creek] had decided the Shenandoah Valley campaign and begun the ruin of the Confederate cavalry. It had given Lincoln the victory he needed for reelection. Lowell had triumphed, even in death."

There was a mystic effect of Lowell's sacrifice—one that reaches out and touches us even today from the life and death of this man. It is the mystic effect of duty well performed. Any act well done is done forever.

Lincoln, above all people, understood the nature of duty and the redemptive sacrifice it often entails. In March of 1865, just weeks before his assassination, he gave his great Second Inaugural Address, in which he tried to make sense of the sacrifice made on such an epic scale during the War between the States. Of course, Lincoln viewed the required sacrifice as deeply related to our country's sin of slavery:

> Fondly do we hope, fervently do we pray, that this mighty scourge of war may speedily pass away. Yet, if God wills that it continue until all the wealth piled by the bondsman's two hundred and fifty years of unrequited toil shall be sunk, and until every drop of blood drawn with the lash shall be paid by another drawn with the sword, as was said three thousand years ago, so still it must be said "the judgments of the Lord are true and righteous altogether."

Redemption was very much on Lincoln's mind throughout the war, and even more so as the war dragged on and on. On the battlefield at Gettysburg, Pennsylvania, in his now famous address, he had sought to redeem "the fearful deaths."

He asked of those assembled:

> that we here highly resolve that these dead shall not have died in vain—that this nation, under God, shall have a new birth of freedom—and that government of the people, by the people, for the people, shall not perish from the earth.

30

Toby and I were walking in the cemetery that overlooks the little village of Lenox—almost within sight of Kripalu Center. I'd taken him to visit the grave of Annie Haggerty Shaw, the wife of the aforementioned Rob Shaw—Lowell's best friend who had been killed heroically leading America's first battalion of Black soldiers. Annie Shaw had been buried in the cemetery in Lenox, just a stone's throw from my home—and once I understood the nature of her loss and her own sacrifice, I often visited her grave. Toby and I placed a bouquet of wildflowers at the base of the Celtic cross that marked it.

I told Toby the story about how Annie Haggerty Shaw had herself been grievously wounded by the loss of her husband. After Rob Shaw's death, Annie seems to have purposely slipped into obscurity. She never remarried, young as she was. I have a sense that she never really recovered from her loss.

Toby and I sat down next to the grave, and remained in silence for a few moments. He picked at long stems of grass and wound them absentmindedly around his fingers.

"You know what, man. I identify with this lady.

"Honestly, I'm not sure I'll ever be quite the same." I had actually wondered about this. Toby looked older since his return from New York. He was quieter. More reflective. Being in the fire had changed him.

"Those three months ripped open my heart," he said. "It's a duty I wish I hadn't been given."

31

Did Toby pay too high a price? Did Lowell?

In his old age, Walt Whitman became the voice of lament for all that had been lost during America's great conflict. Whitman himself, after his years in the Civil War hospitals, would never be the same. And yet he also understood what had been gained. To the end, Walt Whitman insisted that the dead be not forgotten. Indeed, this would be the dharma of his old age. "Lose not my sons," he wrote late in life. "Lose not an atom." In one of his last poems, written when he was seventy-one years old, Whitman finds himself sitting alone in the twilight of the day in front of the meager fire in his boardinghouse, remembering: Remembering the dead. Remembering their faces; their noble sacrifice. And spreading his love over their sacred memories.

> *Each name recall'd by me from out the darkness and*
> *death's ashes,*
> *Henceforth to be, deep, deep within my heart recording,*
> *for many a future year,*
> *Your mystic roll entire of unknown names, or*
> *North or South,*
> *Embalm'd with love in this twilight song.*

In another late poem, he fully bares his heart to "his sons":

> *The moon give you light,*
> *And the bugles and the drums give you music,*
> *And my heart, O my soldiers, my veterans,*
> *My heart gives you love.*

CHAPTER 6

SOJOURNER TRUTH

Trust in the Mystic Power of the Naked Truth

I am pleading for my people,
A poor downtrodden race,
Who dwell in freedom's boasted land,
With no abiding place.

I am pleading that my people
May have their rights restored;
For they have long been toiling,
And yet have no reward.

— One of Sojourner Truth's many "home-made" hymns

"Stop the speech, I say. Stop it now."

A well-dressed, clearly prominent white man was calling from the back of the church hall. He was rude. Boorish. Possibly drunk.

There had been hecklers throughout the talk, yes, and they were not entirely unexpected at a meeting of this kind. But something else was happening here. Tensions in the hall seemed perilously close to exploding into violence. There were catcalls and shouts back and forth, as some members of the audience tried to silence the heckler.

This edgy drama was playing itself out in the year 1858, in a little white clapboard church in rural Indiana. The simple church sat squarely in the center of the village known as Silver Lake. At the podium in the church hall stood an imposing Black woman. She stood almost six feet tall and had a lean, weathered, and intelligent face. Her body, too, was slim—clearly strong, even rugged. She was dressed in a simple black dress with a loose-fitting white blouse and apron. She spoke in a deep, guttural voice that was known to entrance an audience.

This was the famed preacher and self-liberated slave known as Sojourner Truth. In the years leading up to this dramatic moment, Truth had developed an almost epic reputation around the United States as a take-no-prisoners speaker, abolitionist, and women's rights advocate. She was accustomed to conflict at her talks. The scene in which she was caught up at Silver Lake was nothing new to her.

2

The man at the back of the church would not relent. "You, sir, are an imposter," he shouted. "You pose as a woman, but it is obvious you are a man! No woman could speak like that."

Sojourner Truth stared down from the podium at the gaggle of rowdy white men at the rear of the hall. The heckler was one T. W. Strain, a local Indiana physician and a well-known mouthpiece for the pro-slavery Democrats in that area of the state.

It soon became clear that the crowd at the back of the hall was eager for a fight. Many of them had come intentionally to support Dr. Strain and to heckle Truth. (We would learn later that Strain had bet $40—a very large sum in 1858 dollars—that Sojourner Truth was, in fact, a man.)

At this point in the tussle, the organizers of the event made a vain effort to extract Sojourner Truth from the building. She would have none of it. Shots were fired near the back of the hall. Some audience members fled, as if for dear life.

Through it all, Strain continued to shout: "You are a fraud. Reveal yourself."

3

In order to fully understand what was happening here, we need a little context.

In the years leading up to the Civil War, many of America's Midwestern states had enacted so-called Black Code laws. These laws limited the movement of Blacks within a state, preventing them from living in certain "red-lined" areas. The laws restricted essential opportunities for Blacks—preventing them from voting, from testifying in court, and even from securing a school education for their children.

Now a handful of abolitionists in the state of Indiana feared that Black Code laws would be passed in their own state. In the fall of 1858, Sojourner Truth was asked by the well-known abolitionist Josephine Griffing to come and represent the 11,000 Blacks then living in Indiana, and to testify against the passing of these repressive laws. Truth gladly accepted the invitation. She used the opportunity to organize an extensive tour of the area. Pro-slavery mobs followed and heckled Truth wherever she went throughout the course of her tour. She was undaunted.

When she appeared at Silver Lake, Sojourner Truth was just coming to the end of her monthlong tour. Over the course of weeks of intense preaching, the interest in her message had grown substantially. The church hall in little Silver Lake was packed. In attendance were Blacks, whites, men, women, abolitionists, and women's rights activists who had come from miles around to hear Sojourner Truth preach.

4

Things in the church hall were coming to a head. Emboldened by his group of pro-slavery Democrats, Dr. Strain continued, and added a new demand: "We demand that you bare your breasts to a delegation of the women in the room—to prove yourself." Strain, without any authority to do so, spontaneously called for a vote on the matter, and there was a boisterous "aye" that came mostly from the crowd of men gathered at the back of the Hall. According to eyewitness accounts, no negative vote was called for.

The room froze. Not a single woman stepped forward to take on the task of examining Truth's anatomy.

5

Sojourner Truth now took command. She pulled herself up to her full height and calmly addressed the crowd.

"Well, Children, you know these breasts have suckled many a white babe, and most of those babes are grown to adulthood. Well, I dare say they turned out better than the men I see snapping and growling like dogs at the back of this room."

The crowd roared its approval. Strain was not pleased.

"Oh, I have no shame for this Black body, Children. No shame. Here. I'll show these breasts to the whole congregation."

To everyone's shock, Truth began to unbutton her blouse. A cry went up from the audience. As she pulled down her blouse to expose her breasts, Truth said, "Oh, Children, I am not ashamed to bare myself to you. The shame of this moment is on you."

The hecklers were stunned into silence. One young heckler edged closer, presumably to get a better look, and as he pushed people out of his way, Sojourner Truth addressed him directly. "Come closer, young man. Come on. Would you like to suck?"

The audience sat wide-eyed. Dr. Strain and his hecklers were quiet. By this point, no one had enough juice to take on this woman. Strain's group of angry men slowly exited the back of the church, and the meeting continued—with Truth in control.

No tonnage of dynamite could have had as powerful an effect on the room that day in Indiana as Sojourner Truth's unforgettable testimony. Supporters and hecklers alike had come face-to-face with living evidence that many of their preconceptions—about Black women, about women in general, about slavery—were wrong. Sojourner Truth had turned the moment entirely upside down. Says biographer Nell Irvin Painter of this scene, "What had been intended as degradation became a triumph of embodied rhetoric . . . In it, the image of her older woman's black body, a body that transcends shame through hardship, defeats the juvenile pricks of philistines."

Who exactly was this force of nature staring down at murderous mobs of angry men and disarming them with her "embodied rhetoric"?

6

Sojourner Truth was born Isabella Baumfree in Swartekill, New York, in 1797. She was born into slavery. (Note, please, that slavery in the United States was not only a Southern phenomenon. Though most of us are not aware of it, there were more than 30,000 enslaved people in the state of New York in the early 19th century.) Isabella's childhood in slavery was all too predictable. As soon as she was able to work—at about the age of nine—she was sold away from her mother (though not too far away in the first instance). Isabella, or "Belle" as she was called, then went on to change "masters" multiple times before her eighteenth birthday. Her early life was dominated by an unfathomable series of losses. Before she was half grown, Belle had already lost both of her parents and at least ten siblings. As a girl and young woman, she had endured the full hell of enslavement, including frequent beatings, rape, and ongoing sexual abuse.

Belle finally liberated herself when, in a bold move at the age of twenty-nine, she literally walked away from her final "master" with her infant daughter in her arms. When telling the story of her self-emancipation, she would always emphasize the fact that she *walked calmly away*. She did not run.

7

Where did young Isabella get the courage to stand up for herself in the face of the withering oppression she endured? One word: Mother. Isabella Baumfree was heir to a long tradition in the enslaved community. Mothers passed down a secret spiritual knowledge and strength to their daughters. Isabella's devoutly spiritual mother, whom she called Mau-Mau, had given her a spiritual education. Though illiterate, at her mother's knee young Belle had developed a masterful understanding of the Bible and the core tenets of Christianity, and she could recite or sing large sections of the scriptures by heart. Her developing spirituality encompassed, but also transcended, Christianity, because her mother brought to Isabella a wealth of Afrocentric spirituality as well. This native tradition was grounded in nature, in the rhythms of the Earth, in a deep trust in intuition, and in unseen forces that guide the world.

One aspect of Belle's spiritual training in particular gave her the strength to challenge "masters," to confront men in general, and eventually to challenge even the State. Under her mother's tutelage, young Isabella developed a passionate and quite sophisticated life of prayer. Following a long tradition of enslaved women in North America, the young Isabella built herself a "rural sanctuary," which she later describes in her own *Narrative* as "an island in a small stream, covered with large willow shrubbery, beneath which sheep had made their pleasant winding paths." This would be her own sacred temple in the woods. Here, she was safe. Protected. This was her own form of refuge. From this rural sanctuary the young Isabella prayed fervently, "begging," in her own words, "to be delivered from the evil, whatever that might be." There in her sanctuary, she developed a life of prayer that would serve her for the rest of her life.

8

Belle's spiritual development would bear dramatic fruit when she was in her midforties, when she experienced a particularly intense spiritual awakening. This awakening happened in the year 1843, and it was a turning point for Baumfree. On June 1, Pentecost Sunday, Isabella heard the Spirit of God calling on her to go forth and "preach the truth." She told her friends: "The Spirit calls me, and I must go," and she immediately left to make her way north from New York City, traveling from town to town, preaching, and speaking about the soul-killing experience of enslavement. Isabella slowly made her way up through the Connecticut River Valley toward Northampton, Massachusetts, where she eventually settled.

When she left home, Isabella traveled light. "When I left the house of bondage," she later said, "I left everything behind. I wasn't going to keep anything of Egypt on me, and so I went to the Lord and asked Him to give me a new name. And the Lord gave me Sojourner, because I was to travel up and down the land, showing the people their sins, and being a sign unto them. Afterward I told the Lord I wanted another name, because everybody else had two names; and the Lord gave me Truth, because I was to declare the truth to the people."

After her awakening, the woman now called Sojourner Truth felt called by God to take a vow of poverty, and so, as she herself said, she traveled only on "faith and charity." When asked how she provided for herself, she said, "I take no heed of that . . . Child don't you know that all there is of Sojourner is devoted to the Lord? And do you think he will leave me unprovided with what I need? God will send me where I am needed."

Truth believed that she was led by the Holy Spirit in her work, and she had a remarkable ability to call upon her impressive spiritual powers. She sang, she chanted, she preached, she exhorted—all with a spiritual authority that seemed undeniable to those who were lucky enough to be in the same room with her. In particular, Truth loved composing hymns—like the hymn cited as the epigraph to this chapter. She had an entrancing singing voice—which she used to great effect. And just as she used her voice, she used her body, her breasts, a finger lost during slavery, and a back crisscrossed with the scars of the whip, to bear witness against slavery.

Sojourner Truth spent her thirties and forties in various spiritual communities in New York and Massachusetts, nurturing her faith and her speaking skills. Eventually she became one of the most powerful itinerant preachers of 19th-century America. Much of what Truth would eventually preach from the pulpits of churches like the little church in Indiana would be her own life's story—the story of her brutal enslavement, and of her own self-emancipation. Eventually Truth would raise the task of telling her life story into an art form. She would often begin the tale like this:

> Well, Children, I was born a slave in Ulster County New York. I don't know if it was summer or winter, fall or spring. I don't even know what day of the week it was. They don't care when a slave is born or when he dies, just how much work they can do.

Truth told the story of her abuse at the hands of many masters, of course. But most importantly, she always told the story of her spiritual awakening, and of the experiences she'd had as a result of allowing herself to be led only by the Holy Spirit.

9

Throughout the Bhagavad Gita, as we have seen, Krishna exhorts Arjuna to turn his entire life over to Him—to God. This, of course, is precisely what Sojourner Truth had actually accomplished by middle age. One of Krishna's most important speeches to Arjuna is found in the final chapter of the Gita, and is spoken as a kind of summary of Krishna's advice. Krishna exhorts:

> *Be aware of me always, adore me, make every act an offering to me, and you shall come to me; this I promise, for you are dear to me. Abandon all supports and look to me for protection. I shall purify you from the sins of the past; do not grieve. (Gita 18:65–66)*

"Abandon all supports and look to me for protection." This is a critical phrase in the Gita. What does it mean? It means "surrender to me." Let go of your ego, of conventionality, of tradition. Let go of your preconceptions, your routinized way of being in the world. Depend only upon the Divine Voice, upon Divine inspiration—as Gandhi did, and as Thoreau did in his own way when he listened for his own "distant drummer."

Because she was truly "led by the Spirit," one never really knew what Sojourner Truth might say or do, and she freely acknowledged that she often did not know herself. She was once heard to say that she had showed up for one of her own speeches simply out of "curiosity to hear what I'll say." Her spiritual flexibility and fluidity are signs of being led by the spirit—as they were for Gandhi.

10

We have already had a brief taste of how Truth worked with a crowd. Her bold technique of surprise, raw truth, and direct confrontation threw congregations into a psychological grinder. In showing up with all of the parts of her self—her Blackness, her history as a slave, her undeniable intelligence and courage, her stunning spirituality, her deftness in argument—Sojourner Truth caused widespread confusion wherever she went. She forced her audiences to reconsider what they thought about Blacks, abolition, and women in general. In this way, Sojourner Truth herself provoked "the disorienting dilemma" in many of those who heard her.

11

Stories of Sojourner Truth's month in the Midwest abound to this day in many of the rural communities she touched so deeply. This is true, for example, in Kalamazoo, Michigan. At one point during the Indiana tour, Truth was speaking to a large group of college students at Kalamazoo College. The students entered the hall with jests and jokes. Spitballs flew from one corner to another. When Sojourner Truth took the podium, the students hissed and booed. They thumped on their seats. They broke into unrestrained laughter. The Kalamazoo faculty was no doubt appalled by this behavior, but seemed unable to quiet the melee.

Truth stood calmly and faced down the students until the room stilled. Then she spoke:

"Well, Children," she said, "when you go to heaven and God asks you what made you hate the colored people, have you got your answer ready?"

Truth paused for effect. And, naturally, she had her own answer ready.

"When God asks me what made me hate the white people," said Truth, "here is what I will say." She then calmly opened the collar of her dress, pulled it down to her shoulders and turned around so that the whole audience could see the "perfect network of scars made by the slave master's lash."

Again, the room was stunned. Writes Margaret Washington of the reaction to this witness, "The overwhelming effect produced a 'baptism of tears' that replaced the hisses and scoffs."

In fact, Truth often displayed the scars on her back. Here, this is what slavery looks like! The "home-made hymn" that serves as the epigraph to this chapter ended with the following verse:

Whilst I bear upon my body
The scars of many a gash,
I am pleading for my people
Who groan beneath the lash.

Sojourner Truth's dharma would be to witness *in her own body* to the truth of slavery and the truth of a spiritually transcendent womanhood. We have many accounts that a direct physical encounter with Truth changed people. She came around behind their defenses. Her vivid presence made a kind of attack directly aimed at the limbic system of her audience. She would confront, confuse, disorient. She would make her audiences question many of their own assumptions.

12

As we have seen, the contemplative traditions universally found *grasping* (or *raga* in Sanskrit) to be the very root of human suffering. The traditions use different words to describe what they meant: grasping, clinging, craving, holding on, "protecting." But they all refer to the same phenomenon, or as the texts have it, the same "affliction."

Okay, *grasping*. It's a little vague. Grasping to what, we might ask? The ancient yoga texts, including the Bhagavad Gita, provide us with many different lists of the *objects* of grasping and clinging. These lists almost always begin with "grasping to sense pleasures"—one of the most oft-repeated phrases in the Gita. And why is this "grasping to sense pleasures" a hindrance? Grasping to "self-satisfaction" (the language often used in the Gita) is a hindrance because it obscures the deeper, more subtle mystic knowledge of Truth. Grasping to sense pleasures, teaches Krishna, creates precisely the same kind of suffering as anger. In Chapter 1, we saw that anger has some very positive characteristics. But it is a slippery slope. Anger easily becomes obsessive. It feeds on itself. And in its obsessive form, anger eventually burns up—or destroys—its host. So, too, with sense pleasures. Our attachment to these pleasures easily becomes obsessive. They then burn us up, thereby obliterating our capacity to perceive subtler spiritual truth.

Just as a fire is covered by smoke and a mirror is obscured by dust, just as the embryo rests deep within the womb, knowledge is hidden by selfish desire—hidden, Arjuna, by this unquenchable fire for self-satisfaction, the inveterate enemy of the wise. (Gita 3:38–39)

So, the peril of grasping to sense pleasures is a central aspect of the Gita's message. But Krishna will go on to teach that grasping to sense pleasures is only just the beginning of our "afflicted states." There are other, much more elusive, less obvious, forms of grasping that cause us just as much suffering, and these, too, are clearly spelled out for us in the texts. In particular, these lists always include three other major objects of grasping: (1) grasping to "exalted views of the self," (2) grasping to "rites and rituals," and (3) grasping to "views and beliefs."

In this chapter we will be especially interested in the last of these: "grasping—or clinging—to views and beliefs." In the yoga tradition, this form of grasping is considered one of the deepest causes of social suffering. (This hindrance is sometimes called *ditthi* in Sanskrit.)

13

Clinging to views and beliefs. What exactly does this mean?

It's quite straightforward. Each of us holds a plethora of "views" about what is "true." We have, for example, some view about God (Does God exist or not? What is his or her nature?), about the ultimate meaning of life, about how the world works, about what we should strive for, about why we should get up in the morning. (We hold these views, by the way, even if we are not conscious of them.) This plethora of views that we hold will inevitably include views and beliefs about race—about what race means, whether race matters, and why and how. Likewise, it will include beliefs about gender—about what gender means, and whether gender matters and why and how.

The audience at Truth's event at Silver Lake clearly had a wide range of views about race and about gender. Dr. Strain and his rowdies had deeply held views and beliefs about Blacks, and in particular about Black women. No woman, much less a Black woman, could preach with the kind of skill, power, and authority that Truth demonstrated. Therefore, she *must* be a man.

The problem with views and beliefs, of course, is that human beings tend to cling to views about the world even when they are demonstrably wrong—when they do not comport with reality at all. This seems to be especially true when these beliefs are part of a cohesive and highly charged religious system. Wrongheaded as they are, these views are powerful. They've had a mammoth impact on how human beings have behaved lo these many centuries. In the view of the contemplative traditions, most of the world's suffering is, in fact, caused by strongly held views and beliefs that are erroneous.

When Mohandas Gandhi undertook his seven-month pilgrimage around India, he saw human suffering on a vast scale. And he realized that at the very root of this suffering were a number of completely inaccurate views of the world. For example: the astonishingly pervasive view that Indian people could not govern their own country because they were an inferior race; the corresponding view that the white, Anglo-Saxon races were destined to rule the world because they were intrinsically superior; and, devastatingly for India's future, the view that the Muslim faith is inferior to the Hindu faith, or vice versa.

All of these beliefs about the world were grossly inaccurate. And yet the British (almost universally) and Indians (in part) clung to them for dear life. Gandhi would routinely confront the absurdity of these views through his own personal witness. Nothing provoked him to rage more easily than illogical belief systems.

Likewise, on a daily basis Sojourner Truth faced massive misconceptions about Blacks, about women, about slavery itself. Her very presence was a repudiation of these views. As a result, she drove audiences crazy. Dr. Strain and his crew were presented with a human being whose actions conflicted with their views of how things are. And what do we do when confronted with an obvious truth that completely conflicts with our deeply cherished worldviews? Will we get angry? Resistant? Cling to our belief stubbornly? Or will we look at the truth of things? Will we become interested in what is actually so?

In times of great social upheaval, like the time in which Sojourner Truth lived, the aspect of *grasping* that is most dramatically unmasked is this very thorny "clinging to views and beliefs."

14

Sojourner Truth's dharma of challenging deeply held views and beliefs is part of a long tradition. During every time of social and political upheaval—when the world is going through a reassessment of reality—powerful figures like Sojourner Truth inevitably rise up. These figures will confront the world in an altogether new way, with a truth that the world has been too blind to see. These figures are by their very nature radical. They are bold. Shocking. Uncompromising. Throughout the history of Western civilization, we have tended to call these truth-tellers *prophets.* Sojourner Truth had the dharma of the prophet.

In an earlier chapter, I used the image of an egg to portray the development of the human self. Building on the analogy, I have said that the maturing self initially grows within the safe container of the egg's shell (referring here initially to the mother's womb, and then her safe, embracing arms). But eventually, in order to keep growing, the little being inside the shell must break through the shell itself, and burst out into a bigger world. The prophet's vocation is precisely to break the spiritual and psychological shell, freeing the growing being into a larger world. Gandhi and Thoreau both had prophetic dharmas. Their words are still cracking shells today.

Prophetic callings have remarkably similar dimensions across all cultures. First, they require prophets to *witness to a truth that the prophet knows firsthand*, but that the people by and large reject. As a result, they require those who are called to a prophetic dharma to *walk by faith and not by sight*—as Sojourner Truth did. And finally, prophetic dharmas universally require those who are called to come to terms with being disliked, or even hated. "A prophet is only without honor in her own country," goes the saying. The life of a prophet is a difficult life, and one meant for difficult times.

Almost always, as in Sojourner Truth's case, the prophetic vocation is the result of a vivid appearance by the Holy Spirit. In the Christian tradition, an entire book of the Bible recounts the work of the prophets and seers of the New Testament. The Acts of the Apostles describes the work of the Holy Spirit in creating prophets: "But ye shall receive power, after that the Holy Ghost is come upon you; and ye shall be witnesses unto me both in Jerusalem, and in all Judea, and in Samaria, and unto the uttermost part of the earth."

15

So, the duty of the prophet is precisely to provoke a disorienting dilemma in her auditors—to challenge conventional views of reality so powerfully as to provoke individuals to spiritual crises. The prophet *intentionally* disrupts what we think of as the orderly and predictable space-time continuum. And nothing is more disorienting than the disruption of the way we experience space and time.

The prophet disrupts Ordinary Psychological Space: The prophet draws people to move into a new, more fluid psychological space of possibility, which we sometimes call "liminal space." (The word *liminal* comes from the Latin root *limen,* which means "threshold.") This liminal space is the "crossing over" space—a space wherein one has left something behind, but is not yet fully inhabiting the next thing. It's a transition space. The prophet herself learns to live in this larger space, and to encourage others to do likewise. In this way, for example, our friend Emily Dickinson was a prophet. Her poetry shook people up. "I dwell in possibility," she wrote. Thoreau was a prophet as well, wasn't he? His cabin at Walden Pond was a classic example of liminal space. In his own time, visitors to Thoreau's cabin came away changed in ways they could barely describe. And Thoreau's literary masterpiece, *Walden,* is still a central "scripture" for seekers hungry for liminality.

The prophet disrupts Ordinary Time: Those with prophetic dharmas—like Gandhi, Thoreau, and Sojourner Truth—reveal to us in their own lives an altogether new experience of time itself. As we have seen, Thoreau was particularly aware of and interested in this phenomenon. The ancient Greeks, too, were deeply interested in this transformed experience of time, and they examined it closely. Finally, the Greeks developed two altogether different words for time: *chronos* and *kairos*. Chronos refers to chronological or sequential time, or what we might call "horizontal time." This is the predictable, steady, inalterable flow of measured time. Think of the slow, systematic ticking of a clock. "Tomorrow, and tomorrow, and tomorrow," wrote Shakespeare in his play *Macbeth*, "creeps in this petty pace from day to day, to the last syllable of recorded time."

Mystics in all ages, however, discern an altogether different dimension of time than *chronos*—a dimension the Greeks came to call *kairos*. We might call this "vertical time." In vertical time we have an experience of timelessness. Absolutely everything exists in the *now*, in the so-called eternal present. Kairos, for the ancient Greeks, signified a time full of possibility—a time when everything could be rearranged, because nothing was static. A *kairos* moment was considered a particularly opportune time for action.

In 1985, a group of Black South African theologians wrote a response to the then recent crackdowns by the apartheid government. It was called the Kairos Document, and it began, "The time has come. The moment of truth has arrived." The document was pervaded with a strong sense that the time was ripe for change: the fate of South Africa was balanced on a knife's edge, and small actions might have the power to change the path of history.

In the world's most powerful scriptures, time is often transcended in precisely this fashion. It is all happening right here. All of it: past, present, and future. We can now see that Arjuna and Krishna are living in a *kairos* moment. Krishna's role is precisely to rearrange Space and Time for young Arjuna.

16

In a *kairos* moment, everything is unusually fluid. Those static or calcified institutions that resist fluidity, resist life, resist new truths, resist reinvention—those very institutions are always challenged in a *kairos* moment, and are often upended. In Sojourner Truth's "moment," it was the calcified and rigid Christian Church that was most often challenged.

Truth herself was absolutely relentless when confronting the stolidity and pretentiousness of the Christian church and its ministers. She perceived that they were clinging for dear life to views and beliefs that were simply not true. And with disastrous results. As a result of her challenge to Church authority, Sojourner Truth was constantly being attacked by those she called "men of the cloth," who usually tried to assail her with their imagined superior command of scripture. But Truth could rarely be bettered in her knowledge of scripture. When challenged by what she called "men in black carrying bibles," she almost always won the day. Regarding the quotation of scripture as part of an argument, she would quip, "Pshaw, Child, the Bible is a riddle anyone can play on."

And play she did. In one now famous interchange, Sojourner Truth challenged a minister who was squabbling with her at one of her talks. Pointing at the troublesome clergyman, Truth addressed the entire audience: "Then that little man in black there, he says women can't have as much rights as men, 'cause Christ wasn't a woman! Where did your Christ come from? Where did Christ come from? From God and a woman! Man had nothing to do with Him."

Truth said of the devout Christians who challenged her based on their reading of theology: "Most of the suffering in the world is caused by people who read books." And then, to follow up: "I don't read such small stuff as letters . . . I read men and nations. I can see through a millstone, though I can't see through a spelling book."

In her talks, Sojourner Truth was especially critical of Black clerics. Writes Margaret Washington, "She mercilessly satirized Black male clerical opposition to women speaking in public. She was once heard to say that 'big Greek-crammed, mouthing men,' for many a long century, 'had been befogging the world, and getting its affairs into the most terrible snarl and confusion.' Yet when women spoke, ministers 'cried shame on women.' She urged her Black sisters to seize their special mission, move forward . . . she asserted that 'women, not men, were peculiarly adapted to fill the talking professions.'"

As it turned out, Sojourner Truth almost always knew the Bible better than her interlocutors. This, of course, infuriated her audiences even more.

At one church gathering, we are told, Sojourner Truth was sitting in the back of the meeting hall as one of her sister preachers was up front excoriating the clergy for their role in sustaining slavery. There were both Black and white clergymen present in the room that day, and one of the white men just couldn't take it anymore. He rose, red-faced, and demanded to be heard. The speaker invited him to the platform.

The outraged minister introduced himself as "an orthodox minister of the gospel" and launched into his argument. "I came here this afternoon to hear some of the eloquence which I understood was so abundant at these meetings; but instead . . . I have thus far listened to little save insults heaped upon the clergy."

The longer he talked, the more the fury rose within him. "I can find a better use for my leisure hours than attendance upon gatherings where the only speakers are women and jackasses."

The hall was silent.

Then Sojourner Truth "slowly rose from one of the rear seats" and addressed the chairwoman of the meeting. "That gentleman tells us he's a minister of the gospel, and so he probably knows what's in the scripture.

"There was another minister, a long time ago, named Balaam," said Truth, warming to her topic. "He got mighty mad, too, at an ass that spoke. But, Missus Chairman, I'd like to remind the gentleman that it was the ass and not the minister that saw the angel."

Sojourner Truth referred to a story that the clergyman certainly would have known. The Moab prince Balaam planned to kill the children of Israel on their trek to the Promised Land. Even though God had expressly forbidden the destruction of his blessed people, Balaam nonetheless saddled his ass to ride against the Israelites. God, who was by now pissed off, sent the archangel Michael to stand in the road with a sword and block the path of the ass. Balaam, blinded to spiritual realities, could not see the angel because he had no "spiritual vision." But the ass did have spiritual vision. He could see Michael and his sword, and turned off the road, away from the Israelites—thus saving them. So, the moral of the story: because of Balaam's lack of vision, God had to work through an ass.

Says Margaret Washington of the incident: "Sojourner's metaphor implied that like the ass in the Bible, Abolitionists and women had a second sense and supernatural visionary power, while blind proslavery ministers perverted God's will, as did Balaam."

Sojourner Truth provoked people to look at the suffering caused by their beliefs, and finally at some point to ask themselves whether their deeply held beliefs about the world were accurate. Churchmen were forced to ask themselves (usually when alone in the dim light of their parish offices): Could the entire church of God be so off base as to have gotten this one entirely wrong? Could we be wrong about slavery? About the very personhood of Blacks?

I wonder if you are holding tightly to any views and beliefs that simply do not comport with reality. Most of us are. Have a look around you. You will see tightly held but irrational views on display just about everywhere: How about this one, which I recently heard argued quite strenuously on an otherwise intelligent television program: "Women are temperamentally unfit for scientific inquiry; they are more suited for the arts and humanities."

17

Wherever Sojourner Truth went, she carried a banner covered in activist slogans and would plant it in a public place to attract crowds. Chief among the slogans was this one: "Truth is powerful and will prevail."

When she was unfamiliar with the place in which she found herself, Truth would simply loosen her grip on her horse's reins and "let God drive." As a result, she often found herself wandering into unexpected towns and cities, and into new predicaments of all kinds. She welcomed these. Sometimes, as she herself put it, she "stayed lost" on purpose.

As she aged, Truth's message grew broader, deeper, sharper. She moved from a recitation of her own experience in slavery—now a quarter of a century and more behind her—to a condemnation of American slavery as an institution and of white people as a whole. Midway through her career, the Sojourner began to perceive the *structural* conflicts in the United States that enabled the suffering of enslavement to continue, including the conflicts built into the United States' Constitution itself—the Great Dilemma I mentioned in the

Prologue to this book. Truth grew increasingly angry, and "though she was careful not to alienate her audiences with her anger," writes Nell Irvin Painter, "she began more and more to let it show."

After years of peaceful agitation, Sojourner Truth became somewhat more "Old Testament." She identified more and more with the Old Testament prophets. She preached that God would rain down destruction on the unrepentant nation for its sins against her people. God had spoken to her in a vision, she told Joseph Dugdale, and He had revealed to her the importance of certain neglected scriptures, particularly the accounts of the prophet Isaiah, whom Truth adopted as a role model. Later in her life, she often quoted Isaiah's dark prophecies, like this one, written in Isaiah 59, decrying the people's widespread collusion with evil:

> None calleth for justice, nor any pleadeth for truth; they trust in vanity, and speak lies; they conceive mischief, and bring forth iniquity. They hatch cockatrice's eggs, and weave the spider's web; he that eateth of their eggs dieth, and that which is crushed breaketh out into a viper.

Truth said to one angry mob: "It seems that it takes my black face to bring out your black hearts; so it's well I came." At another point she said, "You are afraid of my black face, because it is a looking glass in which you see yourselves."

After the Civil War began in 1861, Truth warned that the Confederacy was arming Blacks to fight against the Union, and she implored the federal government to conscript Blacks to fight *for* the Union. A friend reported that the increasingly militant Truth "was armed (stretching out her long bony arm) to fight for the North, and if she was ten years younger (she is now seventy), she 'would fly to the battlefield, and nurse and cook for the Massachusetts troops, *her boys*! and if it came to the pinch, put in a *blow* now and then.'"

Eventually, Truth made her way to Washington, where she was granted an appointment with President Lincoln. The two tall, gaunt Americans found much in common in each other's background of poverty and privation. We are told that they sat together for a long while as Sojourner Truth—now abandoning her nonviolent creed—pleaded with Lincoln to enlist Northern free men of color to help fight the war. Astonishingly, Truth returned repeatedly to the White House to renew her plea. Her arguments, combined with the manpower needs of the Union Army, eventually won over Lincoln and Congress. At that point, Sojourner Truth decided to remain in Washington, where she worked night and day nursing wounded soldiers and caring for the emancipated slaves who then poured into the capital.

18

In spite of the intense suffering of her early life, Sojourner Truth remained resilient and healthy for most of her life. "It is the mind that makes the body," she had always maintained. "New ideas, new thoughts bring a new mind and renew the whole system, preventing the body from becoming withered up." With Emily Dickinson, Truth insisted upon the mystic view that *the body is in the mind*, not the other way 'round.

In the last years of her long life, however, Sojourner Truth's health failed. She was cared for by two of her daughters. Like Walt Whitman in old age, Truth often sat in her comfortable chair and reviewed her life. Even in retirement, the Sojourner never lost her fire, or her conviction that she had her own unique destiny. A last glimpse of this unquenchable spirit is provided by Truth's friend Hallie Quinn Brown—a daughter of enslaved parents who became a prominent American educator and writer. Brown describes a scene in which Sojourner is reminiscing about her long and eventful life. A little girl sat watching and listening, fascinated by this old woman's stream-of-consciousness recital of her history. At a pause in Truth's monologue, the little girl asked, "Sojourner, did you see Adam and Eve?"

The elderly woman simply said, "No, Child." Then pondering the larger import of the question, she shot back: "And I ain't goin' to die, honey. I'm goin' home like a shootin' star!"

Several days before she died, a reporter came from the *Grand Rapids Eagle* to interview her. "Her face was drawn and emaciated and she was apparently suffering great pain. Her eyes were very bright and mind alert although it was difficult for her to talk."

Truth died early in the morning on November 26, 1883, at her Battle Creek home. Her funeral was held at the Congregational-Presbyterian Church. We are told that over a thousand people attended the service, and some of the most prominent citizens of Battle Creek acted as pallbearers. She was laid to rest in the city's Oak Hill Cemetery. Her simple tombstone reads:

Sojourner Truth

In Memoriam

Born A Slave In
Ulster Co. N.Y.
In The 18th Century

Died in Battle Creek
Mich.
Aged about 105 years

But just to keep things interesting, at the end of this simple inscription is a curious question. It reads:

Is God Dead? S.T.

Was this done at Sojourner Truth's request? We do not know. It would have been very much like her if it had been—provocative to the end. But the background of the inscription requires one further story.

Throughout her long career, Sojourner Truth had often sparred with Frederick Douglass, the famous ex-slave and abolitionist. In one now famous exchange, Douglass was giving a speech in Boston's Faneuil Hall, and was declaring his hard-won belief that America would never put a voluntary end to Black bondage and that armed revolt was the only solution. This kind of massive revolt, he acknowledged, would result in wholesale slaughter. Sojourner Truth was sitting at the rear of the speaker's platform that evening. She rose to confront Douglass, her six feet of height almost dwarfing him. She spoke in her deepest voice. "Frederick," she called out loudly until he stopped his talk. And then she added the zinger: "Is God dead?" Douglass was stunned. The audience rose, and an avalanche of applause is said to have swept through the Hall.

Therefore: "Is God Dead," on the tombstone.

Over the decades, Truth and Douglass developed a profound respect for one another. As prophets, they were cut from the very same cloth, disrupting the old order and insisting on living in a perpetual *kairos* moment. Douglass was extremely moved upon hearing of his "sister's" death, and offered a moving eulogy for Sojourner Truth at a memorial service in Washington, DC. He said:

> Venerable for age, distinguished for insight into human nature, remarkable for independence and courageous self-assertion, devoted to the welfare of her race, she has been for the last forty years an object of respect and admiration to social reformers everywhere.

In 2009, a memorial bust of Truth was unveiled in Emancipation Hall in the U.S. Capitol Visitor Center. Sojourner Truth is the first African American woman to have a statue in the Capitol building.

LESSON FOUR

ALWAYS REMEMBER THAT YOU ARE "NOT THE DOER"

In the final hour of their night together, Krishna and Arjuna have walked to the river to wash themselves and to carry back some water for their ritual ablutions and final cup of tea. The light has begun to dawn on the Eastern horizon. There is a chill in the early morning air, and it has left dew on the field of Kuru. The campfire is burning down to its last embers.

As they sit together for a moment on the banks of the Saraswati River, Krishna has one final lesson to impart. He looks squarely into the eyes of his friend.

"Arjuna, you must remember always to surrender to me. Have me in your mind. Have me in your heart. This will keep you safe."

Krishna is particularly insistent on this point, and he holds Arjuna's gaze until he is sure that he has communicated it clearly.

Then Krishna continues: "When you surrender fully to Me, then you are not the Doer. You are in my hands. I am the great Doer. You don't have to figure everything out by yourself, Arjuna. Just keep me at your side. Always with you. In this way, you simply become a channel for the Divine Mind."

Krishna warns of the dangerous siren song of the ego:

> *Deluded by identification with the ego, a person thinks, I am the Doer. (Gita 3:27)*

No, says Krishna.

> *Those who know the Truth, whose consciousness is unified around Me think always, I am not the Doer. (Gita 5:8)*

Arjuna will begin to see that through his own small calling he can become a channel for the Divine Mind. He will see how he can join his actions of body, speech, and mind with something vast and beautiful. He will see that it is only through his sincere effort to align with dharma that his own being—his own personality—will be perfected. In living out his dharma, he will encounter a transformed version of human possibility—a possibility he had never before imagined. A greater possibility than his own consciousness could envision.

As the sun peeks over the horizon, now, the whole field of Kuru seems lit up as if from within. Anticipation hangs in the very air.

Arjuna and his Divine friend turn back toward their camp to do their ritual ablutions and their morning worship.

CHAPTER 7

MARIAN ANDERSON

Trust in the Mystic Power of the Gift

The master sees things as they are
Without trying to change them.
She lets things go their own way, and
Resides at the center of the circle.

— Lao Tzu, Tao Te Ching
a new English version by Stephen Mitchell

The concert was scheduled to begin at 5 P.M., but crowds began descending on the Lincoln Memorial six hours before that. In spite of the overcast skies and the brisk April wind that whipped up off the Potomac River, concertgoers arrived en masse. They arrived singly and in pairs. They arrived in large groups bussed in from out of state. It seemed that absolutely everyone had come. There were families, children in strollers, elderly folk in wheelchairs and with canes, Boy Scout troops, soldiers. Initially they huddled close to one another and to the steps of the monument. As the throng grew, it gradually spread around both sides of the great reflecting pool and back as far as the base of the Washington Monument, almost a mile away.

By the time the concert was to begin, at least 75,000 souls had gathered to hear one of the greatest American singers of the 20th century—or any century, for that matter—and to participate in an event the likes of which they would not see again in their lifetimes.

It was Easter Sunday, the 9th of April, 1939. Marian Anderson was about to step out onto the wide front terrace of the Lincoln Memorial to present a free open-air concert to America, and—through the forest of microphones that were set in front of her—to the world.

Anderson's rich contralto voice and vocal mastery had already become a legend in the capitals of Europe. "The kind of voice one hears only once in a hundred years," said Arturo Toscanini. She had sung for kings and queens and in every important classical hall in Europe. And yet, because she was an African American, she had been denied access to sing in the most important hall in the capital of her own country. Constitution Hall was the largest concert venue in Washington, DC. The Daughters of the American Revolution (DAR), a supposedly patriotic organization, owned the hall and had ruled that no Black artists would be allowed to appear there.

Fair-minded people across the country exploded with anger. Speaking for the National Association for the Advancement of Colored People (NAACP), Walter White wrote, "Barring a world-famed artist because of color from a building named by the Daughters of the American Revolution 'Constitution Hall' violates the very spirit and purpose of the immortal document after which the hall is named." Strikes and pickets were organized. Committees were formed to support Anderson. Artists and politicians rallied around her.

But the DAR held fast.

Eleanor Roosevelt, wife of the president of the United States, had long been a member in good standing of the Daughters of the American Revolution, and when the DAR refused to budge on this issue, Roosevelt publicly resigned her membership. "You had an opportunity to lead in an enlightened way," she wrote to the DAR president general, "and it seems to me that your organization has failed." Roosevelt's husband, Franklin Delano Roosevelt, agreed with the sentiment: Anderson must sing. "I don't care if she sings from the top of the Washington Monument," he told Secretary of the Interior Harold Ickes, "as long as she sings." Together, Ickes and the Roosevelts came up with a plan: Constitution Hall be damned. She would sing on the steps of the Lincoln Memorial. For the world.

By the time the concert got under way, the skies above Washington had begun to clear, and the sun broke through the clouds to bathe the reflecting pool and the Lincoln Memorial in light. A deep hush settled over the crowd as a small, elegant Black woman, wrapped in a long mink coat, walked with enormous dignity to the side of the grand piano. She tucked her orange and yellow scarf closer to her neck. And then, in her trademark gesture, she clasped her hands together and looked out over the expanse of the crowd fading away into the distance. She took a deep bow and stepped closer to the microphones.

Anderson began to sing.

My country, 'tis of thee
Sweet land of liberty,
To thee we sing;
Land where my fathers died,
Land of the Pilgrims' pride,
From every mountainside
Let freedom ring!

There were not a lot of dry eyes. Few in the crowd had ever really listened carefully to the words of the purportedly familiar anthem, and coming from Anderson, the words came newly alive.

My native country, thee,
Land of the noble free,
Thy name I love;
I love thy rocks and rills,
Thy woods and templed hills;
My heart with rapture thrills,
Like that above.

Let music swell the breeze,
And ring from all the trees
Sweet freedom's song;
Let mortal tongues awake;
Let all that breathe partake;
Let rocks their silence break,
The sound prolong.

2

This was a crossroads moment for just about everyone involved: for Marian Anderson, for Mrs. Roosevelt, for Harold Ickes, and for the thousands who attended. But most of all, for racial justice in America. This one moment has echoed down through the decades. Until the end of her life, Marian Anderson said that almost on a daily basis she has heard the refrain from someone: "You know, I was there on that Easter Sunday."

What had happened? Here was a single, small, powerfully dignified African American woman. Here was a highly trained and masterful artist. Here was a woman simply doing her dharma full-out. She did not see herself as an activist. She was not out to change the world. She only demanded the right for her voice to be heard. God had given her a gift, and she knew that it was meant to be used.

Marian made it clear that her life was not dedicated to political activism. She wrote in her autobiography, "It would be fooling myself to think that I was meant to be a fearless fighter; I was not, just as I was not meant to be a soprano instead of a contralto." She refused to admonish the DAR to the press, who hounded her for comment and hoped for some dirt. No, she said, "I particularly did not want to say anything about the DAR. As I have made clear, I did not feel that I was designed for hand to hand combat, and I did not wish to make statements that I would later regret."

But when presented with the idea of the massive open-air concert in lieu of the Constitution Hall event, she realized that it would be a "moment of statement." She realized after a good deal of soul-searching that it was something she must do. "I had become, whether I liked it or not, a symbol, representing my people. I had to appear. I could not run away from this situation."

And appear she did. And all she brought with her into the arena was the mastery of her own gift.

In her autobiography, Anderson describes the moment she stepped out onto the broad terrace of the Memorial. "All I knew then as I stepped forward was the overwhelming impact of that vast multitude. The crowd stretched in a great semicircle from the Lincoln Memorial around the reflecting pool on to the shaft of the Washington Monument.

I had a feeling that a great wave of good will poured out from these people, almost engulfing me. And when I stood up to sing our National Anthem I felt for a moment as though I were choking. For a desperate second I thought that the words, well as I know them, would not come."

"I sang," she wrote. "I don't know how."

Her thrilling contralto voice poured forth from her "like a prayer," said one observer.

Our fathers' God, to Thee,
Author of liberty,
To Thee we sing.
Long may our land be bright,
With freedom's holy light,
Protect us by Thy might,
Great God our King.

3

I have now read dozens of stories of the response of the crowd to this moment. It appears that thousands of concertgoers were transformed by the event in a way they could barely describe.

Todd Duncan, an acclaimed American opera singer—and fellow African American who had himself faced years of racial discrimination—was standing near Anderson. Shortly after the event, he attempted to capture his complex feelings about the event: "Number one, I never have been so proud to be an American. Number two, I never have been so proud to be an American Negro. And number three, I never felt such pride [as] in seeing this Negro woman stand up there with this great regal dignity and sing."

4

Marian began the program with several well-known classical pieces, and closed it with her unique rendition of three African American spirituals, including her trademark, "My Soul's Been Anchored in the Lord."

When Marian sang her last note, it hung in the air for a long moment. Onlookers remember it as a moment of transcendent quiet—a moment of union for the massive crowd. And then, suddenly, the spell was broken. The crowd surged forward, roaring their acclaim. Walter White, a middle-aged Black man and executive secretary of the National Association for the Advancement of Colored People, pushed his way to a microphone and begged the crowd to restrain itself, fearing that Marian Anderson would be crushed by the crowd's force.

"As I did so," he later wrote, "but with indifferent success, a single figure caught my eye in the mass of people below which seemed one of the most important and touching symbols of the occasion. It was a slender black girl dressed in somewhat too garishly hued Easter finery. Hers was not the face of one who had been the beneficiary of much education or opportunity. Her hands were particularly noticeable as she thrust them forward and upward, trying desperately, though she was some distance from Miss Anderson, to touch the singer. They were hands that despite their youth had known only the dreary work of manual labor. Tears streamed down the girl's dark face. Her hat was askew, but in her eyes flamed hope bordering on ecstasy. Life which had been none too easy for her now held out greater hope because one who was also colored and who, like herself, had known poverty, privation, and prejudice, had, by her genius, gone a long way toward conquering bigotry. If Marian Anderson could do it, the girl's eyes seemed to say, then I can, too."

5

What was happening here?

Simply this: when we enact our dharma, our sacred calling, with every ounce of Soul Force we have, the result leads to a transformation of the "field" around us. Marian was aware that the only gift she had to offer to that crowd was her mastery of song, and she gave it generously. As a result, she achieved an effect on the cultural, political, and spiritual "field" that activists dream of.

The authors of the Bhagavad Gita were well aware of the "field effect" of dharma that Anderson experienced that day. They included a commentary on this in Chapter 13 of the Gita, a chapter usually entitled "The Field and the Knower of the Field." In the present chapter on Marian Anderson, we will examine this particular mystical quality of dharma. How, precisely, do dharmic actions transform "the field"?

6

In order to understand the field effect of mature dharma, we must look more deeply at the rigorous training that accompanies every type of artistic mastery. Surprisingly, perhaps, this is described in detail in the Bhagavad Gita.

Much of the actual technique for mastering one's dharma is laid out in Chapter 6 of the Gita. This chapter describes the practice of meditation, the one and only actual "technique" Krishna gives to Arjuna. Krishna's instructions in that chapter pertain to the mastery of *any* art that requires the systematic training of concentration and attention—the prime métier of yoga technique.

Krishna teaches Arjuna:

> *Those who aspire to the state of yoga should seek the Self in inner solitude through meditation. With body and mind controlled they should constantly practice one-pointedness, free from expectations and attachment to material possessions. (Gita 6:10)*

Krishna then goes on to describe the practice of meditation—or attentional training—in detail. In 6:10 we have both of the key nuggets of his teaching. There are two keys to mastery of meditation, says Krishna, and to the mastery of any dharma: "one-pointedness" and "non-attachment to the outcome."

First, "one-pointedness." What does Krishna mean by this? He means training the mind—training the attention—to come back over and over again to the task, the role, the job, the art, the dharma to be mastered. He means focus. He means concentration. He means gathering the attention together into a powerful, laser-like stream of mental energy. And he means eventually becoming deeply absorbed in the object—or task—of interest. When we do become thus concentrated and thus absorbed, the task itself opens and reveals itself to us in entirely new ways. Through one-pointedness we begin to see into the very heart of the mystery of the craft we are mastering. And we begin to enter into the mystical realm of its power.

And second, "non-attachment to the outcome." What does this mean? This is one of the central and most paradoxical aspects of mastery. Krishna teaches that grasping and craving for a *particular outcome* only interferes with that very outcome. Why? Because grasping creates an anxiety that forces us out of the moment, out of the body and breath, to reach for some other imagined moment—to reach for some idealized moment that we crave. This mind state of grasping assures that we will not in fact be fully present in the body and breath, and in the mind—and this can only derail our performance. Mastery, teaches Krishna, depends not on our hopes and dreams but on regular, systematic, and deliberate practice of our craft, so that we can be completely unified in our performance, and so that we can be "all there" in the very moment of execution.

Marian herself describes this in her autobiography. As we've already seen, Marian, reflecting back upon her Lincoln Memorial experience, wrote, "I sang. I don't know how." And then she adds, "There must have been the help of professionalism I had accumulated over the years. Without it I could not have [carried out] the program." She relied on her mastery of craft. Not on her momentary feelings of inspiration. Not on her wishes and hopes for a successful outcome. None of that. But on her *well-trained capacity to give her full and undivided attention to the moment at hand.*

7

Marian's entire life story is the story of one woman determined to master a craft that she loves, and to which she feels called. As we shall see, her story involves Krishna's two central principles: first, immense amounts of training in concentration and one-pointedness (almost to a supernormal degree); and then, gradually learning to let go of grasping to outcome and to rely instead on craft.

Marian devotes an entire chapter of her autobiography to a thorough description of the rigorous training she went through in mastering the art of singing. She entitles the chapter "Learning How." Learning how to sing. In her book, Anderson describes years of deep concentration on the most subtle details of voice production.

But where did it all begin? Marian's entire journey began with the discovery of the gift. Even as a child, it was clear to everyone that Marian had a magnificent "raw instrument" in her contralto voice. Marian herself was quite aware of the gift. She loved to sing. She was good at it. It connected her to people—to people she loved, even to people whom she did not know. Marian felt a responsibility to this gift. And fortunately for Marian, she was raised by a devout mother who believed that Marian's gift for music was a gift given by God. She believed that the gift must be recognized, nurtured, and matured. She believed that when we receive a gift, it must be given back to the world tenfold.

So yes, Marian had a gift. But that was only the beginning. She understood that she must bring that gift to a mature master of the art of singing who could help her nurture it. She found that, gift or not, in order to sing professionally, she would have to build her voice from the ground up. Systematically. Deliberately. Like any craft. As she describes it in her autobiography, her intensive training over the course of many years sounds much like boot camp for the voice.

Marian describes how one of her early teachers—a respected teacher named Giuseppe Boghetti—worked with her voice. First, he identified the one single note that was her "best natural tone." She writes, "The E-flat was my best tone, according to Mr. Boghetti, because it was perfectly placed. He contrived vocal exercises starting from that tone, moving up and down, and he reminded me that all the other tones must be produced in the same way. His objective was to provide me with an even, unbroken vocal line from the lowest tone to the highest."

Marian's progress with the exercises was painfully slow. "First I did nothing but hum [the exercises] until I could feel the vibration. Then I would attempt to place the tone exactly where I was humming." Early on, she failed more often than she succeeded. But she kept coming back to the training exercises again and again. The process wore on her.

Marian describes the process of learning to breathe all over again, with increasing subtlety of control—of learning to make her voice agile. She describes developing considerable discipline in her practice schedule, returning again and again to complex problems in the voice, and learning over long stretches of time to master each of them.

If we look closely, we will see that all of this discipline was really about the training of *attention*—about bringing attention to one part of the vocal apparatus and then moving it at will to another aspect. These are just two of the complex facets of human attention, facets which we might call "sustaining" and "shifting." Finally, having mastered both sustaining and shifting, Marian's challenge was to "widen" the attentional stream—so as to become aware of all the parts working seamlessly together.

All forms of mastery—athletic, musical, artistic, scientific—require the very same forms of attentional training. Each one requires the refining of awareness in ways that particularly suit the task: sustaining, shifting, widening, narrowing, and so forth.

By the time of her Lincoln Memorial appearance, Marian Anderson had become a master of her craft.

8

The yoga tradition from which the Bhagavad Gita springs details the stages of attentional mastery with great precision. The training of mental and physical concentration unfolds in three distinct stages, and in reading her autobiography we can see Marian passing through each of these in turn. In Sanskrit, these three stages are called *dharana*, *dhyana*, and *samadhi* (roughly: concentration, absorption, and union).

The first stage of concentration is called *dharana*—taken from the same root as the word *dharma* itself, *dhr*, which means to "hold fast," or "to hold together." At this early stage of concentration training, says yoga scholar I. K. Taimni, "the mind is confined within a limited sphere defined by the object which is being concentrated upon . . . the mind is interned, as it were, within a limited mental territory and has to be brought back immediately if it strays out."

In other words, in the early phase of training, we simply train the mind to ignore potential distractions. The mind remains "interned," as Taimni says, or "secluded," as other yoga scholars have it. This allows the attention to dive more deeply into the object of concentration—in this case the various aspects of the physical apparatus that produce the voice.

Let's look more closely for a moment at this phenomenon of human concentration. The capacity for concentration, as we all can observe almost daily, is a naturally arising aspect of mental functioning. Let's say, for example, that we're sitting in a concert listening to a lovely Bach violin concerto, and all of a sudden our mind becomes locked onto the beautiful melody in the violin. For just a few moments, the mind is entirely caught up with that beautiful series of sounds. The mind is deeply concentrated. All aspiring artists and craftspersons simply take advantage of this naturally arising capacity of the mind and train it to become more sustained and more pliant to the will. Then they apply this almost supernormal capacity to concentrate to all the parts of the body and mind involved in their particular task.

Over time, and as a result of this training of attention, singers develop a supernormal awareness of muscles and groups of muscles that are not normally brought under conscious control. As you can imagine, this is only accomplished through sustained concentration on the most minute details of voice production.

9

I myself have seen this vocal training up close and personal.

Kripalu Center, as I have said, is located in the rolling hills of the Berkshire Mountains in western Massachusetts. And as it turns out, our 250-acre campus is just across the street from the campus of the Tanglewood Music Festival—which is the longtime summer home of the Boston Symphony Orchestra.

A component of Tanglewood's vast summer operations is the so-called Tanglewood Music Center (TMC), a rigorous summer academy for advanced musical training that hosts around 150 of the top young musicians in the world. These young musicians come to the TMC for eight weeks in the summer, usually after they have completed their conservatory training and before joining the great orchestras and musical ensembles of the world. Their time at Tanglewood is a kind of final intensive training ground for study and practice.

Tanglewood is, of course, a legend in the music world. There is a host of musical greats associated with its name: Leonard Bernstein. Serge Koussevitzky—the quasi-mythical conductor of the Boston Symphony Orchestra, who founded Tanglewood—composer Aaron Copland, soprano Phyllis Curtin, cellist Yo-Yo Ma. Many of the musicians who now inhabit the upper reaches of the classical music universe worldwide have done their final training here.

For three summers I was lucky enough to be on the faculty of the Tanglewood Music Center, teaching yoga and meditation to a cohort of the young TMC Fellows, right along with their intensive musical training. Our team offered regular daily meditation training and group meditation, as well as yoga classes; we also offered the cohort of young musicians full access to our campus and our classes, our dining hall, and all of our facilities. Over the course of those three summers, we studied the effects of this intensive training with our team of researchers from Harvard Medical School under the guidance of the world's most prolific yoga researcher, Dr. Sat Bir Khalsa of Harvard Medical School.

For us as researchers, the results were astounding. We looked carefully at those three stages of attentional training I have mentioned. And we watched the training of young musicians in awe as we saw that these highly trained musicians went through the exact same series of stages of concentration that we find in the yoga scriptures.

First, of course, we observed dharana. The effort in early training—as we saw in Marian's account—is simply learning to come back again and again to the object of mastery (in this case, of course, voice production) while minimizing distractions. We noticed that there were two attentional skills trained in this first phase: "aiming" and "staying." First, the capacity to aim attention, and then, the capacity to hold attention on the object for considerable periods of time. Most of the young musicians had already achieved this stage in their early training.

But then there is the question of "minimizing distractions." We discovered an interesting finding in our research on this component. Students, eager to develop deep states of concentration, soon began to identify any behaviors that *distracted* from or interfered with their concentration training, and started—without the slightest prompting from us—to modify these behaviors. For example, over the course of the summer training program, many students noticed that how they ate affected their capacity to sustain concentration that day. If they ate heavy food for breakfast or lunch, they felt it inhibiting their performance in subtle ways later in the day. They noticed that drinking alcohol or taking drugs also interfered. They restrained these behaviors—all in the service of craft. They noticed that how they slept made a difference. They stopped staying up late.

What was going on here? Well, we realized that the meditation and yoga we were teaching these young musicians simply made them more and more *aware* of those behaviors that interfered with mastery—and motivated them to modify them. As a result, these students were drawn more deeply into the mysteries of the highly concentrated mind. The training, it turned out, was self-reinforcing.

10

Okay, we have begun to train the mind in dharana, the first stages of concentration. Now what? Well, with training, at a certain point an altogether new stage of concentration will begin to arise intermittently. Yogis called this *dhyana*, or meditative absorption. As the aiming and staying capacities of the mind and body mature, we may penetrate momentarily into this new state of absorption. When we penetrate into the state of dhyana, a sense of easy flow will saturate our experience. The mind flows seemingly effortlessly into the object. This is often compared in the yogic texts to the image of oil being poured from one vessel into another. In this phase, the mind "streams into the object." And more: the mind experiences a visceral, alive connection with the object (in this case, the voice and sound production) and seems capable now of penetrating to its very core, to its very essence.

With dhyana, several new features appear in consciousness. First of all, there is the achievement of a new quality of "steadiness," or *sthira*. Once stabilized, the practitioner can hold his concentration for long periods of time. But something else arises as well at this stage. And this is where the magic really begins. With dhyana, there is a remarkable change in the mind's *perception* of the object. As the mind becomes more one-pointed, the object itself seems to become more subtle. Consciousness now becomes absorbed in the *pure perceptual features* of the object. Though mental and bodily events now occur moment by moment in uninterrupted succession, attention remains fixed on each discrete moment. Awareness of one event is immediately followed by awareness of another without break.

This new level of absorption and its features are absolutely required in the development of mastery. For the singer, for example, each individual note is seen "bare" and separate from each other note—no matter how fast they are sung. Marian discovered this very phenomenon in her training, and along with it, she discovered an altogether new level of control. But, strangely, to the artist this control "feels like no control at all." There is a quality of effortlessness to it.

With the emergence of this stage of training, we observed that our young Tanglewood students periodically experienced an altogether new level of joy, rapture, and bliss in their singing experience. And over time, some of these students discovered that after sustained practice, all subject-object separation disappeared, and the subject (the "I," the "self") became immersed in the object (the voice). All that existed at this point was the object as illumined by and revealed to consciousness. In these magical moments, the mind's awareness of itself—the most subtle form of distraction—has disappeared. At this stage there arises a mystical *identification* with the intended object. I *am* the object. *I am* the music. There is no separation between me and the music, or between me and the world.

11

Dr. Khalsa and I and others on the team talked daily with the music students and began to hear them talk about the changes in perception that seemed to result from their attentional training. Our music students struggled to articulate the experiences they were having with these deeper states of concentration, and often could simply find no words to describe them.

Yogis discovered in this second phase of concentration (again, dhyana) the beginnings of another supernormal power that they would come to call, simply, "knowing." When the mind becomes concentrated on a discrete object—let's say, in this case, voice production—it begins to "know" the object in a special way. In this phase, knowing becomes more subtle and more complex. We see and feel connected to the object of awareness in what can only be described as a mystical fashion.

Students began to talk about relating more intimately to the music. One talked about her increasing zeal for what she called her "duty to the music." She told us, "What arises is the feeling of knowing the very soul of the music. A sense of its sacred quality." (In fact, anyone who knows Tanglewood knows that it is somehow saturated with this oft-remarked-upon sense of the sacred. The summer TMC session begins every year with the singing of Randall Thompson's magnificent hymn "Alleluia." Generations of students—including the aforementioned Bernstein and others—have seen Tanglewood as a kind of hallowed ground, where deeply spiritual experiences take place routinely.)

Our summer music students noticed another outcome that is mentioned in the yoga scriptures: as concentration takes the mind to more subtle levels, a deep new quality of interest arises. Rapture and joy fill one's being. We see here the beginnings of "the unitive experience." There is a sense of the self becoming unified. In other words, the self that is accustomed to internal states of fragmentation, alienation, self-estrangement, and anxiety will inevitably find a deep quality of refreshment in the experiences of "seclusion" that accompany a deeply absorbed mind. In some contemplative traditions (particularly in Buddhism), these stages of concentration are called "the experiences of delight," precisely because they create profound states of well-being.

And now what happens? Well, because the concentrated mind experiences such profound states of well-being, these states become very compelling to us. We want more. We want to return to these states more often. And so we train even more intensively. I saw this phenomenon over and over again during our summer program. Again: training in mastery is self-reinforcing.

12

When we gave our Tanglewood students time to reflect on their experience—which we did often—we discovered that students were generally aware of these mystical states, though they struggled to find words to describe them. They noticed that throughout the summer, these states would arise and pass away. We began to talk about these as "Tanglewood moments."

These states of deep concentration—known for so many centuries in the East—have now been studied by Western psychologists as well. The first psychologist to catalogue these states in detail, research psychologist Mihalyi Csikszentmihalyi, has dubbed them "flow states." In his research, these states of "flow" are found to have certain reliable characteristics:

- A relaxed but intense concentration on the task at hand
- An intense attentiveness to a small target area
- Dissociation to everything else
- A total involvement in the moment, and a complete "present orientation"
- The absence of self-consciousness
- A subtle and high-speed attunement to feedback
- The regular experience of time distortion ("time slows down")
- The occasional disappearance of "time" altogether
- A compelling merger of action and awareness
- The marked absence of any craving for a particular outcome

13

As I've said, our young students struggled to articulate their experiences with flow states. Margot Schwartz, for example, was a young violinist who had just finished her studies at Yale and had joined our

Tanglewood training group. She described this state of flow in her own words: "I'm present and involved, but I'm not clinging to some particular outcome. I can allow the music to move through me without trying to hold on to it."

Michael Kelly, a young singer who had just completed his studies at Juilliard, said: "As a singer, you discover that you can't make it happen. You have to prepare skillfully, of course, but then you have to let it happen. You have to let go of the sound."

To my delight, these students had discovered one of the central features of mastery: non-grasping. Says Schwartz: "There is a curious paradox here that most performers eventually figure out: the more we grasp for perfection, the less likely it is to happen."

In a mere ten weeks of training, our young students began to have an experience of what yogis call "witness consciousness." We talked about this quality of mind briefly in our opening chapters on Gandhi. "The Witness" is an aspect of awareness that stands absolutely still at the center of the whirlwind of thoughts, feelings, and sensations. The Witness is a seeing and knowing presence that is always steady and equanimous. Yogis discovered that there is a deep part of the consciousness that "knows" and "sees" and that is entirely steady and trustworthy—even in the midst of great physical and mental challenge. "This part of the awareness is beyond willpower, beyond force, beyond grasping, and it's totally reliable. You can have faith in this inner skillfulness," says Margot Schwartz.

This is precisely what Marian Anderson relied upon that day on the steps of the Lincoln Memorial. Her mastery—her gift, her dharma—was, in effect, *under its own power.* "You can have faith in this inner skillfulness."

14

Finally, in the quest for mastery, there may arise an entirely new mystical experience—a more advanced stage of absorption that the yogis came to call samadhi. It is an experience that is notorious for being inexplicable.

In samadhi, the boundaries of time and space that ordinarily separate one object from another collapse. "Knowing" is now instant, direct, and immediate. There is a mystical union between subject and object. No seam is left showing. In the Western mystical tradition, this is known as the *coincidentia oppositorium:* the mystic union. The Sanskrit word *samadhi* literally means "putting together." With this experience of samadhi, "I" and "the world" have been "put together." It is the state that mystics in all traditions—from St. Teresa of Avila in the West to Rumi in the East—penetrate over and over again.

There is one particularly interesting feature of this level of mastery. Yogis call it *samapatti*, or coalescence. As this new mind state emerges, objects are no longer perceived as separate. And as they are directly "known" by consciousness, they are found to be "made of the same stuff" as everything else in the created world. At this level of consciousness, all created things are seen to have the same properties, the same nature, the same essence.

When this feature arises in consciousness, it has a profound effect on the personality. No longer does the sense of self set one apart from the rest of nature. This experience of "coalescence" permanently changes the mind. In this state of coalescence, says the Gita,

> *The Master sees the Self in every creature and all creation in the Self. With consciousness unified through meditation, they see everything with an equal eye. (Gita 6:29)*

In the Bhagavad Gita, Krishna calls this experience "the vision of sameness." It gives rise to a new and effortless quality of loving-kindness toward the self and toward all beings. The reasons for this are obvious: one knows oneself to be one with all created things. So with the appearance of "coalescence" comes a profound transformation of our relationship with the object world. Violence and hatred are no longer possible.

Mihalyi Csikszentmihalyi, our Western researcher, comments on this very experience. "Loss of self-consciousness can lead to self-transcendence, to a feeling that the boundaries of our being have been pushed forward." Our young musicians commented on this phenomenon as well. "It's as if I'm not really doing it at all," said

Michael Kelly. "When I am in the zone, there is a sense that 'I' am just a conduit. That the performance is coming from somewhere beyond me." And after his experiences of a summer spent doing yoga and meditation, he added, "I have no doubt that yoga cultivates this."

As we have seen, Krishna makes this point over and over again in the Gita. When immersed in mastery of dharma, he says, "You are not the Doer." You are momentarily freed of the bondage of self.

15

Remember our list of the characteristics of "Awake Mind" from Chapter 2 of this book? We can now begin to see how these are cultivated, and perhaps we can even begin to see fragments of these in our own experience. It might be useful to revisit them here in brief.

- Awake Mind stands still at the center of the whirlwind of life, and is not shaken by the vicissitudes of life.
- This Mind sees not only the present but the past and future, transcending the space-time continuum.
- Awake Mind can directly know the subtle interior life of all sentient beings. The Witness directly "knows" the very essence of all created things.
- This Mind perceives the inherent interconnectedness of all things, and sees that no event is unrelated to any other.
- Awake Mind perceives all the potential events in the Universe in each aspect of the Universe. This wisdom function sees the holographic quality of phenomenal reality.

16

As one might expect, a remarkable number of stories of "unitive experience" began to circulate after Marian Anderson's Lincoln Memorial concert. Some members of the audience described "being part of a seamless whole." In other words: not separate. Some described "a deep sense of well-being." To a person, these descriptions always include a profound sense of the presence of "a mystical whole."

Todd Duncan's written reminiscence reflects on his experience of mystical interconnection. He remembers a heightened consciousness in which he felt every facet of his experience as a part of the mystical whole. He wrote, "In back of me were the Tidal Basin and Washington Monument. Under my feet was the grass. To the side of me the walls were the beautiful trees. The ceiling was the sky. And in front of me were those wonderful majestic stairs going up to the Lincoln Memorial. And there stood Miss Anderson . . . The highlight of the day were the first words that she sang."

17

Now, let's return to our study of the "field effect."

What Csikszentmihalyi and others have noticed is that in musical expression, the heightened consciousness of the artist herself "saturates the field." The audience—those in the audience who are ready and able—actually *begin to participate with the performer in that heightened state of consciousness*, and themselves experience a state of absorption, or "union," right along with the performer.

As it turns out, performers can often intuit this collective state of union as it is happening. It is a state just beyond words, though many have tried to capture it. Canadian champion figure skater Toller Cranston described an experience when "the audience was still, watching intently, anticipating. [At one point] I felt an electric shock run through the crowd. They understood. In that brief instant we fused. Reality no longer existed and time became suspended. We opened *the gateway to tomorrow* that night and passed through. We could feel it; we could feel the birth pangs. It was something beyond reality."

As Cranston indicated, once we touch that state of consciousness, nothing is ever quite the same. We can't ever go back to a rigid belief in our complete separateness. We know that union exists. We are haunted by that. It changes our lives.

We've each had at least a taste of this, haven't we? We've each been entranced by mastery, and by the consciousness that saturates the field in the moment of its execution. We are perhaps entranced as the soccer player dribbles down the field and scores the perfect goal. We are entranced by the pianist absorbed in the Beethoven sonata; the chess player at the board; or by almost any event in the Olympics.

18

Marian Anderson describes an experience of "field effect" in a thrilling concert she gave in Vienna fairly early in her career. When she walked onto the stage of one of the great halls of Vienna, she was disappointed to find that the house was only about a third full. However, after a particularly emotional rendition of Bach's "Komm, süsser Tod" ("Come, Sweet Death"), the field changed. Marian could feel it in the moment, she writes. And she could see it in the almost miraculous tripling of the size of the audience. But it was only later that she found out what had actually happened. At the intermission of Marian's concert—after she had sung "Komm, süsser Tod"—audience members excitedly called around the city and raved to their friends about what they had just heard. Music lovers raced to the hall. At the same time, another huge concert was going on nearby, and Marian's audience rushed to encourage members of that other audience to come over and hear what was happening at Marian's concert.

Marian's description of the field effect that day is characteristically humble. She wrote, "I like to feel that the work I do is sufficiently prepared so that it is pleasing from a vocal standpoint. But beyond that, I know that a pleasing rendition is not all I must give. There are things in the heart that must enrich the songs I sing. If this does not happen—and it does not always happen—the performance is not fulfilled. With 'Komm, süsser Tod' that day in Vienna, I had probably found the key to the heart. And the audience knew. You cannot fool an audience." Yes, she had "probably" found the key to the heart. "Come, Sweet Death" is one of Bach's vocal masterpieces—describing our longing for Heaven and for the sweet finality of rest. It was one of Marian's favorite arias.

19

Krishna taught Arjuna that his own consciousness had the power to change the field around him. Marian independently discovered this very truth. Her own consciousness and mastery had the power to change the field.

So, as we might expect, many things changed after the great concert at the Lincoln Memorial. Writes Russell Freedman: "Thanks to the coast to coast radio hookup, millions of people heard Anderson sing that day. Her voice was carried into hamlets and farmhouses far from any concert hall, and newspapers across the country featured the concert as a front-page story. A headline in the *Norfolk Journal and Guide*, for example, read: 'Marian Anderson Thrills America.'"

Marian Anderson's concert on the steps of the Lincoln Memorial is recognized as a crossroads in the struggle for equal rights. It helped to create the format of the modern civil rights demonstration, and it established the Lincoln Memorial as a moral high ground for generations of protesters. The NAACP, the civil rights organization most closely identified with the concert that day, reaped substantial rewards. Within twelve months, its membership doubled and contributions to the organization skyrocketed. Anderson, who until then had not been associated with any civil rights group, now committed herself to the NAACP and became one of its leading fundraisers.

In 1955, Anderson finally broke the last remaining barrier to Black singers in America. Thirty years after her New York debut, Marian Anderson became the first African American to be a soloist at New York's prestigious Metropolitan Opera.

20

In time, Marian became one of America's most sought-after singers. During World War II, she sang regularly for servicemen and servicewomen at military bases and hospitals. She was generous with her time and her genius.

Finally, in 1943, as a gesture of goodwill, the Daughters of the American Revolution invited Marian to give the opening concert of a series of concerts to raise money for the war effort. The concert would be given in the very Constitution Hall from which she had previously been banned. She accepted the invitation, but on just one condition: that the audience be *completely unsegregated*. This was another new milestone for that hall.

Anderson's appearance on January 7, 1943, was a gala event. Eleanor Roosevelt was there along with a host of dignitaries. The reviews were magnificent. But Anderson's comment about the concert is extremely telling about the experience of mastery. She writes, "When I finally walked onto the stage of Constitution Hall, I felt no different than I had in other halls. There was no sense of triumph. I felt it was a beautiful concert hall, and I was very happy to sing in it." She was not clinging to the approbation of the critics. She was not clinging to the role that she'd played in making the change, or exulting in it. She was just living her dharma. She was living beyond the dualities of fame and ill repute. Beyond the dualities of praise and blame.

Marian Anderson was simply living at the center of her dharma. She did not see herself as in any way different from—or better than—any other person. When asked about that concert in later years, she always said, "The essential point about my wanting to appear in the hall was that I wanted to do so because I felt I had that right as an artist."

21

Marian Anderson embodied a paradox of dharma. She was a change agent who did not confront the world head-on. Rather, she confronted the world quietly, with great dignity, and standing in the very center of her mastery. The dharma itself provided the power. The dharma itself made the change.

"You are not the Doer," says Krishna. "Rest," he says, "in the effortless effort of a dharma mastered."

Lao Tzu writes in the Tao Te Ching of this kind of quiet, paradoxical power—a power that touches and changes the very soul of the times:

> *The master sees things as they are*
> *Without trying to change them.*
> *She lets things go their own way, and*
> *Resides at the center of the circle.*

But wait. What does Lao Tzu mean here? That we should not try to change the world? Not at all. Look deeper. Lao Tzu means that it is not the act of clinging to an exalted sense of "I," "me," and "mine" that changes the world. He means that as we stand squarely in the center of our dharma—our mastery, our calling, our gift—our effort is transformed into a mystical power. And it is *that* power that changes the world. "Reside at the center of the circle," he writes. It is *that* power—the power of dharma itself—that changed the field around Thoreau, Truth, Stowe, Lowell, and now Anderson.

Marian had developed a way of "letting things go their own way"—of standing at the center of her circle. She had apparently learned this from a mother who was a gentle, careful nurturer of her talent. "It's okay, Marian," she would tell her young daughter at the arising of every obstacle. "A way will be found. The Lord will help you find a way. Someone will rise up to help you. Don't press too hard."

"Don't press too hard." Rely on effortless effort. This is Krishna's teaching precisely.

22

It is in pointing people to the true nature of the world—the true nature of life, of reality—that we change the world. "The world is sacred! It cannot be improved," says Lao Tzu. It was the power of mind and consciousness that transformed that vast field of humanity on that chilly day in April. Through mastery, Marian and her audience had entered into the field and had together, even for an instant, become Knowers of the field.

To be clear, none of this means that we do not "try" to change things for the better. Not at all. We bring everything we have to that task. But we must understand where the true power of change happens. And how it happens. We must understand where to most effectively put our effort. Marian's power came through enabling the gift to mature within her. She brought everything she had to that task. She felt her responsibility to the gift, and in becoming, and in *fully being* herself, she changed the world.

Find your own gift, and then set about in life to nurture its maturation in every way you possibly can. As Krishna teaches, the mature gift will take you directly to the corner of the world that needs it most.

CHAPTER 8

JONATHAN DANIELS AND RUBY SALES

Trust in the Mystic Power of Love in Action

Non-violence is our dharma, the central law of our being, written into our every cell. The law of the jungle is all right for animals; violence is their dharma. But for men and women to be violent is to reverse the course of evolution and go against their deepest nature, which is to love, to endure, to forgive.

— Mohandas K. Gandhi

Saturday, August 14, 1965, was a blisteringly hot day in the small town of Fort Deposit, Alabama, where a series of shattering events was about to unfold. We have many descriptions of the day, through newspaper reports and eyewitness accounts.

Early in the morning on this day in August, groups of Black teenagers began to arrive at a small all-Black church near the dusty center of the village. Some arrived on foot or on bicycles. Some arrived in beat-up automobiles driven by apprehensive parents. The kids looked excited. But also, scared. Eventually a group of twenty-five or thirty of the young people huddled together in the cool shade of a tree next to the church.

What was happening? A few dozen Black students had decided to take a stand against racism in the small town of Fort Deposit. The parents of these kids had for decades been understandably afraid to publicly oppose the racist oppression, segregation, and violence that pervaded the culture of this town. In spite of the rising tide of civil rights actions in the South during the mid-1960s, there had never been a single protest in Fort Deposit. Not a peep of organized complaint. But these young people—who were themselves too young to vote—felt the winds of change coming to Alabama. They insisted on making their voices heard.

This small protest was unfolding in the context of big changes in Fort Deposit and the surrounding Lowndes County. The signing of the Civil Rights Act in 1964 had raised expectations and spirits around the county. The work of Dr. Martin Luther King Jr. in their own state of Alabama had inspired the small community. And the presence of a young Black civil rights activist named Stokely Carmichael in their very town had empowered them to speak up.

On this particular Saturday in 1965, the young protesters had chosen to picket three stores where Blacks had been routinely denied service—made to enter through back doors, charged higher prices than whites, and verbally harassed. The three stores were well known by all: the Community Grill, Waters Dry Goods, and McGruder's Grocery Store. The young people had chosen the week's busiest shopping day, Saturday, for their nonviolent protest, hoping to catch the maximum amount of exposure.

The protesters had brought with them homemade cardboard signs that read "Equal Treatment for All" and "No More Back Doors." For most of these kids, it was to be their first demonstration. They were anxious. And with good reason. Fort Deposit was, after all, in the very belly of Lowndes County, a bastion of violent racism and segregation that had for decades been called "Bloody Lowndes."

Twenty-four-year-old Jonathan Daniels and his fellow civil rights worker, Ruby Sales (then just seventeen years old), moved quietly around the group of young protesters as they gathered, reminding them of their training in nonviolent protest. This was to be a completely nonviolent action, they emphasized. The coordinator of the Student Nonviolent Coordinating Committee (SNCC)—the aforementioned Stokely Carmichael—was present, and he asked all the kids to check their pockets to make sure they had nothing whatsoever that resembled a weapon—not an innocent pocketknife, not a nail file. Nothing.

2

Jonathan Daniels was a young white Episcopal seminarian from Keene, New Hampshire. He was what I suppose we would then have called "clean cut": handsome, tall, and lanky, with closely trimmed dark hair and intense dark eyes. He walked and spoke with determination and an air of quiet confidence. And as usual in these situations, he was wearing his seminarian's clerical collar, making it clear that he was a clergyman.

What was this guy doing in the very center of a potentially dangerous protest in small-town Alabama?

Just months earlier, from the safety of his seminary dorm at Episcopal Theological School in Cambridge, Massachusetts, Jon and a group of fellow seminarians had huddled in horror in front of the television, watching the evening news. They had been following a civil rights march in Selma, Alabama. A group of hundreds of protesters had planned to walk the fifty-four miles from Selma to the state capital in Montgomery to protest police brutality. (In particular, the protesters were outraged that a white state trooper had killed an unarmed Black man—Jimmie Lee Jackson—at a peaceful voting rights march and had not been prosecuted.) The march had just begun as the seminarians in Cambridge tuned in. Television cameras rolled as the marchers began to chant. Black civil rights activist John Lewis led the protesters across the Edmund Pettus Bridge out of Selma, and on toward Montgomery—the state capital. But the protesters would not get far. State troopers stopped the marchers on the other side of the bridge and beat them mercilessly. John Lewis himself was almost killed. All of this unfolded on live national television.

At Episcopal Theological School, Jon and his group of friends were stunned. This can happen in America? Really? On live television? What could they do? they wondered. What should they do?

As it turned out, an opportunity was about to present itself. After the unprovoked and illegal attack at the Pettus Bridge, the Reverend Martin Luther King Jr., put out a national call for pastors and seminarians and church people of all stripes to come down to Alabama and stand up to the unprovoked aggression. Perhaps the presence of an international group of clergy would help break the impasse, exhorted King and his advisors.

Young Daniels was in the dining commons at the school on the night when King's urgent call came out. The whole seminary was abuzz with the challenge. Students huddled together in small groups. Who would go? How dangerous might it be? Would the seminary stand behind activist students? Wasn't this kind of activism a core part of a Christian's true calling—to stand up to brutality and racist oppression?

Jonathan thought deeply about the challenge. He wondered: Could he live with himself if he did *not* go? What did his faith mean, after all? He prayed about it all in the safe haven of St. John's chapel that night. He was searching for a sign. He felt torn between his commitment to his studies (and his future career in the church) and the immediate need in Alabama.

This was, of course, an Arjuna moment for Jonathan. Am I called to fight this fight? Or am I called to stay home and pursue my studies? Though he and the world would not realize it until much later, Jonathan had reached the principal crossroads of his life.

As he prayed that night, Daniels meditated on a similar moment in the life of the Old Testament prophet Isaiah, who was called by God to go out into the world and speak against the oppression of his people. Like Martin Luther King Jr., Isaiah's God had put out a call. In the scripture, God cries out: "Who shall I send, and who shall go for me?" The question hung in the air. In the scripture, we are told that Isaiah looked deep into his soul and responded quietly to the challenge. "Here I am, Lord," he said. "Send me." In future years, a documentary would be made about the life of Jonathan Daniels, entitled *Here Am I, Send Me*.

3

Jonathan Myrick Daniels decided that very night that it was indeed his calling to go to Alabama. "I must go," he told his close seminary friend Judy Upham. "I can't live with myself if I don't." As it turned out, Judy decided to go as well. They would both take a leave of absence from their studies at Episcopal Theological School. It all happened quickly. They went back to their dorms to hurriedly pack and to prepare to be away from school for some unknown period of time. Judy and Jon would roll out of Cambridge in Judy's red Volkswagen Beetle at the crack of dawn the next day, headed south, into the storm.

They arrived in Selma, Alabama, just in time to participate in the *second* attempt to march from Selma to Montgomery—this time protesting not only the murder of Jimmie Lee Jackson but also the violence on the Edmund Pettus Bridge. Once they arrived, the two seminarians supported the marchers in every way they could. They used Judy's VW Bug to help ferry marchers and supplies back and forth to the march. After the march was completed—this time successfully—Jon and Judy reached another choice point: To stay in Alabama or to go? As it turned out, most of the Northern civil rights workers—of whom there were dozens—had disappeared after the march. The celebrities who had shown up for the march had gone back to Hollywood. Who would stay, then, and do the work? Another Arjuna moment. Jon and Judy decided to stay.

As it turned out, Jonathan Daniels was a natural for this work. He had many gifts—most of which he discovered there in Alabama in "on the job training." He discovered, for example, that he was good at public speaking; he was good at organizing; he had energy, intelligence, and of course, along with Judy, he had that all-important VW. (Few of the workers had cars.) By midway through his first year in Alabama, Jon was already something of a veteran. He had been leading mass meetings. Speaking to large groups. Canvassing for new voters. And helping integrate Selma's largest Episcopal church, whose rector, shockingly—and apparently without embarrassment—refused to seat Black worshippers for services. Jon Daniels had already worked closely with Stokely Carmichael and had gained Carmichael's trust—as few white workers ever had.

And now here was Jonathan on this hot Saturday in August 1965, in the heart of Lowndes County. Here was Jonathan in "Bloody Lowndes," where Blacks outnumbered whites four to one but no one could remember a time when *any* Blacks had been registered to vote. Not one. Little had changed here since Reconstruction. Most Blacks in Lowndes still worked as sharecroppers on converted plantations, and endured the closest thing possible to slavery.

But of course, as I've said, the rising tide of the civil rights movement had begun to shake things up, to throw light on the situation in which Southern Blacks found themselves, even in Bloody Lowndes.

4

So, it was all of this that had brought Jonathan to Fort Deposit on that Saturday afternoon.

As they gathered at the small church in Fort Deposit, it seems that Jonathan and his group of young adult protesters were unaware that at the other end of the street a nasty scene was developing. A group of angry white segregationists had gathered at a local store. Here were dozens of adult men carrying broken bottles, garbage can lids, and baseball bats. A sense of foreboding spread through the town, and the usually busy Saturday streets quickly emptied, except for the two groups: Black kids and white men. Other white citizens, knowing what was to come, ran for cover.

Geraldine Logan, a Fort Deposit teenager who had been involved in the protest, later put it succinctly: "Everybody was afraid because it was a white folks' town. They used to beat up Black people and hang them on top of Skull Hill." Word had spread quickly around the village: "Stay home." Stokely Carmichael's group, the SNCC, issued a direct warning to all civil rights workers. It read simply: "The [Ku Klux] Klan is very active in the area."

Journalists had also caught wind of the situation, and they began to gather at the scene. There was Bill Price, for example, a New York–based photographer for the *National Guardian*. There was David Gordon, a reporter with the *Southern Courier*—who sat in his car witnessing the scene. Gordon made notes. "The town looked like it was getting ready for a war," he commented later.

The crowd of angry whites pressed closer. Ruby Sales, who had had some experience already in protests and who was assisting Jon Daniels, remembers it clearly, "As frightened as I was—and I was frightened—I felt that it would be a supreme irony if we stopped [these young people] from picketing when we [civil rights workers] had been demonstrating all year."

Ruby Sales was a petite seventeen-year-old Black student from the Tuskegee Institute in Alabama. She had been born into a middle-class Black family and had simply never in her young life experienced the kind of racism she saw in Lowndes County. She'd been raised at the integrated army base of Fort Benning, Georgia, where her father was an officer. Ruby had been stunned to experience violent racism first-hand after joining a Tuskegee student protest in Montgomery in early March. After that, angry and indignant, she left school to work in Lowndes. But she found that being a teenage Black activist in Lowndes was more dangerous than she had even imagined. She received many death threats.

5

Finally, at Jonathan and Ruby's direction, the group of young picketers took a deep breath, broke into three groups, and began to march in the direction of the stores to be picketed.

This was a historic moment in Fort Deposit. As I've said, no Blacks had ever dared to demonstrate there. One reporter understood the deeper meaning of the situation. Observed Bill Price, the photojournalist: "There were these great constitutional principles enshrined in this sort of straggly little march." This elegantly summed up the situation. So many principles were on the line: freedom of speech, the right to peacefully protest, equality under the law, and civil society itself.

Reaching the front of one of the stores, the young people raised their signs over their heads and marched in a circle. Soon they became aware that they were being stalked by the group of angry white men. "I remember looking across the street and seeing a lot of white people with bats," said picketer Geraldine Logan. She put her head down and kept marching. Another young picketer remembers a loud voice coming from the crowd: "Put them niggers in jail for disturbing the peace and parading without a permit."

Just before the group of angry whites could reach the picketers, the police confronted one of the three groups of young people. "What the hell are you doing here?" an officer yelled at them.

"Exercising our constitutional right to picket," said Jonathan Daniels. His voice was calm and self-assured.

"You don't have any rights in Fort Deposit," the officer barked at him angrily. He then proceeded to place the entire group under arrest, with absolutely no legal justification.

6

Before Jonathan Daniels had started classes at Episcopal Theological School the previous fall, he had joined more than 200,000 people at the August 28, 1963, March on Washington. Jonathan stood near the front of the crowd at the Lincoln Memorial as Martin Luther King Jr. delivered his "I Have a Dream" speech. (Jon was standing close to the very spot where Marian Anderson had sung her concert thirty years earlier.) Daniels admired King intensely. He had read his book *Stride toward Freedom*, and was particularly lit up by King's nonviolent approach to activism. After hearing the speech, Jon joined the NAACP, a move that was unusual for a white person. In his first year of seminary, Jon worked with inner-city African American children in an Episcopal parish in Providence, Rhode Island. In the autumn of 1963, Jon had seen Black residents of Boston demonstrate for better housing and schools, and against violent treatment by the Boston police. He had felt the urgent call of the times.

As a young man, Jonathan wrote in his journal that he believed that "self-fulfillment lies in service," a motto he had gotten from his father—a much-loved doctor in his hometown of Keene, New Hampshire. In high school Jon wrote for the Keene High School literary magazine, *The Enterprise*. In an essay titled "Reality," he wrote about his admiration for Henry David Thoreau. He agreed with Thoreau that contemporary life had in many ways blinded us to our souls' deepest needs. He saw, with Thoreau, that conveniences and modern advances caused people to lose sight of "the basic fulfillment of our moral existence." Jon was drawn to Thoreau's emphasis on "what really matters." "Stop right now," Jon wrote in his essay, exhorting his readers, to "examine your lives. Is life just one long, mad social whirl?" Jon was only seventeen years old at the time.

7

Jonathan Daniels's dilemma was, like Arjuna's, how to act in the face of evildoing. He wondered how to decide *when* to take action and *what* action to take. Jon believed that his faith required from him a deep commitment to truth. This view compelled him to see the way things actually are—not just the way we would like them to be.

In the heat of the Alabama summer, the scales fell rather quickly from the eyes of this privileged young white boy from New Hampshire. He experienced a gradual awakening to the reality of violent racism in the South. The 1964 Civil Rights Act was supposed to end segregation and Jim Crow, but it was barely touching the problem. And to Jon's surprise, it hadn't really addressed the all-important issue of voting rights at all.

Authors Rich and Sandra Neil Wallace wrote about the situation in Alabama that summer: "Blacks still couldn't shake hands with whites or eat with them in southern restaurants. If they rode in the same car, blacks had to be in the back seat. And they could never question the character of a white person, even if that person was lying. If they did, they'd be fired from their jobs or worse: beaten, jailed, or killed. In 1965 only 2 percent of the Selma area's black majority was registered to vote."

Jon allowed himself to enter more and more deeply into the reality of racial oppression. For a number of months he lived with a Black family in a housing project. He fell in love with his new family. He continued to extend his stay in Alabama. What was he doing *studying* Christianity in graduate school, when he could be witnessing to its very beliefs? he thought. Here was a young man whose gifts had intersected with the call of the times. For Jonathan and those around him, the meeting of these two powerful forces would be like fire and gasoline.

8

In Fort Deposit, Jonathan and the three small groups of protesters were arrested on trumped-up charges of "parading without a permit and disturbing the peace."

The young picketers surrendered without incident, and were herded onto a filthy garbage truck. Ruby Sales remembered that they were "packed in like cattle, with no room to sit down," and were eventually driven to the Haynesville jail nearby. Remembers Ruby, "We were singing freedom songs and saying, 'We're so glad we got on this garbage truck, 'cause those white men were getting ready to kill us.'"

Eventually the teenagers were ushered into filthy cells, replete with overflowing and blocked toilets and with no source of running water. As soon as the teens were locked in, they began to vent. They were angry with themselves because they had not resisted the white aggression—had not used their fists, had not resorted to violence. "Why didn't we fight back?" they wondered aloud. What had nonviolence achieved in the final analysis? "Next time," they said, "we WILL fight back."

Jon explained to them that they had done exactly the right thing. He was resolute about nonviolence. He told a friend, "I am convinced that in the long run the strategy of love is the only one that will bring real health and reconciliation into this mess . . ." But at the same time, he acknowledged, "Yeah, I get it when Blacks get impatient with this approach."

The teens were not easily mollified. "But we've lost," they complained to Jonathan. "No," said Daniels, and he quoted Gandhi: "Satisfaction lies in the effort, not in the attainment. Full effort is full victory." Jon showed them that their action that day had been powerful in ways that they could not yet see. He reminded them that they had brought everything to the table on the streets of Fort Deposit in a way that had never been done. No, said Jon, arrest was certainly not failure.

This is the unmistakable teaching of the Gita. Krishna teaches over and over again that we must pick up the call of our dharma, do it full-out, and let go of the outcome. The outcome is up to God. Gandhi quoted the passage with these teachings all the time to his own frustrated followers: "In regard to every action, one must know the result that is expected to follow, the means thereto, and the capacity for it. He who, being thus equipped is without desire for the result, and is yet wholly engrossed in the due fulfillment of the task before him, is said to have renounced the fruits of his action."

9

Jonathan Myrick Daniels had studied Gandhi's nonviolent approach in depth.

Gandhi summed up his approach like this:

> Select your purpose, selfless, without any thought of personal pleasure or personal profit, and then use selfless means to attain your goal. Do not resort to violence even if it seems at first to promise success; it can only contradict your purpose. Use the means of love and respect even if the results seem far off or uncertain. Then throw yourself heart and soul into the campaign, counting no price too high for working for the welfare of those around you, and every reverse, every defeat, will send you deeper into your own deepest resources. Violence can never bring an end to violence; all it can do is provoke more violence. But if we can adhere to complete nonviolence in thought, word, and deed, [our] freedom is assured.

As I have said earlier, *satyagraha* was the name Gandhi gave to his new way of overcoming injustice. This means "holding on to truth" or "soul force." *Satya* means "truth" in Sanskrit, and comes from the Sanskrit root *sat*, which means simply "that which is." The idea behind satya is that truth alone exists; for truth is not what holds good just at a certain time and place or under certain conditions, but it is that which never changes. "Evil, injustice, and hatred," Gandhi argued, "exist only insofar as we support them; they have no existence of their own. As long as a people accept exploitation, both exploiter and exploited will be entangled in injustice. But once the exploited *refuse to accept the relationship, refuse to cooperate with it*, they are already free."

For Gandhi, satyagraha means "holding to this truth" in every situation, no matter how fierce the storm. "Because he wants nothing for himself," wrote Gandhi, "the true *satyagrahi* is not afraid of entering any conflict for the sake of those around him, without hostility, without resentment, without resorting even to violent words. Even in the face of the fiercest provocation, he never lets himself forget that he and his attacker are one. This is *ahimsa*, which is more than just the absence of violence; it is intense love. *Satyagraha* is love in action."

Then came Gandhi's magisterial summation of his new approach: "Thus came into being," he exclaimed, "the moral equivalent of war . . ."

10

Martin Luther King Jr. crafted his own synthesis of Gandhian principles along with what he termed the "regulating ideal" of Christian love. As the Montgomery bus boycott unfolded before the Selma marches, King saw firsthand how nonviolent protests draw attention to a just cause rather than detracting from it. He began to be guided more and more by Gandhi's teachings, writing, "While the Montgomery boycott was going on, India's Gandhi was the guiding light of our technique of nonviolent social change." He continued: "Nonviolence is more than simply agreeing that you won't physically attack your enemy. It means seeking truth and love while refusing, through nonviolent resistance, to participate in something one believes is wrong." He connected these ideas to the biblical appeal of Jesus to "love your enemies and pray for those who persecute you."

King would write, "I came to see for the first time that the Christian doctrine of love operating through the Gandhian method of nonviolence was one of the most potent weapons available to oppressed people in their struggle for freedom."

11

Martin Luther King Jr. gradually spelled out the nonviolent principles that would undergird all of his work going forward:

- Nonviolence recognizes the fact that all of life is interrelated.
- The nonviolent resister not only refuses to shoot his opponent, but he also refuses to hate him.
- Nonviolent love gives willingly, knowing that the return might be hostility.
- Nonviolent love is active, not passive.
- Nonviolent love does not sink to the level of the hater.
- Love for the enemy is how we demonstrate love for ourselves.
- Love restores community and resists injustice.

And most importantly, this: Martin Luther King Jr. insisted on seeking redress for injustice *within the rule of law.* Therefore, true love in action means always persuading the opponent of the justice of your cause. It forces the evildoers to see the consequences of their actions. It seeks to win friendship and understanding. With time, it eventually results in redemption and reconciliation. And all of this, said King, slowly but inexorably results in the creation of the beloved community.

12

The young people in Fort Deposit were now packed like cattle into the filthy, stinking jail. There were no functioning toilets. There was filth on the walls and floor. What little food was available was disgusting and practically inedible. There were limited supplies of water. The kids were sleepless, dehydrated, and terrified.

Jonathan worked hard to keep everyone's spirits up. One morning, he passed a note from cell to cell. "We're having a service at 11, so we can sing and pray together." They did just that. Jonathan sang at the top of his lungs, "We shall overcome . . . we shall overcome someday." The young men on the second floor of the jail joined in. Then the women downstairs joined. The voices resonated off the dirty tile walls of the prison and echoed up and down the dusty streets of Fort Deposit.

Night and day, voices from the jail could be heard all over town. The townspeople, still huddled in their homes, were deeply unsettled.

With perspective, we can see now that the scene unfolding in Fort Deposit that day was historic. Blacks had stood up for their rights and picketed there for the first time. At the post office on that very same Saturday, Blacks—who were that day standing in line in large numbers—were actually *succeeding* in registering to vote. This was because the registration process was now, finally, under the protection of a group of federal registrars. For the first time, the segregationists could not stop Blacks from registering.

A court hearing for the young jailed protesters was finally set for Saturday, August 21. But in the interim, none of the jailed protesters was even allowed to make a phone call. The group grew weak from hunger and thirst. The heat in the jail cells during the day was almost unbearable. Astonishingly, this went on for almost a week.

After several days, priests sent from SNCC came to bail Jonathan Daniels out of jail. Daniels refused to go until the protesters could all go together. "We are all bailed out or nobody is bailed out."

In the evenings, as the cells cooled down, Jon pulled his cross out of his pocket, reached for his Bible, and waited for the sun to set. In a voice that could be heard throughout the jail, he said the Episcopal rite of Evensong. Most had never heard the moving Episcopal evening service before. The singing and the prayers, heard around the jail now, kept everyone's spirits up. (Gandhi had routinely said his prayers and chants, both morning and evening, while in jail.)

13

Jonathan Daniels and Ruby Sales were experienced enough to know that they were actually using a Gandhian technique by simply *allowing* themselves to be arrested. Gandhi, in fact, welcomed his arrests and made them as public as possible. He also welcomed appearing before courts. He used court appearances as an opportunity to highlight unfair labor laws and taxation, and to gain the government's ear. Because he truly cared about maintaining law and order in India at all times, there was often little the British government could do to crack down on Gandhi or his supporters—short of arresting him. Between thirty-nine and seventy-five years of age, Mohandas Gandhi would spend a total of nearly seven years in prison. He always brought with him his tattered copy of the Bhagavad Gita. "Act not out of want of respect for the lawful authority," wrote Gandhi, "but in obedience of the higher law of our being, the voice of conscience."

14

In recent years, I have become fascinated by Jonathan Daniels's story. I relate personally to Jon. I myself was a student at the very same Episcopal Theological School just a few years after his tenure there. (Please note, though, that in 1974, my first year at the school, the name was changed from Episcopal Theological School to Episcopal Divinity School.) I studied in all the same classrooms as Jon, and with the same professors. I lived in the same dorms and prayed in the same pews at St. John's Chapel where Jon had prayed.

Stories about Jon's tenure at Episcopal Theological School abound. He was not always well-liked, though he was pretty much universally respected. He was whip smart. He loved to debate issues. He had a contrarian side, a feisty side. He thought deeply and read deeply. Schoolwork came easily to him, even though he was somewhat undisciplined. His mother commented that when he was in high school, he was more into girls and music and his many clubs than he was into academics. Said Jonathan's mother, "He was girl crazy, resentful of all rules, and wrapped up in every activity the school had except classroom work." And, like Gandhi, he had a temper.

Jonathan also had some limitations with which I identify. His severe asthma kept him out of sports, as mine did me. When he discovered that he couldn't play sports, he put together a group of older kids, who read deeply and thought together about current issues. Also, like myself, he was deeply interested in Western classical music.

And finally, Jon was always in love with the church. As a kid, he would sometimes dress up like a priest, and was known to administer "communion" to sick friends. His mother said that as a mere boy, Jon preached serious sermons to "invisible congregants" in the crawl space beneath his New Hampshire home.

In his application to Episcopal Theological School, Jon wrote, "I am quick to see a need and anxious to help. Perhaps because of an intense awareness of my own limitations, I am decidedly more inclined to generosity than to aggression." "Meaning and purpose" were often top of mind for Jon. He gave the valedictory speech at his college graduation (he attended the Virginia Military Institute), wherein he wished his classmates above all "the decency and the nobility of which you are capable" and "the joy of a purposeful life."

15

Jon Daniels, like Gandhi, wrestled with the question of violence.

Early in his first months in Alabama, Jon was tear-gassed while leading another group of teenagers who had staged a peaceful protest in the town of Camden. Jon remembered the scene: "Police rushed in with weapons, and clouds of yellow gas filled the air. I rolled to the ground in a position of nonviolence." Clouds of yellow gas filled the air. His asthmatic lungs seized up, and he coughed uncontrollably. His skin stung with red burns. After this experience, Jon was pissed: "I should gladly have procured a high powered rifle and taken to the woods—to fight the battle as the Klansmen do. I was very, very angry with white people."

But struggling to his feet, he saw injured marchers and had an epiphany in that moment. "I saw that the men who came at me were themselves not free," he wrote later. "It was not that cruelty was so sweet to them (though I'm afraid sometimes it is) but that they didn't know what else to do. Even though they were white and hateful and my enemy, they were human beings, too."

John Lewis had had a similar epiphany, and he wrote about it in his *Walking with the Wind: A Memoir of the Movement*: "If you can understand and feel even in the midst of those critical and often physically painful moments that your attacker is as much a victim as you are, that he is a victim of the forces that have shaped and fed his anger and fury, then you are well on your way to the nonviolent life."

Daniels and Lewis had each—quite independently—arrived at the central insight of the Bhagavad Gita: all human beings are "made of the same stuff" and are caught in the same net of bondage—the bondage of greed, hatred, and delusion. In the Gita, as we have seen, this insight is called "the vision of sameness." It is the understanding that we are all One in the most fundamental of ways. As we saw in the previous chapter, this is precisely the same insight that came to Marian Anderson during her concert at the Lincoln Memorial.

16

Jonathan would have understood that the action that he was part of in Fort Deposit was simply a smaller version of Gandhi's march to the sea to make salt. You will recall our opening chapters and remember the powerful effect of this nonviolent act of noncooperation, and how it ricocheted around India and around the globe. For Gandhi, the response to the "salt action" demonstrated more than anything he had yet seen, what he would call "the mystic power of truth in action."

Let's finish that story now:

On the morning of April 6, 1930, you will recall from the earlier chapters, Gandhi emerged from a bungalow in Dandi. Four thousand satyagrahis awaited him outside. He walked the short stretch out into the sea, and then reached down and scooped up a clump of mud and salt. "With this salt I am shaking the foundations of the empire," he said. Gandhi had broken the salt laws by illegally harvesting salt, with the intention of undermining the British salt monopoly. He had given the signal: massive civil disobedience could now begin across the entire subcontinent of India.

On that very day in April 1930, people all over India began to harvest salt. A *London Times* reporter saw more than 150 people in a dry creek bed somewhere in rural India "busily engaged in scraping salt from the deposits, piling it in mounds, and finally carrying it off in bags." Later that day, British police seized the salt, which amounted to nearly 1,000 pounds. After the British cops left, the volunteers went right back to work. There was plenty of salt to be had.

Just after his action that morning in 1930, Gandhi issued a press statement. Since he had broken the salt laws, he wrote, "anyone could do the same." They had to understand, however, that they could face arrest.

After Gandhi gave the signal, "it seemed as though a spring had been suddenly released," wrote Nehru. Civil disobedience had begun and salt making was exploding around the country. Pamphlets were distributed with instructions on how to manufacture salt. In cities and towns across India, people bought and sold salt illegally, often in packets boldly marked "Contraband Salt."

"Salt in the hands of *satyagrahis* represents the honour of the nation," Gandhi declared.

But salt would be only the beginning. Civil disobedience went well beyond breaking the salt laws. Indians also boycotted foreign cloth. They set fire to heaps of British-made textiles. In Delhi the city's tailors refused to sew foreign cloth.

A massive force had been unleashed in India, and the international press was paying attention. On May 5, 1930, Gandhi was arrested, and as he was led away by guards, he spoke to American reporter Negley Farson of the *Chicago Daily News*. "Have you any farewell messages, Mr. Gandhi?" Farson asked. Gandhi responded happily: "Tell the people of America to study the issues clearly and to judge them on their merits," Gandhi said.

The news of Gandhi's arrest swept through India, and the people responded with strikes, demonstrations, and meetings. People around the world also responded to Gandhi's arrest. In places as far apart as Panama and Kenya, Indians closed their businesses. In the U.S., more than a hundred clergy members sent British Prime Minister Ramsay MacDonald a cable. They begged him to seek a just settlement.

By the end of May, at least 100,000 satyagrahis were in prison in India alone.

The effects of civil disobedience rippled through India and elsewhere, as Gandhi knew they would. The boycott of foreign cloth was so widespread that in Britain, mill after mill had closed its doors indefinitely. In 1930 "the moral equivalent of war" was unleashed upon the world, and the world would never be the same. And today we can trace a straight line from Henry David Thoreau's essay "Civil Disobedience," and his night in jail, to Leo Tolstoy to Gandhi to Martin Luther King Jr. to Jonathan Daniels, Ruby Sales, and the teenagers at Fort Deposit.

Gandhi's march to the sea was impeccably done. And it is now immortal. A thing done well is done forever. That immortal act deeply informed the work of Jon Daniels and Ruby Sales and Stokely Carmichael thirty-five years later and half a world away, in Fort Deposit, Alabama.

17

On day six of the protesters' stay in jail in Fort Deposit, temperatures soared into the 90s. Jon, Ruby, and the young people steeled themselves for another blistering day in jail. But then something surprising happened. The prisoners were shocked when, completely out of the blue, the jailer unlocked their cells and told them they were free to go.

Jonathan and Ruby were suspicious. They didn't want to leave the property. After all, the previous summer, three SNCC volunteers had been murdered in Mississippi immediately after they'd been released from jail. It was obvious that they had been set up.

But Jon and his group were given no choice. Once they left their cells, local police forced the entire group off the property. There were no cars waiting for them. Stokely Carmichael was not there. No officials of SNCC had been notified. No one at all was there to take them home. The streets were deserted. "There was an eerie feeling in the air," Ruby recalled.

Just half a block away from the jail was the little Cash Store, with its tin roof and rough, weather-beaten walls. The group was underfed and thirsty. Jonathan and Ruby and another priest who had been with them—Father Richard Morrisroe, a civil rights worker from Chicago—walked toward the little store, hoping to find some cold drinks for the group.

At the door of the Cash Store, the trio was met by one Tom Coleman. Neither Jonathan nor Ruby had any idea what a dangerous man they were facing. Fifty-four-year-old Tom Coleman was a state highway department engineer who considered himself a special deputy sheriff. He was a vocal segregationist who had killed a Black prison convict in 1959, claiming self-defense. He had shot the man at point-blank range with a 12-gauge shotgun. The local court found him not guilty.

As Jon and Ruby began to enter the small store, Coleman reached for the shotgun he'd rested against the counter. "This store is closed. If you don't get off this goddamned property I'm gonna blow your damned brains out." He aimed his shotgun directly at Ruby Sales and reached for the trigger.

Jonathan pulled Ruby from behind and pushed her to the ground. Just then, Coleman fired. The shot threw Jonathan Daniels up into the air and tore a hole through his chest an inch wide. Clutching his side, Daniels landed on the concrete platform. Coleman then walked directly toward the priest who had been accompanying them, raised his rifle again, and shot the fleeing Father Morrisroe squarely in the back.

Jonathan was dead. Father Morrisroe was critically injured.

Tom Coleman walked calmly back to the city hall and told his friends in the sheriff's office what he had done. He had no remorse. Years later he would declare that he would do it all over again in exactly the same way.

The world was shocked. People around the country woke up. What could they do?

18

The next act in this all-too-common Southern drama would be the murder trial of Tom Coleman.

What ensued was a sham trial the likes of which was entirely routine in the Black Belt South. But there was a difference. This particular trial would play out in front of the whole world, with cameras and national and international press observing its every move. The attorney who "prosecuted" Coleman, Carlton Perdue, was a close friend of Coleman's. No local officials objected. The jury consisted of twelve white men: friends and neighbors—and fellow segregationists—of Coleman's. Again, no officials objected. The presiding judge blatantly violated the law by segregating the jury pool. (Jury segregation had been illegal ever since the Civil Rights Act was put into law in 1964, but the presiding judge simply kept doing it, with no consequences from either local or federal authorities.) Witnesses blatantly lied on the stand, and concocted a fantastical story that Jon Daniels was armed with a weapon and had threatened Coleman's life. No one on either side really believed this.

The Hayneville courthouse and justice system were entirely in the hands of local racists. Violence was in the very air. As Ruby Sales walked into the courtroom to testify, a white man in the courtroom pulled a knife on her, and told her that he would "cut her guts out."

After deliberating for just an hour and twenty-nine minutes, the all-white jury returned the verdict on Coleman: "Not guilty."

The national and international press exploded. Newspapers from around the country voiced outrage. Wrote the *Birmingham News*, "When such an individual is killed in the Deep South, there is little chance of a state court conviction." Civil rights leaders condemned the verdict, calling it "a monstrous farce." One paper declared: "Just as Bloody Sunday [on the Pettus Bridge] had showed the police brutality against African Americans trying to vote, the Coleman trial demonstrated how the Southern justice system did nothing to stop the violence."

19

Jonathan's death and the events that led up to it—and followed it—would now bear fruit in just the way Gandhi and Martin Luther King Jr. had predicted. The gains in the movement were to be the fruit of sacrifice.

With time, those involved would begin to understand: the very heart of Gandhi's doctrine of nonviolent resistance is the demonstrable fact that *voluntary suffering can educate and transform.* "Nonviolence accepts suffering without retaliation," wrote Gandhi. "Suffering can have the power to convert the enemy when reason fails." Gandhi believed that "unearned suffering is redemptive" and has tremendous educational and transforming possibilities. Unearned suffering shone a light on what was actually happening.

As it turned out, of course, Gandhi was right. He did indeed understand the mystic power of love in action. Change came remarkably quickly to Lowndes County after this tragedy—much of it a result of the national scrutiny surrounding Jonathan's death. As I've said, systematic exclusion of Blacks and women from jury pools had gone on for years, unchecked by federal officials. In the wake of Jonathan's death, however, his many defenders brought a lawsuit that would force the federal government into the struggle against the all-white, all-male juries of the South. The case, called *White v. Crook*, revolutionized the Southern jury system. "It was one of a great series of cases which resulted in a transfer of structural power," said civil rights lawyer Charles Morgan.

After Jon's death, civil rights workers bore down on Lowndes County and recruited sympathetic locals to their cause. By the end of 1965, the number of Blacks registered to vote in the county had gone from zero to 2,000, about the same number as registered white voters. Five years later the blatantly racist sheriff, Jim Clark, was voted out of office by the newly empowered Black majority, and a Black man was elected as the county's first African American sheriff.

The civil rights movement of the 1960s was successful not only because of the energy poured into it by hundreds of thousands of people, but also because it courageously sought *redress for racial injustice within the rule of law*. King adopted a game-changing tool—nonviolence—which reduced white backlash and set the stage for civil rights activists and lawyers to fight *within* the justice system.

"Ahimsa is our dharma," wrote Mohandas K. Gandhi, "the central law of our being, written into our every cell . . . The law of the jungle," he continued, "is all right for animals; violence is their dharma. But for men and women to be violent is to reverse the course of evolution and go against their deepest nature, which is to love, to endure, to forgive."

20

I have a vivid memory from my very first day at Episcopal Divinity School in 1974. As I toured the campus, I was struck by a statue of a young man, placed just next to the front door of the community's chapel, the aforementioned St. John's Chapel. It was a statue of a young man kneeling on the ground with his hands raised in supplication and prayer. The figure vividly bespeaks some combination of agony and longing. It occurred to me that the sculptor was trying to portray a fervent longing for freedom and redemption.

It was, of course, a statue dedicated to the life and work of Jonathan Daniels. For some reason, during my tenure at the school—working toward a master's degree in divinity those many years ago—I never heard the full story of Daniels's life and death. And only now do I go back in my imagination to his life at the school, and to the challenging times in which he and I both lived.

As it turns out, Jonathan's life and sacrifice are remembered with statues and plaques not just at Episcopal Divinity School, but all around the world. Along with his hero, Martin Luther King Jr., Jonathan is one of only two 20th-century Americans included in the Chapel of Saints and Martyrs in England's Canterbury Cathedral. He is officially designated as a "martyr" in the Episcopal Church, and his life is celebrated every August 14, the day of his arrest. He is likewise memorialized in Keene, New Hampshire, at the Virginia Military Institute (where he went to college), and countless other places.

21

In this chapter, we've been looking at the mystic power of love in action. Nothing speaks of this more loudly than the next act in this drama.

Fifty-two years after she was the target of Tom Coleman's rage, Ruby Sales was invited to speak at a colloquium on racial justice at Harvard Divinity School. In my own mind she had become practically a figure out of myth and legend. But as it turned out, she was very, very real. There she was: older, heavier, dreadlocked, dressed in a boldly patterned orange top. She sat squarely and confidently in her seat, like a Buddha, eyes serious, staring straight ahead into the crowd with a kind of knowing that sent a current of energy through the room.

I was astonished to hear her story. It turns out that Ruby Sales, the seventeen-year-old activist whom Jonathan Daniels had saved, had herself—inspired by Jon—gone on to study at Episcopal Divinity School and to earn the degree that Jonathan had not been able to complete. She then went on to study at Princeton. And after her exposure to New England elites, Ruby went right back into the front lines in Alabama. By the time she appeared at Harvard, Ruby Sales had spent half a century in the vanguard of civil rights activism, and had become known around the country as a kind of force of nature—a take-no-prisoners preacher, a public theologian, historian, social critic, and educator. In the heat of her experience with Jonathan and with Stokely Carmichael in Lowndes County, Ruby Sales had found her calling, and had now lived it out to the full. Some of the activists and students in the crowd called her "Mama," with a mixture of awe and love.

In an extraordinary dialogue with other Black activists and divinity students that day at Harvard, Ruby Sales reiterated the lesson of Jon Daniels's life. "You cannot have a prophetic voice," she said, "that is shaped by hate." She was asked about Tom Coleman. ". . . I refuse to carry Tom Coleman's hate around. I will not carry that burden." And then she broke out in what almost sounded like a chant: "I love everybody. I love everybody. I love everybody, in my heart," she said, as if singing it. "You can't make me hate you!"

In her talk at the divinity school, I was not surprised to hear Ruby Sales echo an insight that Henry David Thoreau had back in 1846 at Walden Pond. Sales said: "The work that we must do is work that all of us must do. Racism is not a Black problem. It's an American problem. We are not doing missionary work for Black people here. We must all stand together with one another, and work together for the vision of a better America."

Toward the close of her talk, in an extraordinary moment, Ruby Sales turned to the crowd of divinity students and young activists and gave an exhortation I will never forget. She began by saying, "I'm depending on your generation. I'm depending on your taking the ball a little further and redeeming the soul of this nation. You must be audacious."

Then she leaned forward, and in a quieter, more intimate, almost tender voice, she said, "I worry about you." The room quieted.

Ruby continued: "You're too quiet. I worry about your silence. I worry about your lack of passion. I worry about the fact that you feel like you have to be perfect at nineteen. You're too young to be old. I want to see you have a little bit of bravado. Don't be afraid to be wrong, speak out."

"This is a *kairos* moment," Ruby said (referring to the aforementioned Greek notion of a moment of exceptional opportunity). "It is an opportunity for each of us to step forward and put our unique patch on the quilt for an America that is still to be born. I feel so privileged to still be alive to put my own little patch on the quilt of America. This is an opportunity for us to be in the fullness of our humanity."

22

Not long before her appearance at Harvard, Rich and Sandra Neil Wallace—journalists and authors who had been inspired by Jon's story—visited Ruby Sales in her office in Alabama. Sales was at that time the founder and director of SpiritHouse Project—a diverse, intergenerational organization that works for racial, economic, and social justice. The Wallaces recount their conversation with Sales in their book about Jonathan Daniels entitled *Blood Brother: Jonathan Daniels and His Sacrifice for Civil Rights*. In their interview, they asked Sales about Jon Daniels.

"'Jonathan participated in dismantling segregation,' Sales told us. 'When I think of him I think of four things.' He was, she said, unshakeable in his belief for justice; highly passionate, with a temper; intolerant of fools; and willing to make a connection between what he spouted and what he believed."

"Jonathan had never met Black people like the Black people in the South," Ruby told the Wallaces. "I had never met a white person who really cared about what happened to Black people or felt any commitment. This was a new journey for us and it gave us hope. It tenderized our hearts."

In his completely Thoreauvian dedication to action, Jon Daniels had himself written, "It is given to men to lift up the fallen and to free the imprisoned. Not merely to wait, not merely to look on! Man is able to work for the redemption of the world."

Jonathan Daniels and Ruby Sales had understood and had lived out Henry David Thoreau's prophetic words: No matter how small the beginning may seem to be, a thing well done is done forever. Together, Jon and Ruby still live in a *kairos* moment—an eternal present that contains the whole spirit of America's struggle with its Original Dilemma.

AFTERWORD

WHY NOT BE TRANSFORMED INTO LIGHT?

A morning glow has now begun to illuminate the field of Kuru, and the sun's light increases moment by moment. Krishna and Arjuna are standing together, facing the horizon, saying their morning prayers. They stand with arms outstretched and make repeated deep bows toward the rising sun, all the while intoning an ancient chant—the sacred Gayatri Mantra. This is their most sacred chant. Their prayer this morning is especially fervent. *Om bhur bhuvah svah, tat savitur varenyam . . .*

> We meditate on that most adored Supreme Lord, the creator, whose divine light illumines all realms. May this divine light illumine our intellect.

Their ritual prayer, with its repeated bows, slowly becomes more vigorous. As Krishna and Arjuna breathe deeply, the cool morning air in their lungs is soothing and sweet. Droplets of sweat begin to emerge on both their brows.

Halfway through the prayers, Arjuna notices a faint glow around the body of Krishna. Then a penumbra of gold mysteriously begins to surround Krishna's entire physical form. The light grows slowly brighter, until—in a flash—Krishna's mortal body seems to explode into fire. For a moment, the surrounding landscape is lit up.

The hairs stand up on the back of Arjuna's neck as he feels himself drawn into a vortex of energy and light. His own solid body begins to lose its accustomed form. He finds himself both terrified of the light and deeply drawn toward it. As Arjuna is consumed by the glow, he feels an indescribable sense of release—as if sloughing off the physical body and its eons of karma. For a moment Arjuna feels entirely free of any suffering or fear, as if he had taken off a suit of armor that he didn't even know he was wearing.

Deep emanations of bliss and love now flow through Arjuna like waves. There is nothing he can do but surrender. He allows himself to be washed by these waves. His love for Krishna has become unbounded, and for a few moments of rapture, Arjuna feels connected with all beings everywhere.

Bowing down to Krishna, Arjuna cries out:

> *You are the supreme, changeless Reality, the one thing to be known. You are the refuge of all creation, the immortal spirit, the eternal guardian of eternal dharma. You are without beginning, middle, or end; you touch everything with your infinite power. The sun and moon are your eyes, and your mouth is fire; your radiance warms the cosmos. (Gita 11:18–19)*

For a few miraculous seconds, the entire world of mind and matter is dissolved. Everything becomes part of one unified field. The ego and the mortal body are consumed in the flames of consciousness—deconstructing the hard shell of the human self and freeing the soul back into its original Union.

What was happening here?

Arjuna had been granted "the Divine vision."

2

In every age, mystics have beheld the Divine vision, and their descriptions of it are remarkably similar to Arjuna's.

St. Teresa of Avila reached for words to try to describe her own experience of the vision:

> When the soul looks upon this Divine Sun, the brightness dazzles it . . . And very often it remains completely blind, absorbed, amazed, and dazzled by all the wonders it sees.

Moses described his Divine vision on Mount Horeb as a great fire that he beheld in a bush—the "burning bush" that was not consumed by the flames. His face and beard were scorched by it. And as Moses descended the holy mountain, his entire countenance began to glow, so that he had to cover his face when approaching his followers.

For some mystics, the Divine vision lingers. Teilhard de Chardin was a 20th-century French Jesuit who had the gift of "inner sight." He tells us that he constantly saw the world lit up from within by the Divine. "Throughout my whole life," he wrote, "during every minute of it, the world has been gradually lighting up and blazing before my eyes until it has come to surround me, entirely lit up from within."

3

Arjuna can only tolerate a few brief moments of the holy fire.

"Krishna, take it away. Take it away. Too much. Too much!"

The fire continues to burn.

"No, Krishna, please take it away. I need to see you in your mortal body again. Please come back to me in human form."

Slowly, the fire and light begin to dim.

4

Sometime later, Arjuna awakes, as if from a dream. He finds himself lying on the ground at Krishna's feet.

Has he had a dream? A seizure of some kind?

Krishna picks him up and takes him to the foot of a neem tree. He covers Arjuna with a blanket, then sits next to him and hums softly, continuing to chant the Great Mantra: *Om tat savitur varenyam . . .*

For a long while, Arjuna lies curled up in a ball.

5

Finally, Arjuna begins to move.

"You have seen my Divine body, Arjuna," says Krishna. "You have seen what underlies the world of apparent solidity. All of it is saturated with the Divine consciousness—pulsing and flowing, like the waves of a great ocean, a unified field of consciousness, bliss, and being."

Arjuna is speechless. He is still feeling deep waves of love for Krishna. His heart aches in his chest with a longing he has never before experienced.

"This is your true nature, Arjuna. Sat-chit-ananda. Being, consciousness, and bliss."

Krishna speaks again:

> *It is extremely difficult to obtain the vision you have had; even the gods long always to see me in this aspect. Neither knowledge of the Vedas, nor austerity, nor charity, nor sacrifice can bring the vision you have seen. But through unfailing devotion, Arjuna, you can know me, see me, and attain union with me. Whoever makes me the supreme goal of all his work and acts without selfish attachment, who devotes himself to me completely and is free from ill will for any creature, enters into me. (Gita 11:52–55)*

6

The sun is fully risen now. Arjuna and Krishna hear in the distance the call of the conch shell. It is the call to battle.

To Arjuna, it all feels far off and strange. He feels a wave of compassion for those who are about to suffer the hell realm of war. Strangely, he finds himself acting entirely without effort, even without thought. He watches himself as he readies for battle. He is not sure what will happen next. The great Doer is moving him. He has surrendered.

Krishna has readied the chariot. Arjuna picks up his gear, pours water on the vestiges of the fire, and mounts the chariot. Together he and his friend gallop toward the battlefield and disappear beyond the grove of trees.

7

Does Arjuna fight?

Yes, he fights.

But *how* does he fight the battle of good versus evil, of order versus chaos, of dharma versus adharma? This is the real question.

Mahatma Gandhi has famously said that it is impossible for anyone to actually pick up arms after a transformation of consciousness such as Arjuna has experienced. Indeed, even Krishna hints at this at the end of the dialogue when he says,

> *Those who meditate on these holy words worship me with wisdom and devotion. Even those who listen to them with faith, free from doubts, will find a happier world where good people dwell. (Gita 18:70–71)*

A happier world.

At the conclusion of the Bhagavad Gita, all we know for sure is that Arjuna will do God's will with complete certitude and faith. Is it God's will that there should be war? Should Arjuna be an early-day Charles Russell Lowell, doing his duty by strapping on arms and fighting a just war with sadness and love? Or should he be a Jonathan Daniels, determined not to pick up arms but, rather, to take up "the moral equivalent of war"?

Each individual must decide, with God's help, to what particular duty she is called, through discernment, through dialogue, through prayer and meditation, and with complete understanding of the consequences of her actions.

We know, then, that Arjuna will plunge fully into his duty now—his duty in the world. But we know, too, that Arjuna is now in possession of a mystic secret, and this will change everything: God is not just *in* the world. God *is* the world. God is everywhere present. Therefore, act in accord with this knowledge. Teilhard de Chardin wrote:

> Plunge into matter. By means of all created things, without exception, the divine assails us, penetrates us, and holds us. We imagined it as distant and inaccessible, whereas in fact we live steeped in its burning layers.

8

How will Arjuna's duty show up?

My own view is that Arjuna will most likely choose the moral equivalent of war rather than violence. He will choose the Gandhian route, the Ruby Sales route, the Jonathan Daniels route.

In one of his last declarations, Krishna sums up his teaching.

> *Free from self-will, aggressiveness, arrogance, anger, and the lust to possess people or things, [those who hear these teachings] are at peace with themselves and others and enter into the unitive state. United with Brahman, ever joyful, beyond the reach of desire and sorrow, they have equal regard for every living creature and attain supreme devotion to me. By loving me they come to know me*

> *truly; then they know my glory and enter into my boundless being. All their acts are performed in my service, and through my grace they win eternal life. (Gita 18:53–56)*

Those who hear these teachings, then, have equal regard for every creature. This is perhaps the central teaching of the Bhagavad Gita. How can we go to war after this? The Dalai Lama has said that "war is obsolete." Consciousness has made it so.

9

The Bhagavad Gita ends with a flourish, as Sanjaya, our narrator, marvels one final time at what he has seen and heard.

> *Whenever I remember these wonderful, holy words between Krishna and Arjuna, I am filled with joy. And when I remember the breathtaking form of Krishna, I am filled with wonder and my joy overflows. Where the divine Krishna and the mighty Arjuna are, there will be prosperity, victory, happiness, and sound judgement. Of this I am sure! (Gita 18:76–78)*

Through his relationship with his Divine mentor, Arjuna's consciousness has been transformed. He sees with new eyes. His perspective is vast. By the end of the dialogue, Arjuna understands his true nature. He understands the meaning of his dharma, and he sees into the deeper meaning of the battle before him. His very understanding of the world has been transformed.

EPILOGUE

To Each Other Linked

Difficult times: By and large we don't invite them in happily. We run from them, if we can. Or at least we pray to get through them as quickly as possible. "Let this cup pass from me," said Jesus before his crucifixion. But we might take some comfort in this fact: difficult times are very often good for the soul.

Difficult times force us to gather together every scintilla of strength that we have, and to bring that strength forth to meet adversity. "If you bring forth what is within you, what is within you will *save* you." This fine statement is written in the gnostic Gospel of Thomas. And every story in this book witnesses to its truth. Difficult times force us to draw ourselves up to our full height, as Sojourner Truth did before she addressed those crowds of angry men in Indiana. They force us to live in a larger imaginative space—as Gandhi did in order to envision a free India in the early 20th century. As Ruby Sales is doing even now in order to free us all from hate.

The Bhagavad Gita reminds us that difficult times liberate us from the bondage of "I," "me," and "mine." But we must remember, too, that this freedom from the cage of ego does not come easily. Make no mistake, we must be *forced* out of the cave of self. We must be forced out of the womb, out of the egg. This birth of "what is within" is often a brutal, primitive, bloody struggle. Our secret strength comes forth into the greater world screaming and covered with amniotic fluid. Only after a harrowing life of enslavement was Sojourner Truth prepared to surrender her entire self to God. Only after the harrowing of child death was Harriet Beecher Stowe prepared to dig as deeply as necessary to bring forth her powerful writing life.

In the final analysis, the Gita shows us that difficult times inevitably force us to become mystics. Why? Because in difficult times like ours, all of the questions are hard. We must search longer, harder, deeper, for the answers. We must learn to rely on unseen allies, on invisible forces, on mystic strengths. We must rely on hunches—on instinct, as Emerson said—and on the inner voice. Call this inner voice God. Call it Krishna. Or Mohammed. Whatever the case, we know that we must seek out and find the force in the Universe that calls forth the very best in us. Marian Anderson struggled to push the outermost boundaries of her gift because she knew that in her art she had occasionally touched the very face of God—a sublimity that she knew was worthy of her full devotion.

The tale of Krishna and Arjuna teaches us that difficult times force us to discover our dharma, our true nature, the law of our being. And so, in the final reckoning, difficult times perfect us. The full-hearted execution of our dharma matures the hidden seed of humanity within us.

2

If you bring forth what is within you, it will save you. Yes. This is demonstrably true. But the Bhagavad Gita adds an entirely new dimension to Thomas's insight. The Gita declares it on every page: "If you bring forth what is within you, it will save not just you. *It will save the whole world.*" Because when we're fully engaged in our dharma, we are in relationship with the whole world. Difficult times force us to discover the true nature of our radical interdependence.

When Charlie Lowell gave the commencement oration at Harvard University that sultry July morning in 1854, he referred to an ancient tale known even today to most every Indian villager.

When Krishna was just a young boy, the tale goes, his mother asked him to open his mouth wide for her so that she could inspect it. To her astonishment, when she looked, she beheld the entire Universe there. In Krishna's open mouth she saw the sun and the moon, the whirling planets, and all the mountains and rivers of the earth. And she saw that every living creature was there. Every human being was there. All the ancestors. Every single soul was there, and every soul was joined together for eternity.

If you read into the most sublime tracts of every mystic tradition, you will find that the path always ends with the same discovery—the discovery of our profound interconnection. We are woven together into a vast web. Indra's web. Objects—objects like you and me—that appear utterly separate and discrete are actually woven together in the fabric of time and space and are deeply entangled with one another. The entire Universe is more like an interwoven whole than a collection of discrete objects. More like an enormous sweater. Tug on any corner of the sweater and the whole of it is moved. Violate any corner and the whole is violated.

The 19th-century English poet Francis Thompson wrote:

All things by immortal power,
Near or far,
Hiddenly
To each other linkèd are,
That thou canst not stir a flower
Without the troubling of a star.

These hidden connections are at the very heart of the mystic's secret knowledge. Our minds are plunged into the One Mind. Into Brahman. Into God.

Affirms the great medieval European mystic John van Ruysbroeck,

> The image of God is found essentially and personally in all mankind. Each possesses it whole, entire and undivided, and all together not more than one alone. In this way we are all one, intimately united in our eternal image, which is the image of God and the source in us of all our life.

3

As beings that are both human and Divine, we live in a great paradox. We live both *in time* and *beyond time*. American author Annie Dillard wrote: "Ours is a planet sown in beings. Our generations overlap like shingles. We don't fall in rows like hay, but we fall. Once we get here we spend forever on the globe, most of it tucked under. While we breathe, we open time like a path in the grass. We open time as a boat's stem slits the crest of the present."

A boat's stem slits the crest of the present. And now here is the central question of this book: What do we do in this momentarily opened present, in this momentarily opened field of possibility? In this *kairos* moment? While we breathe we must plunge into our work here on the ground. It is the only thing that saves us, truly. Krishna was right: Look to your dharma to save you. Your work on this globe is your opportunity. Your one opportunity. Your dharma is the one place where you can truly pour out all the love that you have in your heart. It is the one place where you can most effectively apply all your energy and your particular genius. It is the one place where you can be as wild and as crazy and as peculiar as you actually are. It is the one place where you will truly know God. All you have to do is be utterly and completely yourself. You don't need to leave anything out.

By the way, there is no guarantee that we will not suffer while doing our dharma. Indeed, we most likely *will* suffer. Every character in this book has suffered. But our dharma brings us to the one place in the world where we will suffer most fruitfully—for ourselves and for the world. And as Dillard observes, if we are lucky, and tenacious, we will have one moment of gleaming mastery and then poof. Tucked under.

Yogis believed that a human birth is auspicious. Why? Because here on earth, in this embodied, human realm, our actions have the power to change everything. Yes, there are God realms. Yogis discovered that those realms really do exist. And there are hell realms as well. Enlightened yogis have seen these things. But the human realm! The human realm is the very best place to achieve full enlightenment. There is a secret possibility here on earth. There is on this mortal coil, apparently, just the right combination of suffering and transformation. Just the right amount of suffering to force us to act well. And just the right amount of transformational energy to guide us to the next step. So while we live, let us indeed act well. Let us bring everything we've got to our work here in the world, today. Of eternal fulfillment, the theologian Paul Tillich has said, "If it is not seen in the present, it cannot be seen at all."

Our effect on the world before we're tucked under is much bigger than we usually think. Don't forget the teachings of the Gita along the way. Through enacting our own personal dharma, we are redeeming not only ourselves but the whole world.

So then, what are you waiting for? Find your own idiosyncratic dharma. And do it full-out, now. No matter how small the beginning may seem to be, what is once well done is done forever!

NOTE TO THE READER

This book contains the stories of seven well-known and well-studied historical figures. In order to help their stories come alive for the reader, some of the scenes involving these figures have been imagined by the author—in complete accord with his understanding of the factual accounts of their history.

ENDNOTES

Epigraph

Sometimes crisis alone . . . Aldous Huxley, *The Perennial Philosophy* (New York and London: Harper Perennial, 2009), 42.

Prologue

My life closed twice . . . Emily Dickinson, *The Poems of Emily Dickinson: Reading Edition*, Ralph W. Franklin, ed. (Cambridge: Harvard University Press, 1999), 631. Used with permission.

A "disorienting dilemma" usually . . . Andrew Stricker, ed., *Integrating an Awareness of Selfhood and Society into Virtual Learning* (Hershey, PA: Information Science Reference, 2017), 162.

A disorienting dilemma is an experience . . . Sue Stein and Shanan Farmer, eds., *Connotative Learning: The Trainer's Guide to Learning Theory* (Dubuque, IA: Kendall/Hunt, 2004), 197.

I measure every Grief I meet . . . Emily Dickinson, *The Poems of Emily Dickinson: Reading Edition*, Ralph W. Franklin, ed. (Cambridge, MA: Harvard University Press, 1999), 248. Used with permission.

Lesson One: Take Refuge

My will is paralyzed . . . Eknath Easwaran, *The Bhagavad Gita: Translated for the Modern Reader* (Tomales, CA: Nilgiri Press, 2007), Gita 2:7–8, 89.

Conflicting sacred duties . . . Barbara Stoler Miller. *The Bhagavad Gita: Krishna's Counsel in Time of War* (New York: Bantam, 1986), (Gita 2:7), 30.

I cannot fight this fight . . . Author's translation of the Bhagavad Gita, 2:9.

Chapter 1: Mohandas K. Gandhi I

I caught a glimpse of him . . . Yogesh Chadha, *Gandhi: A Life* (Ann Arbor, MI: University of Michigan Press, 1997), 204.

We spit anywhere . . . Louis Fischer, ed., *The Essential Gandhi: An Anthology of His Writings on His Life, Work, and Ideas* (New York: Vintage, 1962), 128.

If a stranger . . . Fischer, *Essential Gandhi*, 128.

There is no salvation for . . . Fischer, *Essential Gandhi*, 129.

overbearing, tyrannical, and . . . Fischer, *Essential Gandhi*, 130.

Every moment of Gandhi's . . . Louis Fischer, *Gandhi: His Life and Message for the World* (New York: Signet, 2010), 12.

Anger clouds the judgment . . . Easwaran, *The Bhagavad Gita* (Gita 2:63–64), 96.

Fill your mind with me . . . Easwaran, *The Bhagavad Gita* (Gita 9:34), 177.

The stability of the self . . . Ernest Wolf, commenting on the work of Heinz Kohut, from *Treating the Self* (New York and London: Guilford Press, 1988), 27.

Turning and turning in the widening . . . William Butler Yeats, "The Second Coming," first printed in *The Dial*, 1920, and included in Yeats, *Michael Robartes and the Dancer* (Churchtown, Dundrum, Ireland: Cuala Press, 1920).

What I want to achieve . . . Fischer, *Essential Gandhi*, 4.

I have not yet found Him . . . Arvind Sharma, *Gandhi: A Spiritual Autobiography* (New Haven: Yale University Press, 2013), 159.

Enveloped in smoke . . . Easwaran, *The Bhagavad Gita* (Gita 3:38).

He preferred such old superstitious beliefs . . . Pankaj Mishra, "The Inner Voice," *The New Yorker*, May 2, 2011, 80.

Ritual is the husk of true religion . . . Author's translation of the *Tao Te Ching*, stanza 38.

Dear Lord and Father . . . John Greenleaf Whittier. The hymn is taken from a longer poem by Whittier, entitled "The Brewing of Soma." It is usually sung to the tune "Repton" by English composer Hubert Parry.

Chapter 2: Mohandas K. Gandhi II

It is the still small voice . . . Paul Abein, *William Dean Howells and the Ends of Realism* (New York: Routledge, 2005), 45.

The only tyrant I accept . . . Rajmohan Gandhi, *The Good Boatman: A Portrait of Gandhi* (New York: Penguin, 1997), 202.

When the mind becomes . . . author's translation of the classical Yoga Sutra.

You do not need to leave . . . Patricia Hamp, *The Art of the Wasted Day* (New York: Penguin, 2019), 30.

Realize that which pervades . . . Easwaran, *The Bhagavad Gita* (Gita 2:17), 90.

The body is mortal . . . Easwaran, *The Bhagavad Gita* (Gita 2:18, 2:20), 90.

The Brain—is wider than . . . Emily Dickinson, Poem 598, in Franklin, ed., *The Poems of Emily Dickinson*, 269.

Though God is everywhere . . . Huxley, *The Perennial Philosophy* (New York: Harper, 1945), 2.

The seed of God is in us . . . Huxley, *Perennial Philosophy*, 39.

The higher the moral purity . . . Sharma, *Gandhi*, 160.

refused to be bound . . . Sharma, *Gandhi*, 182.

When meditation is mastered . . . Easwaran, *The Bhagavad Gita* (Gita 6:19–20), 142.

You sit in your room . . . Betsy Kuhn, *The Force Born of Truth: Mohandas Gandhi and the Salt March, India*, 1930 (Minneapolis: Twenty-First Century Books, 2011), 60.

I could tell [the people] nothing . . . Kuhn, *Force Born of Truth*, 68.

Next to air . . . Kuhn, *Force Born of Truth*, 68.

There is no article . . . Kuhn, *Force Born of Truth*, 69.

The salt tax oppresses . . . Kuhn, *Force Born of Truth*, 68.

It is the formula . . . Kuhn, *Force Born of Truth*, 68.

Gandhi was the most . . . Eknath Easwaran, *Gandhi the Man* (Tomales, CA: Nilgiri Press, 1997), 65.

the workings of his conscience . . . Mishra, "The Inner Voice", *The New Yorker* 87:11 (May 2, 2011), 80.

No one knew . . . Easwaran, *Gandhi the Man*, 65.

With this salt . . . Kuhn, *Force Born of Truth*, 91.

When Gandhi gave the signal . . . Kuhn, *Force Born of Truth*, 93.

Truth is the highest attribute . . . M. K. Gandhi, quoted in Sharma, *Gandhi*, 160.

The little fleeting . . . *Mohandas K. Gandhi: An Autobiography* (Boston: Beacon Press, 1993), 504.

God's voice has been . . . *Mohandas Gandhi, An Autobiography or My Experiments with Truth* (New Haven: Yale University Press, 2018), 26.

A man who struggles long . . . quoted by Annie Dillard, *For the Time Being* (New York: Knopf, 1999), 141.

when [the seeker] cleaves . . . Dillard, *For the Time Being*, 141.

God is . . . Bhagwan Shree Rajneesh, *The Secret of Secrets*, Vol. II (Rajneeshpuram, OR: Rajneesh Foundation International, 1983), 286.

Lesson Two: Peer Carefully into the Chaos for the Sure Signs of Dharma

The reader should be aware that Krishna's "Lesson Two" in this rendering represents a much more contemporary view of dharma than would have existed in the 3rd century B.C.E. when the text was first composed. At the time of the Gita's composition, dharma was determined strictly by birth. Arjuna was a warrior by birth, and this could not be changed. There was much less sense of a "personal self" in the traditional society out of which the Gita emerged. The self was much more of a socially embedded self than a personal self. Today, however, dharma is determined by idiosyncratic gifts and personal preferences, leanings, and opportunities. Most traditional societies do eventually develop the notion of a personal self, much as we have in the contemporary West.

Always look to your dharma . . . Author's translation of the Gita, 2:31.

Chapter 3: Henry David Thoreau

The best place for each . . . Henry David Thoreau, cited in William E. Bridges, *Spokesmen for the Self* (New York: Chandler, 1971), 85.

How does it become . . . Henry David Thoreau, *Civil Disobedience*, Paul Sherman, ed. (Boston: Houghton Mifflin, 1960; originally published 1849).

It was a closer . . . Henry David Thoreau, *The Journal of Henry David Thoreau* (Princeton, NJ: Princeton University Press, 1981), 262.

"Henry, why are you in jail" . . . See account in Laura Dassow Walls, *Henry David Thoreau: A Life* (Chicago: University of Chicago Press, 2017), 209.

The State was nowhere . . . Walls, *Henry David Thoreau*, 210.

the nose aquiline . . . Ellery Channing, quoted in Henry S. Salt, *The Life of Henry David Thoreau* (Chicago: University of Illinois Press, 2000), 53.

Rather than love . . . Henry David Thoreau, *A Week on the Concord and Merrimack Rivers* (Mineola, NY: Dover, 2001).

He is considered . . . Robert A. Gross, "That Terrible Thoreau," in William E. Cain, ed., *A Historical Guide to Henry David Thoreau* (Oxford and New York: Oxford University Press, 2000), 182.

Thoreau didn't want . . . Walls, *Henry David Thoreau*, 186.

In his view . . . Walls, *Henry David Thoreau*, 186.

The oldest Hindoo . . . Henry David Thoreau, in Raymond Alden, *Thoreau's Walden* (Cambridge, MA: Harvard University Press, 1910), 83.

Tell me of those . . . Easwaran, *The Bhagavad Gita* (Gita 2:54), 95.

They live in wisdom . . . Easwaran, *The Bhagavad Gita* (Gita 2:55), 95.

They are forever . . . Easwaran, *The Bhagavad Gita* (Gita 2:71–72), 97.

Depend upon it that . . . Henry David Thoreau, in Harrison Blake, *Letters to a Spiritual Seeker* (New York: Norton, 2004), 49.

To be a philosopher . . . Henry David Thoreau, in Jeffrey S. Cramer, *Walden: A Fully Annotated Text* (New Haven: Yale University Press, 2004), 14.

I went to the woods . . . Henry David Thoreau, *Walden: Or, Life in the Woods* (New York: T.Y. Crowell and Co., 1899), 93.

Mind precedes all . . . The Buddha, cited in S. N. Goenka, *Discourse Summaries* (Igatpuri, Maharashtra, India: Vipassana Research Publications, 2012), 91.

By detachment I mean . . . Easwaran, *Gandhi the Man*, 105.

The spotted hawk . . . Walt Whitman, "Song of Myself," verse 52, in Whitman, *Leaves of Grass* (American Renaissance Books, 2009).

I am a mystic . . . Henry David Thoreau, in Harold Bloom, *Henry David Thoreau* (New York: Chelsea House, 2007), 16.

I cannot for an instant . . . Henry David Thoreau in Cain, *Historical Guide to Henry David Thoreau*, 162.

If the injustice . . . Henry David Thoreau in Walls, *Henry David Thoreau*, 252.

If I have unjustly . . . Walls, *Henry David Thoreau*, 251.

I know this well . . . Henry David Thoreau in Luca Prono, ed., *Henry David Thoreau* (Facts on File e-book, 2014), 48.

It is not so important . . . Henry David Thoreau in Philip Cafaro, *Thoreau's Living Ethics* (Athens: University of Georgia Press, 2010), 179.

Under a government which imprisons . . . Henry David Thoreau, *Civil Disobedience* (Irvine, CA: Xist Publishing, 2016).

A minority is powerless . . . Thoreau, *Civil Disobedience* (Xist).

I believe that if one man . . . M. K. Gandhi in K. Ramakrishna Rao, *Foundations of Yoga Psychology* (Singapore: Springer, 2017), 239.

All of us are one . . . Easwaran, *Gandhi the Man*, 79.

Is there not a sort of blood shed . . . Henry David Thoreau in David R. Weber, *Civil Disobedience in America* (Ithaca, NY: Cornell University Press, 1978), 88.

Every object . . . Sir Charles Eliot, quoted in David Mumford, *Indra's Pearls: The Vision of Felix Klein* (Cambridge, MA: Cambridge University Press, 2002), xix.

Cast your whole vote . . . Henry David Thoreau, *Civil Disobedience* (Xist).

The best place . . . Henry David Thoreau in Bridges, *Spokesmen for the Self*, 85.

I bequeath myself . . . Walt Whitman, stanza 52 of "Song of Myself."

Chapter 4: Harriet Beecher Stowe

I am deeply indebted to Nancy Koester for her superb account of Harriet Beecher Stowe's spiritual life. This chapter relies heavily on her account.

Deep unspeakable suffering . . . George Eliot, *Adam Bede* (London: Wordsworth Editions, 1997), 367.

a deep immortal longing . . . Stowe in Nancy Koester, *Harriet Beecher Stowe: A Spiritual Life* (Grand Rapids, MI: Eerdmans, 2014), 95.

were happy mothers . . . Stowe in her book *Men of Our Times*, in Koester, *Harriet Beecher Stowe*, 57.

A Kentucky slave mother . . . John Rankin, *The Life of Rev. John Rankin: Written by himself in his 80th year c. 1872* (Ripley, OH: Rankin House National Historic Landmark, 2004), 36.

a beautiful, loving . . . Stowe in Jeanne Boynton, Mary Kelley, and Anne Margolis, *The Limits of Sisterhood: The Beecher Sisters on Women's Rights and Women's Sphere* (Chapel Hill: University of North Carolina Press, 1988), 76.

hold [Charley] to my . . . Boynton, Kelly, and Margolis, *Limits of Sisterhood*, 76.

At last it is . . . Boynton, Kelly, and Margolis, *Limits of Sisterhood*, 77.

shrouded, pale, and . . . Boynton, Kelly, and Margolis, *Limits of Sisterhood*, 77.

along with the usual . . . Therese A. Rondo, ed., *Parental Loss of a Child* (Champaign, IL: Research Press Company, 1986), 20.

During the early days . . . Rondo, *Parental Loss of a Child*, 20.

The search for meaning . . . Rondo, *Parental Loss of a Child*, Chapter 1.

Surviving the death . . . Rondo, *Parental Loss of a Child*, Chapter 1.

I measure every grief . . . Emily Dickinson, *The Poems of Emily Dickinson*, ed. Ralph W. Franklin (Cambridge, MA: The Belknap Press of Harvard University Press, 1999), 248.

Deep unspeakable suffering . . . Eliot, *Adam Bede*, 367.

Thinking of [her] . . . Koester, *Harriet Beecher Stowe*, 111.

I am strong . . . Koester, *Harriet Beecher Stowe*, 107.

[Karuna] is the . . . Sharon Salzberg, *Lovingkindness: The Revolutionary Art of Happiness*, (Boston: Shambhala, 1995), 103.

When a person . . . Easwaran, *The Bhagavad Gita* (Gita 6:32), 143.

the crushing of . . . Stowe in Koester, *Harriet Beecher Stowe*, 152.

God hath chosen . . . Koester, *Harriet Beecher Stowe*, 103.

[Compassion] allows us . . . Sharon Salzberg, *Lovingkindness*, 103.

Life is half gone . . . Stowe in Koester, *Harriet Beecher Stowe*, 91.

I have not . . . Koester, *Harriet Beecher Stowe*, 91.

Now by the grace . . . Koester, *Harriet Beecher Stowe*, 91.

Now Hattie, if I could . . . Koester, *Harriet Beecher Stowe*, 110.

[She] rose from . . . Koester, *Harriet Beecher Stowe*, 110.

You must be a . . . Koester, *Harriet Beecher Stowe*, 90.

Having experienced losing . . . Ruth Peck, "The Woman Who Fought with a Pen," in Ruth Peck and Vickie Weaver, eds., *Women Who Shaped America* (Dayton, OH: Xlibris, 2018).

willing to sacrifice . . . Koester, *Harriet Beecher Stowe*, 113.

I feel now that the time . . . Koester, *Harriet Beecher Stowe*, 113.

I have begun . . . Koester, *Harriet Beecher Stowe*, 111.

composed by her . . . Koester, *Harriet Beecher Stowe*, 114.

scenes, incidents . . . Koester, *Harriet Beecher Stowe*, 114.

God wrote it . . . Koester, *Harriet Beecher Stowe*, 114.

Those who follow the path . . . Easwaran, *The Bhagavad Gita* (Gita 5:7–8), 128.

As soon as she . . . Koester, *Harriet Beecher Stowe*, 117.

her frizzy hair . . . Koester, *Harriet Beecher Stowe*, 117.

This child is all . . . Retawnya M. Provenzano, *Memory and Connection in Maternal Grief* (Indianapolis: Indiana University-Purdue University Indianapolis, University Library Press, 2017), 66.

Stronger than all was . . . Harriet Beecher Stowe, *Uncle Tom's Cabin* (Oxford and New York: Oxford University Press, 1877), 35.

Stowe asks the reader . . . Provenzano, *Memory and Connection*, 11.

[She] often assumes . . . Provenzano, *Memory and Connection*, 15.

She witnesses loss . . . Provenzano, *Memory and Connection*, 74.

have a spiritual gift . . . Ann-Janine Morey, "American Myth and Biblical Interpretation in the Fiction of Harriet Beecher Stowe and Mary E. Wilkins Freeman," *Journal of the American Academy of Religion*, vol. 55, no. 4 (Winter 1987), 741.

this secret knowledge . . . Provenzano, *Memory and Connection*, 11.

Written in tears . . . quoting Elizabeth Ammons in Joan D. Hedrick, *Harriet Beecher Stowe: A Life* (Oxford and New York: Oxford University Press, 1994), 57.

those whose sorrows . . . Provenzano, *Memory and Connection*, 76.

Tom suffered in patience . . . Koester, *Harriet Beecher Stowe*, 201.

a mighty force . . . Koester, *Harriet Beecher Stowe*, 224.

millennial vision . . . Koester, *Harriet Beecher Stowe*, 227.

So you are the . . . Koester, *Harriet Beecher Stowe*, 241.

It would be a poor result . . . Eliot, *Adam Bede*, 401.

Lesson Three: Understand That True Personal Fulfillment and the Common Good Always Arise Together

Strive constantly to . . . Easwaran, *The Bhagavad Gita* (Gita 3:19–20), 106.

Chapter 5: Charles Russell Lowell

Please note that the character of Toby Williams who appears in this chapter is a composite character. In Toby's story, names and locations have been changed or modified to protect the privacy of those involved.

I am deeply indebted to Carol Bundy for her inspiring biography of Charles Russell Lowell, cited below. This chapter relies heavily on her account.

To every human being . . . Anna Jackson Lowell, quoted in Carol Bundy, *The Nature of Sacrifice: A Biography of Charles Russell Lowell, Jr., 1835–1864* (New York: Farrar, Straus and Giroux, 2005), 75.

had a curious power . . . Bundy, *Nature of Sacrifice*, 11.

drew their wills . . . An unattributed comment cited by Bundy, from an earlier Harvard memorial biography of Lowell, Bundy, *Nature of Sacrifice*, 11.

There they march . . . William James, quoted in Eliza Richards, *Battle Lines* (Philadelphia: University of Pennsylvania Press, 2019), 120.

Students during Lowell's years . . . Bundy, *Nature of Sacrifice*, 120.

Charlie Lowell and his group of friends . . . Bundy, *Nature of Sacrifice*, 185.

imbued with almost hereditary . . . Bundy, *Nature of Sacrifice*, 186.

were it not for a muddled . . . Bundy, *Nature of Sacrifice*, 186.

Cicero was an early . . . see Marcus Tullius Cicero, Quintus Curtius, tr., *On Duties* (Fortress of the Mind Publications, 2016).

At the beginning . . . Easwaran, *The Bhagavad Gita* (Gita 3:10).

when the Lowells started . . . Bundy, *Nature of Sacrifice*, 52.

Anna believed literature . . . Bundy, *Nature of Sacrifice*, 51.

arousing her pupils to intense . . . Bundy, *Nature of Sacrifice*, 51.

it enables us to benefit . . . Bundy, *Nature of Sacrifice*, 55.

will do more to free . . . Bundy, *Nature of Sacrifice*, 75.

to every man there is . . . Bundy, *Nature of Sacrifice*, 75.

fresher and purer . . . Bundy, *Nature of Sacrifice*, 90. See Bundy for more on Lowell's fascinating graduation oration.

The world always advances . . . Bundy, *Nature of Sacrifice*, 91.

Children are monarchs . . . Bundy, *Nature of Sacrifice*, 75.

generous discontent . . . Bundy, *Nature of Sacrifice*, 82.

I hope he will never . . . Bundy, *Nature of Sacrifice*, 82

The speech was a cry . . . Bundy, *Nature of Sacrifice*, 91.

decades of popular . . . Bundy, *Nature of Sacrifice*, 187.

an affair of instincts . . . Ralph Waldo Emerson, in Lyde Cullen-Sizer and Jim Cullen, eds., *The Civil War Era: An Anthology of Sources* (Wiley e-book, 2008), 44.

a slight, rather shabby . . . Cullen-Sizer and Cullen, *Civil War Era*, 177.

Whenever dharma declines . . . Easwaran, *The Bhagavad Gita* (Gita 4:7–8), 117.

All dreaded . . . Lincoln's Second Inaugural Address. See Ronald C. White, *Lincoln's Greatest Speech: The Second Inaugural* (New York: Simon and Schuster, 2006).

I have always . . . Bundy, *Nature of Sacrifice*, 471.

I was very fond . . . Bundy, *Nature of Sacrifice*, 471.

All the energy had gone . . . Bundy, *Nature of Sacrifice*, 473.

If there is another . . . Bundy, *Nature of Sacrifice*, 472.

He was perfectly willing . . . Walt Whitman, quoted in Roy Morris, Jr., *The Better Angel: Walt Whitman in the Civil War* (Oxford and New York: Oxford University Press, 2000), 223.

This mighty mother of us all . . . George Putnam, quoted in Bundy, *Nature of Sacrifice*, 10. (Note: Carol Bundy begins her biography with a moving description of Lowell's funeral, from which this account is taken.)

A generation of men . . . Bundy, *Nature of Sacrifice*, 11.

Here if ever we might . . . Bundy, *Nature of Sacrifice*, 11.

Some offer wealth . . . Easwaran, *The Bhagavad Gita* (Gita 4:28–33), 120.

Lowell had fallen at the head . . . Bundy, *Nature of Sacrifice*, 12.

Fondly do we hope . . . Abraham Lincoln, Second Inaugural. See White, *Lincoln's Greatest Speech.*

Each name recall'd by me . . . Walt Whitman, "A Twilight Song," in Gary Schmidgall, ed., *Walt Whitman: Selected Poems 1855–1892* (New York: St. Martin's, 2000), 405.

The moon give you . . . Walt Whitman, "A Dirge for Two Soldiers," in Roy Morris, Jr., *The Better Angel: Walt Whitman in the Civil War* (Oxford: Oxford University Press, 2000), 244.

Chapter 6: Sojourner Truth

I am pleading for . . . Sojourner Truth, "A Hymn," quoted in Patricia C. McKissack, *Sojourner Truth: Ain't I a Woman?* (New York and London: Scholastic, Inc., 1992), 102.

"Stop the speech" . . . The scene from Silver Lake, Indiana, in this chapter is taken from multiple scholarly sources, and then reimagined by the author. The author has relied particularly heavily on the recounting of the scene in Margaret Washington, *Sojourner Truth's America* (Urbana and Chicago: University of Illinois Press, 2011), 285, and Nell Irvin Painter, *Sojourner Truth: A Life, A Symbol* (New York and London: W. W. Norton, 1996), 138–140.

What had been intended . . . Painter, *Sojourner Truth: A Life*, 139.

an island in a small stream . . . taken from Sojourner Truth's *Narrative*, co-created with Olive Gilbert during Truth's lifetime. See the excellent section on Truth's relationship with nature, in Jami Carlacio, *"Aren't I a Woman(ist)?": The Spiritual Epistemology of Sojourner Truth* (New Haven: Yale University Press, 2020), 13.

begging to be delivered . . . Sojourner Truth, *Narrative*.

When I left the house . . . Sojourner Truth, purportedly written down by Harriet Beecher Stowe and quoted in Adrian Ramos, *Sojourner Truth: Exploring the Achievements of a Self-Emancipated Slave from Beginning to End* (Middletown, DE: Sea Vision Publishing, 2020), 50.

I take no heed . . . Washington, *Sojourner Truth's America*, 311.

Well, Children, I was born . . . Sojourner Truth in McKissack, *Sojourner Truth: Ain't I a Woman?*, 102–3.

Be aware of me . . . Easwaran, *The Bhagavad Gita* (Gita 18:65–66).

She possessed the bold . . . Washington, *Sojourner Truth's America*, 286.

Well, Children, when you go to heaven . . . this scene at Kalamazoo is also imagined by the author, but relies on several sources, most heavily on Washington, *Sojourner Truth's America*, 286.

When God asks me . . . Washington, *Sojourner Truth's America*, 287.

The overwhelming effect . . . Washington, *Sojourner Truth's America*, 287.

Whilst I bear upon . . . Sojourner Truth, in McKissack, *Sojourner Truth: Ain't I a Woman?*, 102.

Just as a fire . . . Easwaran, *The Bhagavad Gita* (Gita 3:38–39), 109.

But ye shall receive power . . . Acts of the Apostles 1:6.

Pshaw, Child, the . . . Sojourner Truth, quoted in Washington, *Sojourner Truth's America*, 288.

Most of the suffering . . . Washington, *Sojourner Truth's America*, 288.

I don't read such small . . . Washington, *Sojourner Truth's America*, 288.

She mercilessly satirized . . . Washington, *Sojourner Truth's America*, 259.

I came here this afternoon . . . This story is taken from Washington's telling of it in her biography of Sojourner Truth: Washington, *Sojourner Truth's America*, 270.

I can find a better . . . Washington, *Sojourner Truth's America*, 270.

Sojourner's metaphor implied . . . Washington, *Sojourner Truth's America*, 270.

Truth is powerful . . . Sojourner Truth in Washington, *Sojourner Truth's America*, 295.

Truth's message grew broader . . . Painter, *Sojourner Truth*, 134.

Truth grew increasingly angry . . . Painter, *Sojourner Truth*, 155.

None calleth for justice . . . Isaiah 59:4–5.

It seems that it takes my . . . Sojourner Truth, in Painter, *Sojourner Truth*, 181.

Was armed (stretching out) . . . Painter, *Sojourner Truth*, 180.

It is the mind . . . Sojourner Truth in Washington, *Sojourner Truth's America*, 305.

Her face was drawn and . . . "Sojourner Truth," Wikipedia.

Venerable for age . . . Frederick Douglass, quoted in Bruce Bliven, *A Mirror for Greatness* (New York: McGraw Hill, 1975), 169.

Lesson Four: Always Remember That You Are "Not the Doer"

Deluded by identification with . . . Easwaran, *The Bhagavad Gita* (Gita 3:27), 107.

Chapter 7: Marian Anderson

The master sees things . . . Lao Tzu, Stephen Mitchell, tr., *Tao Te Ching: A New English Version* (New York: Harper Perennial, 2006), Verse 29.

The kind of voice . . . Arturo Toscanini, in Russell Freedman, *The Voice That Challenged a Nation: Marian Anderson and the Struggle for Equal Rights* (Boston and New York: Houghton Mifflin Harcourt, 2004), 41.

Barring a world-famed . . . Walter White, in Freedman, *Voice*, 53.

You had an opportunity . . . Eleanor Roosevelt, in Freedman, *Voice*, 54.

I don't care if . . . Franklin D. Roosevelt, in Freedman, *Voice*, 57.

It would be fooling . . . Marian Anderson, *My Lord, What a Morning: An Autobiography* (Urbana and Chicago: University of Illinois Press, 1984), 188.

I particularly did not want . . . Anderson, *My Lord, What a Morning*, 189.

I had become . . . Anderson, *My Lord, What a Morning*, 189.

All I knew then as I . . . Anderson, *My Lord, What a Morning*, 191.

I sang, I don't know . . . Anderson, *My Lord What a Morning*, 191.

Number one, I have never . . . Todd Duncan, in Freedman, *Voice*, 65.

As I did so, but with indifferent . . . Walter White, in Freedman, *Voice*, 69.

Those who aspire . . . Easwaran, *The Bhagavad Gita* (Gita 6:10).

I sang. I don't know . . . Anderson, *My Lord, What a Morning*, 191.

The E-flat was my best . . . Anderson, *My Lord, What a Morning*, 50.

First I did nothing . . . Anderson, *My Lord, What a Morning*, 50.

the mind is confined . . . I. K. Taimni, *The Science of Yoga* (London: Theosophical Publishing House, 1961), 277.

flow states . . . see Mihalyi Csikszentmihalyi, *Flow: The Psychology of Optimal Experience* (New York: Harper Perennial, 1991).

The Master sees the Self . . . Easwaran, *The Bhagavad Gita* (Gita 6:29).

Loss of self-consciousness . . . Csikszentmihalyi, *Flow*, 65.

In back of me were . . . Todd Duncan, in Freedman, *Voice*, 65.

the audience was still . . . Toller Cranston, in Michael Murphy, *In the Zone: Transcendent Experience in Sports* (New York: Penguin, 1995), 117.

I like to feel that the . . . Anderson, *My Lord, What a Morning*, 156.

Thanks to the coast to coast . . . Freedman, *Voice*, 71.

It helped to create . . . Freedman, *Voice*, 71.

When I finally . . . Anderson, *My Lord, What a Morning*, 193.

The essential point . . . Anderson, *My Lord, What a Morning*, 193.

The master sees . . . Lao Tzu, Mitchell tr., *Tao Te Ching*, Verse 29.

It's okay, Marian . . . Anderson, *My Lord, What a Morning*, 76.

Chapter 8: Jonathan Daniels and Ruby Sales

Ruby Sales is a major character portrayed in this chapter. Her life and work are vividly portrayed in the many talks and interviews available by and about her on YouTube. The quotations from her talk and the panel discussion at Harvard Divinity School are available at https://www.youtube.com/watch?v=7fElaIn0Ij4 (accessed June 2021), but I would urge the reader to watch other appearances catalogued on YouTube as well.

Non-violence is our dharma . . . M. K. Gandhi, in Easwaran, *Gandhi the Man*, 56.

Everybody was afraid . . . Geraldine Logan, in Rich Wallace and Sandra Neil Wallace, *Blood Brother: Jonathan Daniels and His Sacrifice for Civil Rights* (Honesdale, PA: Calkins Creek, 2016), 227.

The [Ku Klux] Klan is very . . . Wallace, *Blood Brother*, 228.

The town looked like . . . David Gordon, in Wallace, *Blood Brother*, 229.

As frightened as I was . . . Ruby Sales, in Wallace, *Blood Brother*, 231.

There were these great . . . Bill Price, in Wallace, *Blood Brother*, 232.

I remember looking across . . . Geraldine Logan, in Wallace, *Blood Brother*, 233.

Put them niggers . . . Wallace, *Blood Brother*, 233.

What the hell are you . . . Wallace, *Blood Brother*, 233.

Exercising our constitutional right . . . Wallace, *Blood Brother*, 233.

You don't have any . . . Wallace, *Blood Brother*, 233.

self-fulfillment lies in . . . Jonathan Daniels, in Wallace, *Blood Brother*, 68.

the basic fulfillment of our . . . Jonathan Daniels, in Wallace, *Blood Brother*, 26.

Stop right now . . . Jonathan Daniels, in Wallace, *Blood Brother*, 26.

Blacks still couldn't shake . . . Wallace, *Blood Brother*, 89.

We were singing freedom . . . Ruby Sales, in Wallace, *Blood Brother*, 235.

I am convinced . . . Jonathan Daniels, in Wallace, *Blood Brother*, 243.

Satisfaction lies in the effort . . . M. K. Gandhi, in Dennis Dalton, ed., *Gandhi: Selected Political Writings* (New York: Hackett, 1996), 41.

In regard to every action . . . M. K. Gandhi, in Arun Mehta, *Lessons in Non-Violent Civil Disobedience* (London: Arjun Mehta, 2014), 122.

Select your purpose . . . M. K. Gandhi, in Easwaran, *Gandhi the Man*, 49.

Evil, injustice, and hatred . . . Easwaran, *Gandhi the Man*, 48.

satyagraha means "holding to . . . Easwaran, *Gandhi the Man*, 53.

while the Montgomery boycott . . . Martin Luther King Jr.

Nonviolence is more than simply . . . Martin Luther King Jr.

I came to see for the first time . . . Martin Luther King Jr.

Act not out of want . . . M. K. Gandhi, in Satya P. Agarwali, *The Social Role of the Gita* (Mumbai: Motilal Banarsidass, 1997), 206.

He was girl crazy, resentful . . . Connie Daniels, in Wallace, *Blood Brother*, 31.

I am quick to see . . . Jonathan Daniels, in Wallace, *Blood Brother*, 57.

the decency and the . . . Jonathan Daniels, in Wallace, *Blood Brother*, 52.

Police rushed in with weapons . . . Jonathan Daniels, in Wallace, *Blood Brother*, 152.

I saw that the men who . . . Jonathan Daniels, in Kerry S. Walters, *The Art of Dying and Living* (Maryknoll, NY: Orbis, 2011), 124.

If you can understand . . . John Lewis and Michael D'Orso, *Walking with the Wind: A Memoir of the Movement* (New York: Simon and Schuster, 2015), 77.

With this salt I am . . . M. K. Gandhi, in Kuhn, *Force Born of Truth*, 91.

busily engaged in scraping salt . . . Kuhn, *Force Born of Truth*, 91.

it seemed as though . . . Nehru, in Kuhn, *Force Born of Truth*, 93.

Salt in the hands of . . . Gandhi, in Kuhn, *Force Born of Truth*, 94.

Have you any farewell . . . Kuhn, *Force Born of Truth*, 98.

This store is closed . . . Wallace, *Blood Brother*, 260.

When such an individual . . . Wallace, *Blood Brother*, 307.

Just as Bloody Sunday . . . Wallace, *Blood Brother*, 307.

Nonviolence accepts suffering . . . Martin Luther King Jr., *Stride Toward Freedom: The Montgomery Story* (Boston: Beacon e-book, 2010).

It was one of a great series . . . Charles Morgan, in Wallace, *Blood Brother*, 310.

Ahimsa is our dharma . . . M. K. Gandhi, in Easwaran, *Gandhi*, 56.

You cannot have a prophetic . . . All of the material quoted here about Ruby Sales's remarkable talk at Harvard Divinity School, April 27, 2017, was captured on videotape and is available at the time of this writing on YouTube as "Spiritual Activism: A Conversation With Ruby Sales."

Jonathan participated in . . . Ruby Sales, in Wallace, *Blood Brother*, 313.

Jonathan had never met . . . Ruby Sales, in Wallace, *Blood Brother*, 314.

Afterword

Om bhur bhuvah . . . The Gayatri Mantra is taken from the ancient Rig Veda, composed on the Indian subcontinent between 1500 and 1000 B.C.E., and is one of the most sacred mantras in the Hindu tradition.

You are the supreme . . . Easwaran, *The Bhagavad Gita* (Gita 11:18–19), 196.

When the soul . . . St. Teresa of Avila, in Easwaran, *The Bhagavad Gita*, 192.

It is extremely difficult . . . Easwaran, *The Bhagavad Gita* (Gita 11:52–55), 202.

Those who meditate . . . Easwaran, *The Bhagavad Gita* (Gita 18:70–71), 264.

Plunge into matter . . . Pierre Teilhard de Chardin, in Annie Dillard, *For the Time Being* (New York: Knopf, 1999), 171.

Free from self-will . . . Easwaran, *The Bhagavad Gita* (Gita 18:53–56), 262.

Whenever I remember . . . Easwaran, *The Bhagavad Gita* (Gita 18:76–78), 265.

Epilogue

All things by immortal power . . . Francis Thompson, in Lars Skyttner, *General Systems Theory* (World Scientific Publishers, E-book, 2005), 12.

The image of God . . . Ruysbroeck, in Easwaran, *The Bhagavad Gita*, 27.

Ours is a planet . . . Dillard, *For the Time Being*, 203.

If it is not seen . . . Paul Tillich, in Dillard, *For the Time Being*, 89.

INDEX

C

D

E

F

G

H

L

M

N

O

P

R

S

T

U

V

W

Y

ACKNOWLEDGMENTS

This book has been written during what we will probably at some point in the future call "COVID-times." The COVID pandemic has changed our world in ways that most of us could never have predicted. So, during the writing of the book—from 2018 to 2022—I have always been standing on shifting sands. Shifting cultural sands. Shifting emotional sands. I hadn't intended it, of course, but it turns out that I have written a book *about* difficult times *during* difficult times. I can say with complete confidence that no writing project has ever challenged me quite so deeply. The writing of this book has engaged just about everyone and everything in my life for the past four years. It's hard, then, to imagine doing an adequate job of acknowledging the many debts of gratitude I now owe. But let me try.

First of all, the book itself would not have been possible without the love, help, and daily support of my companion, Susan Louise Griffiths. She runs the house, takes care of the dog, and makes the meals, while I'm laboring at the office, and often burning the midnight oil. Susie does all of this without complaint—indeed, with love and a sense of humor. I kid you not. She's an angel.

Secondly, the book would certainly not have happened without the ongoing support and inspiration I receive from my spiritual and professional home base—Kripalu Center for Yoga and Health in Stockbridge, Massachusetts, where I continue to be Scholar Emeritus. I'm deeply grateful to the CEO, the Board, and the staff of Kripalu Center for its ongoing support and encouragement in so many forms.

Ned Leavitt is a seasoned, courageous, and unrelenting lover of the written word and the story. Luckily, he is also my literary agent. In this book project, he has been far more than an agent, though. I would say, perhaps, that he's been "a worthy opponent": Krishna to my Arjuna. The book would not have been born in its present form without his candor, love, and skill.

I must give a deep bow of gratitude to my team from Hay House, including the marvelous Patty Gift, Marlene Robinson, and especially to the gentle, elegant, respectful, and super-smart Anne Barthel, my editor at Hay House, who has now guided me expertly through two books.

Nan Satter did her usual superb job of editing, and, as always, went the second mile with this book—as did our mutual friend, Gail Straub, who is my sister-in-authorship and one of my longest and deepest friendships.

Carol Bundy, author of the superb *The Nature of Sacrifice*, read the chapter on her relative, Charles Russell Lowell, and offered enormously helpful perspective and feedback.

Kim Townsend, my writing professor from Amherst College and dear friend, read the entire manuscript and gave his usual frank and unrestrained praise and criticism.

Nilgiri Press has been most generous in allowing me, once again, to use Eknath Easwaran's brilliant rendering of the Bhagavad Gita, in his now-classic translation and commentary.

And finally, a deep bow of gratitude to my incomparable twin sister, Sandra Cope Stieglitz, to whom this book is dedicated (and of whom I have occasionally written within its covers). Sandy has been a most able, ardent, and truthful critic and supporter throughout my entire writing career, and so this book is dedicated to her with gratitude and love.

ABOUT THE AUTHOR

Stephen Cope is Scholar Emeritus at the renowned Kripalu Center for Yoga and Health in Stockbridge, Massachusetts, and the founder and former director of the Kripalu Institute for Extraordinary Living. He is a Western-trained psychotherapist who writes and teaches about the relationship between Western psychological paradigms and the Eastern contemplative traditions, and is the best-selling author of such books as *The Great Work of Your Life* and *Yoga and the Quest for the True Self*. He is the recipient of numerous awards for his work.

Website: stephencope.com

Hay House Titles of Related Interest

YOU CAN HEAL YOUR LIFE, the movie, starring Louise Hay & Friends
(available as an online streaming video)
www.hayhouse.com/louise-movie

THE SHIFT, the movie,
starring Dr. Wayne W. Dyer
(available as an online streaming video)
www.hayhouse.com/the-shift-movie

***

THE HOPE: A Guide to Sacred Activism, by Andrew Harvey

MORE BEAUTIFUL THAN BEFORE: How Suffering Transforms Us, by Steve Leder

SPIRITUAL PRACTICE FOR CRAZY TIMES: Powerful Tools to Cultivate Calm, Clarity, and Courage, by Philip Goldberg

WISDOM IS BLISS: Four Friendly Fun Facts That Can Change Your Life, by Robert Thurman

***

We hope you enjoyed this Hay House book. If you'd like to receive our online catalog featuring additional information on Hay House books and products, or if you'd like to find out more about the Hay Foundation, please contact:

Hay House, Inc., P.O. Box 5100, Carlsbad, CA 92018-5100
(760) 431-7695 or (800) 654-5126
(760) 431-6948 (fax) or (800) 650-5115 (fax)
www.hayhouse.com® • www.hayfoundation.org

Published in Australia by: Hay House Australia Pty. Ltd.,
18/36 Ralph St., Alexandria NSW 2015
Phone: 612-9669-4299 • *Fax:* 612-9669-4144
www.hayhouse.com.au

Published in the United Kingdom by: Hay House UK, Ltd.,
The Sixth Floor, Watson House, 54 Baker Street, London W1U 7BU
Phone: +44 (0)20 3927 7290 • *Fax:* +44 (0)20 3927 7291
www.hayhouse.co.uk

Published in India by: Hay House Publishers India,
Muskaan Complex, Plot No. 3, B-2, Vasant Kunj, New Delhi 110 070
Phone: 91-11-4176-1620 • *Fax:* 91-11-4176-1630
www.hayhouse.co.in